The Critical Reception of Charles Dickens
1833–1841

GARLAND REFERENCE LIBRARY
OF THE HUMANITIES
(VOL. 900)

The Critical Reception
of
Charles Dickens
1833–1841

Kathryn Chittick

.

Garland Publishing, Inc. • New York and London
1989

Library of Congress Cataloging-in-Publication Data

Chittick, Kathryn, 1953–
    The critical reception of Charles Dickens, 1833–1841 / Kathryn
Chittick.
    p. cm.—(Garland reference library of the humanities ; vol.
900)
    Bibliography: p.
    ISBN 0-8240-5620-5 (alk. paper)
    1. Dickens, Charles, 1812–1870—Criticism and interpretation—
Bibliography. 2. Dickens, Charles, 1812–1870—Bibliography.
I. Title. II. Series.
Z8230.C45   1989
[PR4581]
823'.8—dc19   88-33644
                                                                          CIP

Printed on acid-free, 250-year-life paper
Manufactured in the United States of America

ACKNOWLEDGEMENTS

The research on this material has made me indebted to many people. Much of my first research into Dickens was tactfully guided by Professor K. J. Fielding, whose immense knowledge of Victorian literary history has long been invaluable to students of the period. I have also benefited from the work and advice of Philip Collins and John Sutherland. My discussions with Roy Graham shaped much of my thinking, and to him I owe my earliest and longest intellectual debt.

Merrill Distad was helpful at the first, and also at the last, in guiding me through the mazes of Victorian serials bibliography and has taught me much about the field. Kent Thompson helped me with the research, and his enthusiasm and patience were a timely support.

I am happy to acknowledge the financial assistance of the Social Sciences and Humanities Research Council of Canada, the University of New Brunswick, Queen's University, and Trent University. The Harriet Irving Library at the University of New Brunswick gave me generous access to its splendid Dickens collection. I am also grateful to the staff of the British Library at Bloomsbury Colindale for allowing me to work with its unrivalled holdings in Victorian serials.

Trina Calhoun and Marg Tully produced early versions of the script with commendable accuracy. For longstanding practical assistance and encouragement, I thank Susan Anderson, Laurie Gehrling, and Mary Chittick. Mary Dempster and Carol Gillis offered welcome last minute help. Zailig Pollock gave generously of his time and scholarly advice. And I am especially grateful to Stephen Brown for his acute critical eye and invaluable suggestions.

Finally, I wish to offer my particular thanks to the reading room staff of the National Library of Scotland. Their cheerful assistance has greatly speeded my task and made my summers in Edinburgh times of instruction and delight.

Kathryn Chittick
16 October 1988

TABLE OF CONTENTS

PREFACE

This bibliography brings together a number of reviews of the
early Dickens which appeared in contemporary magazines,
newspapers, and quarterlies during the eight years between
1833 and 1841. Dickens saw his first sketch printed in
December 1833, when he was twenty-one; by December 1841, after
having put out fifteen works, he decided to take a sabbatical
from writing. But to say thus simply that he had produced a
quantifiable number of works is to mislead. Such a manner of
referring to Dickens's productions as discrete volumes
distorts the continuity of his daily experience as a serial
journalist. What it also overlooks is the fact that not until
1841 did Dickens write the work he had always considered his
first literary production. As a young journalist in 1833, he
had proposed to write a three-volume historical novel (Gabriel
Vardon, later Barnaby Rudge) in his spare time. Pickwick
intervened, and his "novels" turned out to be serial prose
fictions which were only transformed into literary commodities
when bound between cloth covers at the close of their serial
runs. The year 1841 is significant because it marks the end
of Dickens's initial fame and the beginning of the realization
by both Dickens and his reviewers that the serial phenomenon
of publishing and reviewing associated with the "Pickwick
periodicals" had not only made him famous but also altered the
genre of the novel--something to which Pickwick originally
bore no relation.

The periodical publishing of the 1830s is connected to
the creation of a novel form that is topically oriented (or
what we have come to call "Victorian") in a number of ways.
Dickens not only produced his work in serial form but was
continually reviewed by his journalistic peers and colleagues
in serials on a daily, weekly, and monthly basis. He often
knew his reviewers and replied to them in the prefaces he
appended to his works at the end of their serial runs. The
chronologically oriented organization in this bibliography
attempts to recreate that ongoing literary discussion. The
collection of periodicals and articles here is long but
nonetheless selective. The Waterloo Directory of Victorian
Periodicals, the most comprehensive list of nineteenth-century
periodicals we have, indicates the existence of over 30,000
titles between the years of 1824 and 1900; this is
acknowledged to be but a fraction of the real number. The
listing in the New Cambridge Bibliography of English
Literature, an earlier effort in serials bibliography, offers
fewer titles but greater detail. Both these reference works,
along with the Wellesley Index, have been fundamental to my
research.

In choosing among periodicals to consult for reviews of Dickens's work between the years of 1833 and 1841, however, I began with the Key Serials Project published in the Victorian Periodicals Review in Fall 1980, which lists 426 serials selected for their significance to the period by various scholars in the field of Victorian studies; it is hoped that eventually the Project will produce detailed analytic bibliographical descriptions of these "key" serials and a manual of the procedure for uniform periodical description. After eliminating provincial newspapers and those publications whose dates fell outside the period under study, I found it necessary to look at approximately 120 periodicals. A list of these titles is provided at the end, of this volume and includes their NCBEL column numbers and Waterloo Directory reference numbers. Readers will notice that there are a number of serials for which no reviews are noted. These serials do not feature reviewing, and I have thought it important for purposes of bibliographic description to indicate this fact about them, and to show that in such cases the issues for the years studied have been checked. What has turned out to be more surprising is the number of specialized journals (for example, the Mark Lane Express, an agricultural journal) which did take generous and regular notice of an anonymous cockney sketch writer.

The bibliography is divided into three parts. The first is a chronological listing of the periodical criticism, which begins with an overview of such criticism from 1814 to 1841, and then, concentrates on those reviews, excerpts, and essays that deal directly with Dickens for the years 1833 to 1841. The next section gives the reviews of Dickens according to the titles of his works. The third and final section gives detailed information about the volumes and issues canvassed and any specifically pertinent facts about the nature of each periodical and its reviewing. I have also appended a bibliography of critical works. Readers are referred to such standard reference works as the Wellesley Index, the Waterloo Directory, and British Literary Magazines for further information.

The chronological arrangement of reviews, both of Dickens and others, forms the core of this study. Some readers may quarrel with the decision to include all the notices from newspapers, which are often little more than excerpts with a few mindless effusions appended. One finds these again and again, under the headings of "Literature," "The Magazines" or "Magazine Day," and "Notices of New Publications." Lower still in the critical canon are those

columns headed "Miscellaneous" and "Varieties," which treat
Dickens's work essentially as convenient filler. As Fraser's
Magazine justly says, "No author can...count on being reviewed
in the newspapers; because, generally speaking, they only
resort to the practice in particular cases, in order to fill
up their pages when parliament is not sitting" ("On the
Present State of Literary Criticism in England" [FM 21 no 121
Feb 1840: 199]). Fraser's notes that such inclusions often
depend on an author's politics and friendships. Two papers
are cited as exceptions to this rule, the Sun and the Morning
Advertiser, and this is confirmed by my own research; the Sun,
in particular, gives full and fair-minded reviews that are
often better than those found in the magazines. I have paid
special attention to the Sun critic, because there is reason
to believe that Dickens himself did so.

In the other cases, I decided to pay attention to the
"filler," because the phenomenon of Dickens's excerptibility
becomes a major point of discussion in the serious reviews of
his work. Critics of the day recognized that his mode of
publication and its reception were creating significant
changes in the form of the novel itself. The beginnings of
the Victorian novel, perhaps best dated from the years 1847-
48 (Vanity Fair, Jane Eyre, Wuthering Heights, Mary Barton
and Dombey and Son), are to be found in the expectations set
up by these humble paragraphs from Pickwick and Nickleby. One
is reminded of Fraser's grumbling in the article quoted above
from February 1840, that there are no serious belle-
lettristical works published any more in England like those
in the French and German literatures; the English seem to have
become "a mere novel and romance-reading people," or more
specifically, "a people only reading monthly scraps of the
Nickleby school." Even as late as 1840, Fraser's evidently
did not count Dickens's work as "Literature," and much as this
bibliography relies on Fraser's inimitable criticism, it is
also a record of all the unlikely ways in which Dickens's
writing came to be part of the literary canon.

Format

The first number following the name of the periodical refers to the volume, if there is one; "ns" denotes a new series. This is followed by the number ("no"; numbers = "nos") of the issue, and the date (day/month/year). The months of the year are abbreviated into the first three letters, except for June, which is written as "Jne," to avoid any confusion with "Jan" for January. Quarterlies, monthlies, and weeklies with continuous page numbering, have a page number after the colon. Daily newspapers and some weeklies usually had eight pages, unnumbered. Excerpts, especially when under their own headings, could appear anywhere in the columns of the paper.

I have generally tried to follow each entry with some indication of its topic, if this is not apparent from the heading. In the "Overview," this consists of a few words in parentheses, followed by the name of the writer, if known, in square brackets. In the second section, which consists predominantly of reviews of Dickens's works, each entry ends with an abbreviation referring to the work being reviewed or excerpted. These are:

MM – the Monthly Magazine.
      The early entries denote general comments upon the magazine; later, the entries refer specifically to Dickens's tales, although usually there are also passing comments on the magazine's other contents. Dickens had nine tales in the magazine between December 1833 and February 1835. They are:

Dec 1833: "A Dinner at Poplar Walk"
Jan 1834: "Mrs. Joseph Porter 'over the way'"
Feb 1834: "Horatio Sparkins"
Apr 1834: "The Bloomsbury Christening"
May 1834: "The Boarding House"
Aug 1834: "The Boarding House. No. II"
Oct 1834: "The Steam Excursion"
Jan 1835: "Passage in the Life of Mr. Watkins Tottle. Chapter the First"
Feb 1835: "Passage in the Life of Mr. Watkins Tottle. Chapter the Second"

SB - <u>Sketches by Boz</u>.
This refers to the sketches in their collected form.
Dickens's various newspaper sketches appeared originally
in:

<u>Bell's Weekly Magazine</u> (7 Jne 1834)

<u>Morning Chronicle</u>   Street Sketches. Nos I-V.

(26 Sep; 10, 23 Oct; 5 Nov;
15 Dec 1834)

<u>Evening Chronicle</u>   Sketches of London. Nos I-XX.

(31 Jan; 7, 19, 28 Feb; 7, 17
Mar; 7, 11, 16, 23 Apr; 9, 19
May; 6, 18, 30 Jne; 14, 21, 28
Jul; 11, 20 Aug 1835)

<u>Bell's Life in London</u> Scenes and Characters. Nos
I-XII.

(27 Sep; 4, 11, 18, 25 Oct;
1, 22, 29 Nov; 13, 27 Dec 1835;
3, 17 Jan 1836)

<u>Library of Fiction</u>   (Apr; Jne 1836)

<u>Carlton Chronicle</u>   (6 Aug 1836)

<u>Morning Chronicle</u>   Sketches by Boz. New Series.

(18 Mar 1836);Nos I-IV   (24
Sep; 4, 11, 26 Oct 1836)

A few other sketches appeared for the first time with
the publication of the collected <u>Sketches by Boz</u> by John
Macrone (established 1834). The First Series was published

February 1836; the Second Series, December 1836. It was not
customary for sketches in newspapers to be reviewed; I have
not found any reviews of the "Sketches" except as they appear
in magazines or in volume form. The longest silence about
Dickens's work comes during those months when he is publishing
the "Street Sketches," "Sketches of London," and "Scenes and
Characters" in the Morning Chronicle, Evening Chronicle, and
Bell's Life in London, respectively (September 1834–January
1836); this is broken only by the reviews of the Monthly
Magazine tales published in October 1834, and January and
February 1835.

PP - Pickwick Papers.
        Parts I–XX, published from April 1836 to November 1837,
        with a break in June 1837 (death of Mary Hogarth,
        Dickens's sister-in-law). Published as a single volume
        on 17 November 1837. Publisher: Chapman and Hall
        (established 1831).

SUTH - Sunday Under Three Heads.
        Published June 1836, by Chapman and Hall.

SG - The Strange Gentleman.
        Burletta at St. James's Theatre. Opened 29 September
        1836. Selected reviews.

VC - The Village Coquettes.
        Burletta at St. James's Theatre. Opened 6 December 1836.
        Selected reviews.

ISHW - Is She His Wife?
        Burletta at St. James's Theatre. Opened 3 March 1837.
        Selected reviews.

BM - <u>Bentley's Miscellany</u>.
Dickens signed a contract with Richard Bentley
(established 1829 in partnership with Henry Colburn;
in business on his own after 1832) to edit the magazine
in August 1836; it began publication in January 1837.
From February 1837, entries under this heading include
the monthly instalments of "Oliver Twist" (not published
June [death of Mary Hogarth], October 1837 or September
1838 [disputes with Bentley]). After a number of
quarrels with Bentley, Dickens resigned as editor of
the <u>Miscellany</u> in January 1839; W. H. Ainsworth became
the new editor, and his sensationalistic serial "Jack
Sheppard" became the magazine's leading article. Seen
as another "Newgate novel," it was strongly associated
with "Oliver Twist," which continued alongside, even
after publication in volume form in November 1838, with
its last instalment appearing in April 1839. Dickens
published other articles in the issues for January and
October 1837, and September 1838 ("The Mudfog
Association").

SYG - <u>Sketches of Young Gentlemen</u>.
Published anonymously 10 February 1838, by Chapman and
Hall.

MJG - <u>Memoirs of Joseph Grimaldi</u>.
Edited, with an introduction by Dickens. Published 26
February 1838, by Bentley.

NN - <u>Nicholas Nickleby</u>.
Parts I-XX, published from April 1838 to October 1839.
Published as a single volume on 23 October 1839, by
Chapman and Hall.

OT   -   <u>Oliver Twist</u>.
Published in three volumes on 9 November 1838. Second edition published 17 December 1838, by Bentley. "Third edition," the first with a preface, published 15 May 1841, by Chapman and Hall.

SYC -   <u>Sketches of Young Couples</u>.
Published anonymously 10 February 1840, by Chapman and Hall.

MHC -   <u>Master Humphrey's Clock</u>.
Dickens agreed to "edit" a new miscellany, this time for Chapman and Hall, on 31 March 1840; publication began on 4 April 1840, and continued weekly thereafter. From 25 April 1840 to 6 February 1841, entries under this heading refer to the instalments of "The Old Curiosity Shop." "Barnaby Rudge" appeared from 13 February to 27 November 1841; its last instalment concluded the publication of <u>Master Humphrey's Clock</u>. The two novels were published, each in one volume, on 15 December 1841; the serial as a whole had already been published in three volumes at intervals (15 October; 12 or 15 April; and 15 December 1841).

PNP -   <u>Pic Nic Papers</u>.
Edited by Dickens, as part of a charitable effort to raise money for the widow of John Macrone, his first publisher. Published in three volumes on 9 August 1841, by Henry Colburn.

I. CHRONOLOGICAL LIST OF REVIEWS

A. Overview of English Literature   1814-1841

"Waverley: or, 'tis Sixty Years Since" Quarterly Review 11
      no 22 Jul 1814: 354-77 [J.W. Croker]

"Thoughts on Novel Writing" Blackwood's Magazine 4 no 22 Jan
      1819: 394-96   [J.G. Lockhart]

"On Critics and Criticism" Blackwood's Magazine 8 no 44 Nov
      1820: 138-41   [David Moir, prob.]

"Melmoth the Wanderer"   Blackwood's Magazine 8 no 44   Nov
      1820: 161-68 (review - Melmoth the Wanderer by Charles
      Maturin)

"Periodical Literature" Westminster Review 1 no 1 Jan 1824:
      206-49 [James Mill]

"On the Reciprocal Influence of the Periodical Publications
      and the Intellectual Progress of this Country"
      Blackwood's Magazine 16 no 94 Nov 1824: 518-28 [William
      Stevenson]

"Lives of the Novelists" Quarterly Review 34 no 68 Sep 1826:
      349-78   (review - Sir Walter Scott, Lives of the
      Novelists) [J.G. Lockhart]

"Characteristics of the Present State of English Literature"
      Athenaeum no 1   2 Jan 1828: 1-2

"Periodical Criticism" Athenaeum no 1 2 Jan 1828: 10-12 (re
      the Quarterly Review's remarks on the novel)

"The Drama" Athenaeum no 1   2 Jan 1828: 12-14

"Sketches of Contemporary Authors"
      Athenaeum no 3   16 Jan 1828: 33   General Remarks (I)
      no 4   23 Jan 1828: 49-50   Francis Jeffrey (II)
      no 5   29 Jan 1828: 65-66   Robert Southey (III)
      no 7   12 Feb 1828: 97-99   William Cobbett (IV)
      no 8   19 Feb 1828: 112-15   William Wordsworth (V)
      no 9   22 Feb 1828: 129-30   Thomas Moore (VI)
      no 11   29 Feb 1828: 161-63   Henry Brougham (VII)
      no 13   7 Mar 1828: 193-94   Percy Bysshe Shelley(VIII)

```
no 14  11 Mar 1828:  217-19  Sir Walter Scott (IX)
no 16  18 Mar 1828:  249-50  James Mackintosh (X)
no 19  28 Mar 1828:  289-91  Maria Edgeworth (XI)
no 23   8 Apr 1828:  351-52  Lord Byron (XII)
no 34  18 Jne 1828:  527-29  James Mill (XIII)
no 40  30 Jul 1828:  623-24  George Crabbe (XIV)
```

"Unpublished Lectures on Periodical Literature"
    Athenaeum no 18 25 Mar 1828: 273-75 (I)
```
      no 20   1 Apr 1828:  305-07  (II)
      no 22   8 Apr 1828:  335-37  (III)
      no 24  15 Apr 1828:  367-69  (IV)
      no 26  23 Apr 1828:  399-400  (V)
      no 28   7 May 1828:  431-32  (VI)
```
    [the Rev. Henry Stebbing]

"On Female Authorship" Athenaeum no 42 13 Aug 1828: 655-56

"The English Periodical Press" Athenaeum no 44 27 Aug 1828:
    695-96 [Theodore Elbert]

"Hallam's Constitutional History" Edinburgh Review 45 no 95
    Sep 1828: 96-169 (remarks on parliamentary reporting)
    [Thomas Babington Macaulay]

"Mr.Colburn's List" Athenaeum no 47 17 Sep 1828: 735-36

"A New-Year-Day's Dream" Athenaeum no 62 31 Dec 1828: 973-
    75 (state of literature in 1828)

"Pelham: The Disowned" Westminster Review 10 no 19 Jan 1829:
    173-91 (review - Pelham by Edward Lytton Bulwer;
    comments on contemporary taste)

"Newspaper Press" Westminster Review 10 no 19 Jan 1829: 216-
    37 (useful account of contemporary press) [Gibbons
    Merle]

"Journals and Reviews" London Review 1 no 1 Feb 1829: 1-9

"Sir Walter Scott's Novels" London Review 1 no 1 Feb 1829:
    11-14

"Weekly Newspapers" Westminster Review 10 no 20 Apr 1829:
    466-80 [Gibbons Merle]

"Noctes Ambrosianae - No. XLII" Blackwood's Magazine 25 no
153 Apr 1829: 525-48 (the contemporary periodical
press) [John Wilson]

"Signs of the Times" Edinburgh Review 49 no 98 Jne 1829:
439-59 [Thomas Carlyle]

"Our 'Confession of Faith'" Fraser's Magazine 1 no 1 Feb
1830: 1-8 (opening editorial; definition of periodical
literature) [William Maginn]

"Dramatic Taste" Fraser's Magazine 1 no 1 Feb 1830: 125-28
(decline of the drama)

"Lawrie Todd" Fraser's Magazine 1 no 2 Mar 1830: 236-42
(review - Lawrie Todd by John Galt)

"Fashionable Novels" Fraser's Magazine 1 no 3 Apr 1830: 318-
35 (review - The Dominie's Legacy by Andrew Picken)
[William Maginn, perhaps with J.A. Heraud]

"Mr.Edward Lytton Bulwer's Novels; and Remarks on Novel-
Writing" Fraser's Magazine 1 no 5 Jne 1830: 509-32
[William Maginn with J.A. Heraud]

"Literary Recollections" Athenaeum no 146 14 Aug 1830: 497
(review - Literary Recollections by the Rev. Richard
Warner; the end of literary anonymity)

"Galt's Life of Byron" Athenaeum no 149 4 Sep 1830: 552-55
(review - Colburn and Bentley's National Library series)

"Galt's Life of Byron" Edinburgh Review 52 no 53 Oct 1830:
228-30 (review - Colburn and Bentley's National Library
series) [Henry Brougham]

"Place-Men, Parliament-Men, Penny-a-Liners, and Parliamentary
Reporters" Fraser's Magazine 2 no 9 Oct 1830: 282-94
[William Maginn, perhaps with J.A. Heraud]

"Galt's Life of Byron" Fraser's Magazine 2 no 9 Oct 1830:
347-70 (review - Colburn and Bentley's National Library
series) [J.A. Heraud and William Maginn prob.]

"The Sock and the Buskin" Fraser's Magazine 2 no 10 Nov
1830: 458-66 (state of the drama)

"The Annuals" Fraser's Magazine 2 no 11 Dec 1830: 543-54

"Gleig's History of the Bible" Athenaeum no 174 26 Feb 1831:
    129 (review - Colburn and Bentley's National Library
    series)

"The Novels of the Season" Fraser's Magazine 3 no 13 Feb
    1831: 95-113 [William Maginn]

"The Metropolitan: A 'Prospect'-Ive Puff of a New Periodical"
    Fraser's Magazine 3 no 16 May 1831: 493-95 [William
    Maginn?]

"Autobiography of Edward Lytton Bulwer, Esq." Fraser's
    Magazine 3 no 18 Jul 1831: 713-19 [William Maginn?]

"The Novels of the Season - Batch the Second" Fraser's
    Magazine 4 no 19 Aug 1831: 8-25 [William Maginn]

"Influence of the Newspapers" Fraser's Magazine 4 no 20 Sep
    1831: 127-42; continued in 4 no 21 Oct 1831: 310-21

"Our Weekly Gossip" Athenaeum no 207 15 Oct 1831: 666-67
    (depression in literary affairs during Reform crisis)

"Our Weekly Gossip" Athenaeum no 208 22 Oct 1831: 692
    (depression in literary affairs during Reform crisis)

"Our Weekly Gossip" Athenaeum no 212 19 Nov 1831: 755
    (depression in literary affairs during Reform crisis)

"Epistles to the Literati - No I to E.L. Bulwer" Fraser's
    Magazine 4 no 23 Dec 1831: 520-28 (Edward Lytton
    Bulwer) [William Maginn, prob.]

"Progress of Misgovernment" Quarterly Review 46 no 92 Jan
    1832: 544-622 (effect of Reform agitation on book
    trade) [John Fullarton]

"Maritime Romances, and Parliamentary Novels" Fraser's
    Magazine 4 no 24 Jan 1832: 661-71

"Our Weekly Gossip" Athenaeum no 220 14 Jan 1832: 34-35
    (crisis in the book trade)

"Our Weekly Gossip" Athenaeum no 221 21 Jan 1832: 50 (crisis in the book trade)

"Historical Romance No. I: Sir Walter Scott and His Imitators" Fraser's Magazine 5 no 25 Feb 1832: 6-19 [J.A. Heraud, prob.]

"Our Weekly Gossip" Athenaeum no 223 4 Feb 1832: 82-83 (crisis in the book trade)

"Historical Romance No. II: Sir Walter Scott and His Imitators" Fraser's Magazine 5 no 26 Mar 1832: 207-17 [J.A. Heraud, prob.]

"Our Weekly Gossip" Athenaeum no 227 3 Mar 1832: 146 (the magazines)

"Our Weekly Gossip" Athenaeum no 231 31 Mar 1832: 210-11 (useful knowledge trend in publishing)

"The Waverley Novels" Edinburgh Review 55 no 109 Apr 1832: 61-79 [Thomas Henry Lister]

"The Puffing System" Examiner no 1263 15 Apr 1832: 274-75 (advertising and reviewing in the book trade)

"Our Weekly Gossip" Athenaeum no 235 28 Apr 1832: 274-75 (crisis in the book trade)

"On Youthful Authorship" Athenaeum no 237 12 May 1832: 305-06

"Our Weekly Gossip" Athenaeum no 237 12 May 1832: 307 (growth of periodical literature during Reform crisis)

"Our Weekly Gossip" Athenaeum no 238 19 May 1832: 322 (paucity of imaginative works)

"Our Weekly Gossip" Athenaeum no 239 26 May 1832: 338-39 (growth of newspaper reading during Reform crisis)

"Our Weekly Gossip" Athenaeum no 241 9 Jne 1832: 371 (the magazines)

"Our Weekly Gossip" Athenaeum no 242 16 Jne 1832: 386 (revival of book trade)

"Gallery of Literary characters" Fraser's Magazine 6 no 31
      Aug 1832: 112 (Edward Lytton Bulwer) [William Maginn]

"Our Weekly Gossip" Athenaeum no 249   4 Aug 1832: 507
      (growth of periodical literature)

"Gallery of Literary Characters" Fraser's Magazine 6 no 32
      Sep 1832: 249 (Allan Cunningham) [William Maginn]

"Our Weekly Gossip" Athenaeum no 254   8 Sep 1832: 588-89
      (Leitch Ritchie's Library of Romance new fiction series)

"Gallery of Literary Characters" Fraser's Magazine 6 no 33
      Oct 1832: 313 (William Wordsworth) [William Maginn]

"Miss Edgeworth's Tales and Novels" Fraser's Magazine 6 no
      25   Nov 1832: 541-58

"Reviews: The Library of Romance: Volume I" Athenaeum no 270
      29 Dec 1832: 836-37 (review - Leitch Ritchie's Library
      of Romance new fiction series)

"Report from the Select Committee on Dramatic Literature with
      the Minutes of Evidence: Ordered by the House of Commons
      to be printed, 2nd August, 1832" Westminster Review 18
      no 35   Jan 1833: 31-43 (state of the drama)

"Du Journalisme" Westminster Review 18 no 35   Jan 1833:
      195-208   [Gibbons Merle]

"New Year's Day Address to Contributors and Readers" Fraser's
      Magazine 7 no 37 Jan 1833: 1-15 (state of periodical
      literature) [William Maginn]

"Gallery of Literary Characters" Fraser's Magazine 7 no 37
      Jan 1833: 80 (Prince de Talleyrand) [William Maginn]

"Illustrated Books" Spectator 6 no 239   26 Jan 1833: 91
      (the book trade)

"Gallery of Literary Characters" Fraser's Magazine 7 no 38
      Feb 1833: 159   (James Morier)

"Life and Genius of George Cruikshank" Monthly Magazine 15
      no 86 Feb 1833: 129-47

"The Art and Mystery of Fashionable Novel Writing" Monthly
    Magazine 15 no 86   Feb 1833: 173-76

"General Bankruptcy of Literature" Tait's Edinburgh Magazine
    2 no 11 Feb 1833: 662 (stalemate of fiction trade and
    growth of periodical literature)

"Our Weekly Gossip"   Athenaeum no 275   2 Feb 1833: 74-75
    (crisis in the book trade)

"Mr. Leigh Hunt; Mr. Banim; Mr. E.L. Bulwer: Bookselling and
    Publishing" Literary Gazette 17 no 837 2 Feb 1833: 75
    (poverty of authors)

"Sense and Sensibility" Sun no 12,607 5 Feb 1833 (Bentley's
    Standard Novels edition of Sense and Sensiblity by Jane
    Austen)

"Our Weekly Gossip" Athenaeum no 276 9 Feb 1833: 90 (growth
    of periodical literature)

"Review of New Books"   Literary Gazette 17 no 839   16 Feb
    1833: 102-03   (review - Bentley's Standard Novels
    series)

"Our Weekly Gossip" Athenaeum no 278   23 Feb 1833: 122
    (barrenness of contemporary literature)

"Gallery of Literary Characters" Fraser's Magazine 7 no 39
    Mar 1833: 267   (Countess of Blessington) [William
    Maginn]

"The Leading Newspaper Press" Cobbett's Political Register
    79 2 Mar 1833: cols. 564-70

"Our Weekly Gossip" Athenaeum no 283   30 Mar 1833: 202
    (crisis in the book trade)

"Gallery of Literary Characters" Fraser's Magazine 7 no 40
    Apr 1833: 436 (William Dunlop) [William Maginn]

"Recollections of a Chaperon" Quarterly Review 49 no 97
    Apr 1833: 228-47 (review - Recollections of a Chaperon
    by Arabella Sullivan, and other fashionable novels)
    [J.G. Lockhart]

"Progress of the People - The Periodical Press" Edinburgh
    Review 57 no 115 Apr 1833: 239-48 [Henry Brougham]

"The Magazines" Morning Post no 19,446   5 Apr 1833
    (popularity of writing for periodicals)

"The Puffing System" Examiner no 1316   21 Apr 1833: 245
    (contemporary critical standards)

"Magazine Writing" Tait's Edinburgh Magazine 3 no 14 May
    1833: 256-58

"Gallery of Literary Characters" Fraser's Magazine 7 no 41
    May 1833: 602 (Benjamin D'Israeli) [William Maginn]

"Our Weekly Gossip" Athenaeum no 288   4 May 1833: 281-82
    (the magazines)

"The Puritan's Grave, A Novel. Constance, A Novel. The
    Buccaneer, A Romance" The Times no 15,162 11 May 1833
    (status of the novel)

"Review of New Books" Literary Gazette 17 no 851   11 May
    1833: 297 (Colburn's Modern Novelists series)

"The Bondman: A Story of the Times of Wat Tyler" Bell's New
    Weekly Messenger (Reviewer) 2 no 72 12 May 1833: 37
    (review - Leitch Ritchie's Library of Romance series)

"Our Weekly Gossip" Athenaeum no 290 18 May 1833: 315 (the
    publishing of fiction)

"Gallery of Literary Characters" Fraser's Magazine 7 no 42
    Jne 1833: 706 (Thomas Carlyle) [William Maginn]

"On the Morality of Authors" Monthly Repository 7 no 77 Jne?
    1833: 305-13

"Modern Novelists and Recent Novels" New Monthly Magazine 37
    no 150 Jne 1833: 135-42

"Gallery of Literary Characters" Fraser's Magazine 8 no 43
    Jul 1833: 64 (Samuel Taylor Coleridge) [William
    Maginn]

"On Periodical Literature" Tait's Edinburgh Magazine 3 no 16
Jul 1833: 491-96

"Recollections of a Chaperon" Edinburgh Review 57 no 116 Jul
1833: 403-11 (review - Recollections of a Chaperon by
Arabella Sullivan; status of the novel)

"Our Weekly Gossip" Athenaeum no 300 27 Jul 1833: 499 (new
periodicals)

"Gallery of Literary Characters" Fraser's Magazine 8 no 44
Aug 1833: 190 (George Cruikshank) [William Maginn]

"A Collection of Literary Portraits from Fraser's Magazine"
Literary Gazette 17 no 866 24 Aug 1833: 539 (decline
of "serious" literature)

"Our Weekly Gossip" Athenaeum no 305 31 Aug 1833: 589
(current state of publishing)

"Gallery of Literary Characters" Fraser's Magazine 8 no 45
Sep 1833: 290 (David Moir) [William Maginn]

"French and English Authorship" Tait's Edinburgh Magazine 3
no 18 Sep 1833: 727-28

"Fashionable Novelism" Tait's Edinburgh Magazine 3 no 18
Sep 1833: 729-31

"Magazine Day" Sun no 12,785 2 Sep 1833 (New Monthly
Magazine)

"On Criticism" Weekly True Sun ns 2 8 Sep 1833: 9-10 [Leigh
Hunt]

"Common Novel Readers" Athenaeum no 307 14 Sep 1833: 618
(defence of the novel)

"Of the False Medium Hostile to Men of Genius" Literary
Gazette 17 no 868 7 Sep 1833: 563-65 (the calamities
of authors) [R.H. Horne]

"Of the False Medium Hostile to Men of Genius" Literary
Gazette 17 no 869 14 Sep 1833: 580-82 (the calamities
of authors) [R.H. Horne]

"Of the False Medium Hostile to Men of Genius" Literary
    Gazette 17 no 870 21 Sep 1833: 596-98 (the calamities
    of authors) [R.H. Horne]

"Gallery of Literary Characters" Fraser's Magazine 8 no 46
    Oct 1833: 433 (Letitia E. Landon) [Francis Mahony]

"Bulwer and His Book" Monthly Magazine 16 no 94 Oct 1833:
    374-82 (review - England and the English by Edward
    Lytton Bulwer)

"Chit-Chat" Metropolitan Magazine 8 no 30 Oct 1833: 123-28
    (magazine literature)

"Biographical and Critical History of the Literature of the
    Last Fifty Years" Athenaeum no 313 26 Oct 1833: 713-21
    [Allan Cunningham]

"Gallery of Literary Characters" Fraser's Magazine 8 no 47
    Nov 1833: 576 (Harriet Martineau) [William Maginn]

"Literary Reform" Dublin University Magazine 2 no 11 Nov
    1833: 530-35 (satire of contemporary authorship)

"Novel Writing" Athenaeum no 315 9 Nov 1833: 752-53

"Biographical and Critical History of the Literature of the
    Last Fifty Years"
    Athenaeum no 316 16 Nov 1833: 769-77
               no 318 30 Nov 1833: 809-15
               no 320 14 Dec 1833: 849-55
               no 322 28 Dec 1833: 890-94
               [Allan Cunningham]

"Gallery of Literary Characters" Fraser's Magazine 8 no 48
    Dec 1833: 70 (Grant Thorburn) [William Maginn]

"Notes on Periodicals" New Monthly Magazine 39 no 156 Dec
    1833: 424-31 [S.Carter Hall]

"Genius of Galt" Monthly Magazine 17 no 97 Jan 1834: 25-28
    (review - Stories of the Study by John Galt)

"Gallery of Literary Characters" Fraser's Magazine 9 no 49
    Jan 1834: 64 (Captain John Ross) [William Maginn]

"Johnstone's Edinburgh Magazine: The Cheap and Dear Periodicals" Tait's Edinburgh Magazine 4 no 22 Jan 1834: 490-500 (growth in weeklies)

"Colburn's Modern Novelists" Spectator 7 no 289 11 Jan 1834: 33 (letter to the editor)

"Spectator's Library" Spectator 7 no 289 11 Jan 1834: 38-39 (Tait's Edinburgh Magazine and cheap literature)

"Our Weekly Gossip" Athenaeum no 325 18 Jan 1834: 50 (the magazines)

"Allan Cunningham's Fifty Years" Fraser's Magazine 9 no 50 Feb 1834: 224-40 (review - "Biographical and Critical History of the Literature of the Last Fifty Years" by Allan Cunningham)

"On the Decline and Fall of the Empire of Fashion" Tait's Edinburgh Magazine ns 1 no 1 Feb 1834: 54-59

"Gallery of Literary Characters" Fraser's Magazine 9 no 50 Feb 1834: 146 (Sir Egerton Brydges) [William Maginn]

"Progress of Publication" Spectator 7 no 292 1 Feb 1834: 112 (increasing cheapness of periodicals)

"Monthly Review of Literature and Art" Monthly Magazine 17 no 99 Mar 1834: 331-32 (Bentley's Standard Novels series)

"Notes on the Newspapers" Monthly Repository ns 8 no 87 [Mar] 1834: 172-73 (social position of journalists)

"Gallery of Literary Characters" Fraser's Magazine 9 no 51 Mar 1834: 300 (Daniel O'Connell) [William Maginn]

"Gallery of Literary Characters" Fraser's Magazine 9 no 52 Apr 1834: 435 (Theodore Hook) [William Maginn]

"Literature in 1834" New Monthly Magazine 40 no 160 Apr 1834: 497-505 [S. Carter Hall]

"Address" Leigh Hunt's London Journal 1 no 1 2 Apr 1834: 1-2

"Gallery of Literary Characters" Fraser's Magazine 9 no 53
May 1834: 536 (Charles Westmacott) [William Maginn]

"Gallery of Literary Characters" Fraser's Magazine 9 no 54
Jne 1834: 644 (Leigh Hunt) [William Maginn]

"Miss Edgeworth's Helen: Mr. Morier's Ayesha" Quarterly
Review 51 no 102 Jne 1834: 481-93 (state of the novel)

"High-ways and Low-Ways; or, Ainsworth's Dictionary with Notes
by Turpin" Fraser's Magazine 9 no 54 Jne 1834: 724-38
(review - Rookwood by W.H. Ainsworth; Newgate novels)
[William Makepeace Thackeray, perhaps John Churchill]

"Dick Turpin, with a Few Words on Highwaymen" Monthly
Magazine ns 17 no 102 Jne 1834: 668-75 (review -
Rookwood by W.H. Ainsworth; Newgate novels)

"The New School of Novel-Writing" Chambers's Historical
Newspaper no 20 Jne 1834: 158-59 (silver-fork and
Newgate novels)

"Unsocial Readers of Periodicals" Leigh Hunt's London Journal
1 no 12 18 Jne 1834: 101

"Sir Egerton Brydges's Autobiography" Edinburgh Review 59
no 120 Jul 1834: 439-45 (literary men and popular
politics) [Edward Lytton Bulwer]

"Dacre: A Novel" Edinburgh Review 59 no 120 Jul 1834:
475-86 (review - Dacre by Countess Morley; the state
of the novel)

"Gallery of Literary Characters" Fraser's Magazine 10 no 55
Jul 1834: 48 (W.H. Ainsworth) [William Maginn]

"Review - Literature and Arts" Bell's Weekly Messenger no
1996 6 Jul 1834: 209 (state of periodical literature)

"Our Weekly Gossip" Athenaeum no 352 26 Jul 1834: 554
(publishing affairs)

"Notes of the Month" Monthly Magazine 18 no 104 Aug 1834:
211 (sentimentalism and the cult of useful knowledge)

"Monthly Review of Literature and Art - New Poems" Monthly
    Magazine 18 no 104 Aug 1834: 223-26

"Gallery of Literary Characters" Fraser's Magazine 10 no 56
    Aug 1834: 172   (Thomas Hill) [William Maginn]

"Poetry, and the Decline of the Poetical Genius" Dublin
    University Magazine 4 no 20 Aug 1834: 174-83 [William
    Archer Butler]

"Gallery of Literary Characters" Fraser's Magazine 10 no 57
    Sep 1834: 282 (the Rev. George Robert Gleig) [William
    Maginn]

"Gallery of Literary Characters" Fraser's Magazine 10 no 58
    Oct 1834: 463 (William Godwin) [William Maginn]

"The Annuals" Morning Herald no 19,285 [sic; shd be 16,285]
    30 Oct 1834 (fashionable literature)

"Gallery of Literary Characters" Fraser's Magazine 10 no 59
    Nov 1834: 538 (James Smith) [William Maginn]

"Of Certainty in Taste" Athenaeum no 366 2 Nov 1834: 804-07
    (discussion of aesthetics)   [Sir Charles Morgan]

"Gallery of Literary Characters" Fraser's Magazine 10 no 60
    Dec 1834: 645 (Comte d'Orsay) [William Maginn]

"Notice to the Public" Leigh Hunt's London Journal 1 no 38
    17 Dec 1834: 297 (contemporary magazines)

"Our Weekly Gossip" Athenaeum no 373   20 Dec 1834: 921
    (depression in the publishing world)

"Private History of the London Newspaper Press" Tait's
    Edinburgh Magazine 1 no 12 Supplement 1834: 788-92

"The Printing Machine" Bell's Weekly Magazine 1 (1834):
    83-84   (contemporary periodical literature)

"The True Spirit of Reform" Monthly Repository 9 no 97 Jan
    1835: 1-8

"Samuel Taylor Coleridge" Tait's Magazine ns 2 no 13 Jan
    1835: 3-10 [Thomas De Quincey]

"Gallery of Literary Characters: The Fraserians; or, The Commencement of the Year Thirty-Five" Fraser's Magazine 11 no 61 Jan 1835: 1-27 (Gallery of Literary Characters: group portrait) [William Maginn]

"Literature" John Bull 15 no 734 5 Jan 1835 (current political excitement)

"Gallery of Literary Characters" Fraser's Magazine 11 no 62 Feb 1835: 136 (Charles Lamb) [William Maginn]

"Our Weekly Gossip" Athenaeum no 383 28 Feb 1835: 169 (literature and politics)

"Gallery of Literary Characters" Fraser's Magazine 11 no 63 Mar 1835: 300 (Pierre-Jean de Béranger) [Francis Mahony]

"Last Days of Pompeii" Dublin University Magazine 5 no 27 Mar 1835: 276-93 (review - Last Days of Pompeii by Edward Lytton Bulwer)

"Our Weekly Gossip" Athenaeum no 384 7 Mar 1835: 185 (the magazines)

"Gallery of Literary Characters" Fraser's Magazine 11 no 64 Apr 1835: 404 (Jane Porter) [William Maginn]

"Aristocratic Revelations" Westminster Review 22 no 44 Apr 1835: 314-21 (fashionable novels) [Andrew Bisset]

"Literature" Courier no 13,642 24 Apr 1835 (review - Bentley's Standard Novels and Romances series)

"Our Weekly Gossip" Athenaeum no 391 25 Apr 1835: 322 (depressed state of book trade)

"Gallery of Literary Characters" Fraser's Magazine 11 no 65 May 1835: 529 (Lady Morgan) [William Maginn]

"The Pilgrims of Walsingham" Monthly Review 2 no 1 May 1835: 93-101 (review - The Pilgrims of Walsingham by Agnes Strickland; state of the novel)

"Irving's Tour on the Prairies" Dublin University Magazine 5 no 29 May 1835: 554-72 (sketch writing)

"Gallery of Literary Characters" <u>Fraser's Magazine</u> 11 no 66
   Jne 1835: 652   (Alaric Watts)   [William Maginn]

"Gallery of Literary Characters" <u>Fraser's Magazine</u> 12 no 67
   Jul 1835: 43   (Francis Egerton)   [William Maginn]

"Taxes on Knowledge" <u>British and Foreign Review</u> 1 no 1   Jul
   1835: 157-72   (Lord Brougham's speech)

"State of English Literature" <u>British and Foreign Review</u> 1
   no 1   Jul 1835: 190- 217   (review - <u>The Printing
   Machine</u>)

"Prose Fictions and their Varieties" <u>London Review</u> 1 no 2
   Jul 1835: 476-87 [Edward Lytton Bulwer]

"Gallery of Literary Characters" <u>Fraser's Magazine</u> 12 no 68
   Aug 1835: 154 (Henry O'Brien)   [Francis Mahony]

"Gallery of Literary Characters" <u>Fraser's Magazine</u> 12 no 69
   Sep 1835: 280 (Michael Thomas Sadler) [William Maginn]

"Gallery of Literary Characters" <u>Fraser's Magazine</u> 12 no 70
   Oct 1835: 430   (William Cobbett)   [William Maginn]

"Literature" <u>Courier</u> no 13,801 27 Oct 1835 (review - <u>London
   Review</u> no 3; the place of newspaper writers in society)

"Poetry and Prose"   <u>Athenaeum</u> no 418   31 Oct 1835: 817
   (utilitarianism)

"Gallery of Literary Characters" <u>Fraser's Magazine</u> 12 no 71
   Nov 1835: 540   (Earl of Mulgrave)   [Benjamin Disraeli]

"Literature" <u>John Bull</u> 15 no 777 2 Nov 1835: 350   (Colburn's
   <u>Modern Novelists</u> series)

"Old Bachelors"   <u>Leigh Hunt's London Journal and Printing
   Machine</u> 2 no 87   28 Nov 1835: 416   (Henry Colburn, the
   publisher)

"Gallery of Literary Characters" <u>Fraser's Magazine</u> 12 no 72
   Dec 1835: 650   (Robert Macnish)   [William Maginn]

"Our Weekly Gossip" <u>Athenaeum</u> no 423 5 Dec 1835: 913 (flood
   of novel publishing)

"Our Weekly Gossip" <u>Athenaeum</u> no 425   19 Dec 1835: 950-51
    (revival in literary affairs)

"Our Weekly Gossip" <u>Athenaeum</u> no 426   26 Dec 1835: 968-69
    (growth of periodical literature)

"Guizot's Course of Modern History" <u>Foreign Quarterly Review</u>
    16 no 32 Jan 1836: 407-37 (history in fiction)

"Reduction, or Abolition, of the Stamp-Duty on the Newspapers"
    <u>London and Westminster Review</u> 2 no 4   Jan 1836: 336-55
    [W.E. Hickson]

"Gallery of Literary Characters" <u>Fraser's Magazine</u> 13 no 73
    Jan 1836: 1-79 (Fraserian Report);80 (Female Fraserians)
    [William Maginn with Francis Mahony; William Maginn]

"Gallery of Literary Characters" <u>Fraser's Magazine</u> 13 no 74
    Feb 1836: 224 (Michael Faraday) [William Maginn]

"Novels of the Month" <u>Monthly Review</u> 1 no 2   Feb 1836:
    181-92   (proliferation of mediocre novels)

"The Public Journals: Historical Novels" <u>Mirror</u> 27 no 762
    6 Feb 1836: 88-89

"Gallery of Literary Characters" <u>Fraser's Magazine</u> 13 no 75
    Mar 1836: 30 (the Rev. William Lisle Bowles) [William
    Maginn]

"Gallery of Literary Characters" <u>Fraser's Magazine</u> 13 no 76
    Apr 1836: 427 (Francis Place) [William Maginn]

"French Novels" <u>Quarterly Review</u> 56 no 111 Apr 1836: 65-131
    (history of the novel) [J.W. Croker]

"The Poets of Our Age, Considered as to their Philosophic
    Tendencies" <u>London and Westminster Review</u> 3 no 1
    Apr 1836: 60-71 [William Henry Smith]

"English Literature of 1835" <u>London and Westminster Review</u>
    3 no 1 Apr 1836: 234-64 [signed R.W.]

"Gallery of Literary Characters" <u>Fraser's Magazine</u> 13 no 77
    May 1836: 568 (Sir John C. Hobhouse) [William Maginn]

"The Morning and Evening Papers" <u>Fraser's Magazine</u> 13 no 77
     May 1836: 620-31

"Spirit of Modern Publishers" <u>Monthly Repository</u> ns 10 no 113
     [May] 1836: 271-76 [R.H. Horne]

"Our Weekly Gossip on Literature and Art" <u>Athenaeum</u> no 445
     7 May 1836: 329 (the new <u>Dublin Review</u>)

"Gallery of Literary Characters" <u>Fraser's Magazine</u> 13 no 78
     Jne 1836: 718 (Mrs. S.C. Hall) [William Maginn]

"The Paper Duty and Its Influence on Literature" <u>Monthly
     Review</u> 2 no 2 Jne 1836: 276-79

"The Quarterly Review for April 1836 <u>London and Westminster
     Review</u> 3 no 2 Jul 1836: 300-10 (comparison of French
     and English novels) [Andrew Bisset]

"Gallery of Literary Characters" <u>Fraser's Magazine</u> 14 no 79
     Jul 1836: 68 (Thomas Noon Talfourd) [William Maginn]

"Reviews" <u>Athenaeum</u> no 455 16 Jul 1836: 497-99 (review -
     <u>Essays on English Literature</u> by Chateaubriand)

"Gallery of Literary Characters" <u>Fraser's Magazine</u> 14 no 80
     Aug 1836: 202 (Sir John Soane) [William Maginn]

"Mr. Grantley Berkeley and His Novel" <u>Fraser's Magazine</u> 14
     no 80   Aug 1836: 242-47   (vulgarity in literature)
     [William Maginn]

"Gallery of Literary Characters" <u>Fraser's Magazine</u> 14 no 81
     Sep 1836: 272 (Sheridan Knowles) [William Maginn]

"The Spirit of Criticism on Literature and the Fine Arts"
     <u>Constitutional and Public Ledger</u> 1 no 2 16 Sep 1836

"Gallery of Literary Characters" <u>Fraser's Magazine</u> 14 no 82
     Oct 1836: 457 (Lord Lyndhurst) [William Maginn]

"Gallery of Literary Characters" <u>Fraser's Magazine</u> 14 no 83
     Nov 1836: 595 (Edmund Lodge) [William Maginn]

"The Annuals" <u>Morning Herald</u> no 16,919 11 Nov 1836

"Gallery of Literary Characters" Fraser's Magazine 14 no 84
    Dec 1836: 720 (John Baldwin Buckstone) [William Maginn]

"Literature of the Aristocracy and the Literature of Genius"
    Dublin Review 2 no 3 Dec 1836: 111-29 (review –
    various fashionable novels)

"Mr. Bulwer, and the Lady Novelists" British and Foreign
    Review 3 no 6 Dec 1836: 477-510 (review – various
    fashionable novels)

"The Spirit of Criticism" Constitutional and Public Ledger
    1 no 88 26 Dec 1836

"Books of the Past Year" Court Magazine 10 no 1 Jan 1837:
    4-13

"England Under Seven Administrations" London and Westminster
    Review 5/27 nos 9 & 52 Apr 1837: 65-98 (review –
    England Under Seven Administrations by Albany
    Fonblanque; the social status of journalists) [J.S.
    Mill]

"Literary Gossip on Novels and Drama" Foreign Quarterly
    Review 19 no 37 Apr 1837: 51-61 (whether a novelist
    can also be a dramatist, mentions Boz)

"Germany in 1831; Sketches of Germany and the Germans"
    Quarterly Review 58 no 116 Apr 1837: 297-333
    (comparison to English authors) [Abraham Hayward]

"On Cotemporary [sic; see OED] Criticism" Court Magazine 110
    no 5 May 1837: 201-06

"National and Historical Novels" Court Magazine 10 no 6
    Jne 1837: 272-78

"Editor's Address to the Reader" Monthly Repository 1 no 127
    Jul 1837: 1-2 (Leigh Hunt)

"Newspaper Literature" Edinburgh Review 65 no 132 Jul 1837:
    196-213 (review – England Under Seven Administrations
    by Albany Fonblanque)

"To the Readers of the Constitutional" Constitutional and
    Public Ledger 1 no 249 1 Jul 1837 (last editorial)

"Shakespeare, Ben Jonson, Beaumont and Fletcher" Fraser's Magazine 16 no 95 Nov 1837: 527-36 [William Maginn]

"Confessions of Ralph Restless" New Monthly Magazine 50 no 100 Aug 1837: 473-79 (status of authorship)

"D'Israeli's Novels" Edinburgh Review 66 no 133 Oct 1837: 59-72

"The Conversazione, on the Literature of the Month" New Monthly Magazine 51 no 203 Nov 1837: 418; 427-31 (fiction-writing; cheap literature)

"Novels of the Season" Monthly Review 3 no 3 Nov 1837: 307-27 (history of taste)

"Life of Scott" London and Westminster Review 6/28 nos 12 & 55 Jan 1838: 293-45 (review - Life of Sir Walter Scott by J.G. Lockhart) [William Maginn]

"Parliamentary Patronage of Literature" Sunday Times no 805 25 Mar 1838 (cheap literature)

"Thomas Hood" London and Westminster Review 7/29 no 1 Apr 1838: 119-45

"Authors and Literary Property" Morning Advertiser no 14,677 19 Apr 1838 (letter to the editor)

"Naval Novelists" Fraser's Magazine 17 no 101 May 1838: 571-77 (novels about the Napoleonic wars)

"Lockhart's Life of Scott" Dublin University Magazine 11 no 66 Jne 1838: 667-88

"Lady Blessington's Novels" Edinburgh Review 67 no 136 Jul 1838: 349-57 (status of the novel) [Edward Lytton Bulwer (Bulwer-Lytton)]

"Southey's Poetical Works" Edinburgh Review 68 no 138 Jan 1839: 354-76 (history of taste) [Herman Merivale]

"Tales by the Author of Headlong Hall" Edinburgh Review 68 no 138 Jan 1839: 432-59 (Thomas Love Peacock) [James Spedding]

"Influence and Responsibilities of Periodical Literature"
Christian Teacher ns 1 no 1 1839: 1-20

"Our Weekly Gossip" Athenaeum no 586 19 Jan 1839: 51-52
(decline of the novel)

"Review" Athenaeum no 594 16 Mar 1839: 195-97 (review –
Richelieu, A Play, Odes by Edward Lytton Bulwer
[Bulwer-Lytton]; state of the novel)

"Literary Lionism" London and Westminster Review 32 no 2
Apr 1839: 261-81 [Harriet Martineau]

"Table-Talk No. 75" Morning Post no 21,360 19 Jne 1839
(status of the novel)

"Table-Talk No. 87" Morning Post no 21,400 26 Aug 1839
(poetry criticism)

"Literature of Childhood" London and Westminster Review 33
no 1 Oct 1839: 137-62 (against "mechanical" education)
[Mary Margaret Busk]

"De Kock's Novels" Foreign Quarterly Review 24 no 47 Oct
1839: 168-99 (comparison to Dickens)

"The Periodical Press:The Edinburgh and Other Quarterly
Reviews" Church of England Quarterly Review 6
Oct 1839: 348-83

"New Translations of the Arabian Nights" London and
Westminster Review 33 no 1 Oct 1839: 101-37 [Leigh
Hunt]

"A Newspaper Editor's Reminiscences" Fraser's Magazine 20 no
119 Nov 1839: 588- 603 [Gibbons Merle]

"The Drama" Monthly Review ns 3 no 4 Dec 1839: 457-72
(review – The Sea Captain by Edward Lytton Bulwer
[Bulwer-Lytton]; Love by Sheridan Knowles)

"The Influence of Periodical Literature on the State of the
Fine Arts" Monthly Chronicle 4 Dec 1839: 502-08

"Preface to Our Second Decade" Fraser's Magazine 21 no 121
Jan 1840: 1-31 (retrospective of 1830s) [William Maginn]

"Novel Writing and Newspaper Criticism" Monthly Chronicle 5
    Jan 1840: 33-38 [Samuel Laman Blanchard]

"Thraldom of the British Press" Monthly Chronicle 5 Feb
    1840: 138-50

"On the Present State of Literary Criticism in England"
    Fraser's Magazine 21 no 121 Feb 1840: 190-200

"Un Jeune Homme Charmant" Monthly Review 1 no 2 Feb 1840:
    178-92 (review - Un Jeune Homme Charmant by Paul de
    Kock; comparison of Paul de Kock to Dickens)

"Library Studies - Present Aspects of Poetry" Monthly
    Magazine 3 no 16 Apr 1840: 433-37 (review - Sordello
    by Robert Browning) [signed J.W.M.]

"Style" Blackwood's Edinburgh Magazine 48 no 297 Jul 1840:
    1-17 [Thomas De Quincey]

"Literature" Morning Post no 21,712 27 Aug 1840 (review -
    collected "Table-Talk" criticism)

"New Publications" Morning Herald no 18,133 20 Oct 1840
    (review - book on drama by Leigh Hunt)

"The Church and the Novelists" Church of England Quarterly
    Review 9 Jan 1841: 33-52

"Table-Talk No. 187" Morning Post no 21,832 4 Jan 1841
    (journalism)

"Specimen Leaders of a Would-Be Editor" Fraser's Magazine 23
    no 136 Apr 1841: 433-50 (the contemporary press)

"Henry Fielding" Monthly Magazine 5 no 28 Apr 1841: 412-24
    (contemporary critical standards)

"Literature and Authorship in England" Christian Remembrancer
    ns 1 no 6 Jne 1841: 432-40 (the newspaper press)

"Literature" Observer 12 Dec 1841 (review - Old St. Paul's
    by W.H. Ainsworth)

B. Reviews of Dickens's Works and Related Topics 1832-1842

1832

"A Word or Two on Modern Literature" Bell's New Weekly
   Messenger (Reviewer) 1 no 1 1 Jan 1832: 1 (growth of
   periodical literature)

"The Monthly Magazine for February" Bell's New Weekly
   Messenger (Reviewer) 1 no 7 12 Feb 1832: 28 MM

"Novels" Bell's New Weekly Messenger (Reviewer) 1 no 8
   19 Feb 1832: 29

"The Monthly Magazine for March" Bell's New Weekly Messenger
   (Reviewer) 1 no 10 4 Mar 1832: 40   MM

"Literature" True Sun no 84 9 Jne 1832   MM

"Literature" True Sun no 87 13 Jne 1832 (magazine
   literature)

"The Trade of Book Reviewing" Bell's New Weekly Messenger
   (Reviewer) 1 no 27 1 Jul 1832: 93

"A Glance at the Periodicals" True Sun no 103 2 Jul 1832
   MM

"Notice" Bell's New Weekly Messenger 1 no 31 29 Jul 1832:
   101   (re advertising and reviewing)

"The Metropolitan Magazine, for August, 1832" Bell's New
   Weekly Messenger (Reviewer) 1 no 32 5 Aug 1832: 104
   (growth of periodical literature)

"The Magazines" True Sun no 156 1 Sep 1832   MM

"Literature" True Sun no 188 9 Oct 1832   MM

"Literature" True Sun no 236 4 Dec 1832 (magazine
   literature)

1833

"The Newspapers"   Metropolitan Magazine   6 no 21   Jan 1833:
        53-66

"Ultra Radicalism" Monthly Magazine 15 no 85   Jan 1833: 28-44

"The Magazines"   True Sun no 261   2 Jan 1833   MM

"The Monthly" Bell's New Weekly Messenger (Reviewer) 2 no 54
        6 Jan 1833: 2   MM

"The Newspapers"   Metropolitan Magazine 6 no 22   Feb 1833:
        176-85

"The Monthly" Bell's New Weekly Messenger (Reviewer) 1 no 7
        7 Apr 1833: 28   MM

"The Magazines" Morning Post no 19,576 4 Sep 1833   MM

"The Magazines" Sun no 12,812 3 Oct 1833   MM

"The   Magazines"   Morning Post no 19,630   6 Nov 1833
        (Blackwood's Magazine and the system of publishing
        stories in instalments or "continuations")

"Magazine Day" Sun no 12,863 2 Dec 1833   MM

"The Monthly" Bell's New Weekly Messenger (Reviewer) 2 no 102
        8 Dec 1833: 98   MM

1834

"Magazine Day" Sun no 12,889 1 Jan 1834   MM

"The Magazines" Morning Advertiser no 13,344 3 Jan 1834 MM

"The Monthly" Bell's New Weekly Messenger (Reviewer) 3 no 106
        5 Jan 1834: 2   MM

"True Sun Daily Review" True Sun   no 585   15 Jan 1834   MM

"Magazine Day" Sun no 2915 [sic; shd be 12,915] 1 Feb 1834
        MM

"Review - Literature and Arts" <u>Bell's Weekly Messenger</u> no 1975
    10 Feb 1834: 46   MM

"The Magazines" <u>Morning Advertiser</u> no 13,379 13 Feb 1834 MM

"Magazine Day" <u>Sun</u> no 2940 [<u>sic</u>; shd be 12,940] 1 Mar 1834
    (<u>New Monthly</u>)

"Magazine Day" <u>Sun</u> no 12,966 1 Apr 1834   MM

"The Magazines" <u>Morning Advertiser</u> no 13,421 3 Apr 1834 MM

"The Monthly" <u>Bell's New Weekly Messenger</u> (<u>Reviewer</u>) 2 no 119
    6 Apr 1834: 28   MM

"Literature and Art" <u>Weekly Dispatch</u> no 1696 6 Apr 1834: 106
    MM

"The Magazines" <u>Morning Advertiser</u> no 13,446 2 May 1834 MM

"The Monthly" <u>Bell's New Weekly Messenger</u> (<u>Reviewer</u>) 3 no 123
    4 May 1834: 36   MM

"Literature and Art" <u>Weekly Dispatch</u> no 1700 4 May 1834: 142
    MM

"The Weekly Reviewer" <u>Bell's New Weekly Messenger</u> (<u>Reviewer</u>)
    3 no 127   1 Jne 1834: 43 (review - <u>Rookwood</u> by W.H.
    Ainsworth)

"Literature and Art" <u>Weekly Dispatch</u> no 1713 3 Aug 1834: 252
    MM

"Review - Literature and Arts" <u>Bell's Weekly Messenger</u> no 2000
    3 Aug 1834: 245-46   MM

"Literature" <u>Observer</u> no 2185 10 Aug 1834   MM

"Literature" <u>Sun</u> no 13,096 30 Aug 1834   (Bentley's <u>Standard
Novels</u> series)

"Literature in America" <u>Morning Advertiser</u> no 13,555 6 Sep
    1834   (American periodicals)

"The Magazines" <u>True Sun</u> no 827 1 Oct 1834   MM

"The Magazines" <u>Morning Advertiser</u> no 13,576 1 Oct 1834 MM

"Magazines" <u>Sun</u> no 13,126 4 Oct 1834   MM

"The Magazines" <u>Morning Herald</u> no 16,266 4 Oct 1834   MM

"Literature and Art" <u>Weekly Dispatch</u> no 1722 5 Oct 1834: 332
    (state of the book trade)

"Literature" <u>Observer</u> no 2198 5 Oct 1834   MM

"The Magazines" <u>Sunday Times</u> no 624 5 Oct 1834   MM

"Review - Literature and Arts" <u>Bell's Weekly Messenger</u> no 2010
    12 Oct 1834: 323   MM

1835

"Magazine Day" <u>Sun</u> no 13,202 1 Jan 1835   MM

"Literature and Art" <u>Weekly Dispatch</u> no 1735 4 Jan 1835: 8
    MM

"Review - Literature and Art" <u>Bell's Weekly Messenger</u> no 2022
    11 Jan 1835: 10   MM

"The Magazines" <u>Sun</u> no 13,230 4 Feb 1835   MM

"Reviewer" <u>Bell's New Weekly Messenger</u> 4 no 163 8 Feb 1835:
    85-86   MM

"Literature and Art" <u>Weekly Dispatch</u> no 1740 8 Feb 1835: 54
    MM

"Review - Literature and Art" <u>Bell's Weekly Messenger</u> no 2027
    15 Feb 1835: 50   MM

"Literature, &c" <u>United Services Gazette</u> no 109 7 Mar 1835
    MM

"Our Weekly Gossip" <u>Athenaeum</u> no 388 4 Apr 1835: 266
    (notice of a cockney sporting paper)

"Literature, &c" <u>United Services Gazette</u> no 115 18 Apr 1835
  (Bentley's publishing practices)

"The Library: Bentley's Library of Standard Novels and
  Romance" <u>Sun</u> no 13,296 22 Apr 1835 (reprint of notice
  from <u>Printing Machine</u>)

"Literature" <u>Observer</u> 3 May 1835   MM

"Our Weekly Gossip" <u>Athenaeum</u> no 388   4 Apr 1835: 266
  (review - cockney sporting paper in <u>Court Magazine)</u>

"Magazine Day" <u>Sun</u> no 13,460 2 Nov 1835   MM

"Periodical Literature" <u>Morning Advertiser</u> no 13,963   26 Dec
  1835

1836

"Progress of Publication" <u>Morning Advertiser</u> no 14,003 11 Feb
  1836   SB

"Literature" <u>Morning Chronicle</u> no 20,696   11 Feb 1836   SB
  [George Hogarth]

"Review of New Books" <u>Literary Gazette</u> 20 no 995 13 Feb 1836:
  102   SB

"Literature" <u>Bell's Life in London</u>   14 Feb 1836   (see MC
  11.2.1836)   SB

"Literature" <u>Sun</u> no 13,550   15 Feb 1836   SB

"The Sketches of Boz" <u>Spectator</u> 9 no 399   20 Feb 1836: 182-83
  SB

"Our Library Table" <u>Athenaeum</u> no 434   20 Feb 1836: 145   SB

"Literature" <u>Sunday Times</u> no 696   21 Feb 1836   SB

"Literary Memoranda" <u>Atlas</u> 11 no 510   21 Feb 1836: 123   SB

"Literature" <u>True Sun</u> no 1258   25 Feb 1836   SB

"The Literary Examiner" Examiner no 1456 28 Feb 1836: 132-33
    SB

"Literature and Art" Weekly Dispatch no 1793 28 Feb 1836: 78
    SB

"Notices of New Works" Metropolitan Magazine 15 no 59
    Mar 1836: 77   SB

"Sketches by 'Boz'" Monthly Review 1 no 3 Mar 1836: 350-57
    SB

"Magazines" Morning Advertiser no 14,022 4 Mar 1836   MM

"Literature" Morning Post no 20,363 12 Mar 1836   SB

"Literary Memoranda" Atlas 11 no 516 3 Apr 1836: 220   PP

"A Cabman's Description of His Horse" The Times no 16,071
    7 Apr 1836 PP

"A Cabman's Description of His Horse" Morning Advertiser
    no 14,052 8 Apr 1836   PP

"A Cabman's Description of His Horse" Morning Post no 20,386
    8 Apr 1836   PP

"A Cabman's Description of His Horse" Morning Herald no 16,735
    9 Apr 1836 PP

"Miscellaneous" Literary Gazette 20 no 1003 9 Apr 1836: 233
    PP,LF

"Notabilia: Shabby-Genteel People" Examiner no 1471 10 Apr
    1836: 234-35   SB

"Fact and Scraps - Original and Select: A Cabman's Description
    of His Horse" Weekly Dispatch no 1799 10 Apr 1836: 134
    PP

"A Cabman's Description of His Horse" Sunday Times no 703
    10 Apr 1836   PP

"Literature" Bell's Life in London 10 Apr 1836   PP, LF

"Progress of Publication" Spectator 9 no 407 16 Apr 1836: 373   PP

"New Books" Mirror 27 no 772 16 Apr 1836: 249-51   SB

"Literature and Art" Weekly Dispatch no 1800 17 Apr 1836: 146   (state of the book trade)

"Miscellaneous: A Cabman's Description of His Horse" Mark Lane Express 4 no 225 18 Apr 1836: 126   PP

"Notices of New Books" Metropolitan Magazine 16 no 61 May 1836: 15   PP,LF

"Magazine Day" Sun no 13,615 2 May 1836   PP

"The Magazines" True Sun no 1316 3 May 1836   MM

"Critical Notices" New Monthly Magazine 47 no 185 May 1836: 105   SB

"Literature of the Month" Court Magazine 8 no 5 May 1836: 227 LF

"Literature" Morning Post no 20,413 11 May 1836   PP, LF

"Notices of New Works" Metropolitan Magazine 16 no 62 Jne 1836: 46-47   PP

"The Magazines" Sun no 13,642 2 Jne 1836   PP, LF

"Literature" Morning Chronicle no 20,791 7 Jne 1836   PP

"Literature and Fine Arts" Globe no 10,478 8 Jne 1836   PP

"Reviews of New Books" Carlton Chronicle 1 11 Jne 1836: 10 PP

"Literature" John Bull 16 no 809 13 Jne 1836: 190   PP

"Notices of New Works" Metropolitan Magazine 16 no 63 Jul 1836: 76   PP

"Reviews of New Books" Carlton Chronicle no 4 2 Jul 1836: 57-58   PP

"Literature" Bell's Life in London 3 Jul 1836   SUTH

"Literature and Art" Weekly Dispatch no 1811 3 Jul 1836: 246
    SUTH

"The Magazines" Sun no 13,669 4 Jul 1836   PP

"Miscellaneous" Literary Gazette 20 no 1016 9 Jul 1836: 442
    PP

"Literary Memoranda" Atlas 11 no 531 17 Jul 1836: 457 SUTH

"Reviews of New Books" Carlton Chronicle no 6 23 Jul 1836:
    104-05   SUTH

"Notices of New Works"   Metropolitan Magazine 16 no 64
    Aug 1836: 110-11   PP,LF

"Notices of New Works"   Metropolitan Magazine 16 no 64
    Aug 1836: 111   SUTH

"Miscellany: A Contested Election" Carlton Chronicle   no 9
    6 Aug 1836: 131   PP

"Original Papers: The Literary Men of Town" Carlton Chronicle
    no 9 6 Aug 1836:141   PP

"The Quarterly Reviews" Spectator 9 no 423   6 Aug 1836:
    755-56   (the quarterly reviews)

"Literature" Bell's Life in London 7 Aug 1836   PP

"Literature" Morning Post no 20,491 10 Aug 1836   SUTH

"A Contested Election" The Times no 16,178 10 Aug 1836 PP

"A Contested Election" True Sun ns 15 10 Aug 1836   PP

"A Contested Election" Public Ledger 78 no 24,312   13 Aug
    1836   PP

"Miscellaneous" Literary Gazette 20 no 1021 13 Aug 1836: 520
    PP

"Miscellaneous: A Contested Election"   Mark Lane Express 4
    no 242 15 Aug 1836: 262   PP

"Literature" Morning Post no 20,496 16 Aug 1836   PP

"A Contested Election" Morning Chronicle no 20,843 18 Aug
    1836   PP

"Progress of Publication" Spectator 9 no 425 20 Aug 1836:
    805 PP

"Facts and Scraps, Original and Select: An Election Manoeuvre"
    Weekly Dispatch no 1818 21 Aug 1836: 310   PP

"Notices of New Works"   Metropolitan Magazine 17 no 65
    Sep 1836: 13   PP

"Critical Notices" New Monthly Magazine 48 no 189 Sep 1836:
    102-04 PP

"Magazines" Sun no 13,719 2 Sep 1836   PP

"Literary Examiner" Examiner no 1492 4 Sep 1836: 563-65
    PP

"Literature" Bell's Life in London 4 Sep 1836   PP

"Miscellaneous" Literary Gazette 20 no 1025 10 Sep 1836: 584
    PP

"Literature" John Bull 16 no 822 12 Sep 1836: 295   PP

"The Magazines" Morning Herald no 16,869 14 Sep 1836
    (Metropolitan Magazine)

"Theatricals, &c" Mark Lane Express 4 no 248 26 Sep 1836
    SG

"Newspapers" True Sun ns 57 28 Sep 1836

"Theatres" Morning Chronicle no 20,880 30 Sep 1836   SG

"St. James's Theatre" Morning Herald no 16,883 30 Sep 1836
    SG

"St. James's Theatre" Standard no 2931 30 Sep 1836   SG

"The Theatres" Courier no 14,090 30 Sep 1836   SG

"The Theatres" Globe no 10,576 30 Sep 1836   SG

"St. James's Theatre" Morning Advertiser no 14,202   30 Sep 1836 SG

"St. James's Theatre" The Times no 16,222 30 Sep 1836   SG

"The Theatres" Morning Post no 20,535 30 Sep 1836   SG

"St. James's Theatre"   Constitutional and Public Ledger 1 no 14   30 Sep 1836   SG

"Music and the Drama" Athenaeum no 466 1 Oct 1836: 708 SG

"St. James's Theatre" Morning Post no 20,536 1 Oct 1836 SG

"Theatres" Courier no 14,091 1 Oct 1836   SG

"Drama" Literary Gazette 20 no 1028 1 Oct 1836: 637 SG

"Magazine Day" Sun no 13,744 1 Oct 1836   SG

"The Theatres" Carlton Chronicle no 13 1 Oct 1836: 206 SG

"The Theatres" United Services Gazette no 191 1 Oct 1836 SG

"Particulars of Pie-Making" True Sun ns 60 1 Oct 1836 PP

"Cockney Sportsmen" St. James's Chronicle no 21,316 1 Oct 1836 PP

"Particulars of Pie-Making" The Times no 16,223 1 Oct 1836 PP

"Theatricals" Age 2 Oct 1836: 326   SG

"The Drama" Bell's Life in London 2 Oct 1836   SG

"Amusements: St. James's Theatre"   Bell's Weekly Messenger no 2111 2 Oct 1836: 314   SG

"The Theatres" Observer 2 Oct 1836   SG

"The Drama" Champion no 3 2 Oct 1836: 22   SG

"Theatricals" Atlas 11 no 542 2 Oct 1836: 631   SG

"The Winter Theatrical Campaign" Weekly Dispatch no 1824
    2 Oct 1836: 368   SG

"Theatricals" Sunday Times no 728 2 Oct 1836   SG

"The Drama" Bell's New Weekly Messenger 5 no 249 2 Oct 1836:
    634   SG

"Particulars of Pie-Making" Morning Post no 20,537 3 Oct
    1836   PP

"Magazines" Morning Chronicle no 20,884 5 Oct 1836   PP

"A Shooting Party" True Sun ns 65 7 Oct 1836   PP

"Particulars of Pie-Making"   Morning Advertiser no 14,209
    8 Oct 1836   PP

"Theatricals" Figaro in London no 253 8 Oct 1836: 167-68
    SG

"Literary Examiner" Examiner no 1497 9 Oct 1836: 647-48
    PP

"Miscellaneous: Cure for the Gout. Twopenny Rope" Mark Lane
    Express 4 no 250 10 Oct 1836   PP

"The Law" True Sun ns 72 15 Oct 1836   PP

"Varieties"   Bell's New Weekly Messenger 5 no 251   16 Oct
    1836: 667   PP

"Miscellaneous: Particulars of Pie-Making" Mark Lane Express
    4 no 251 17 Oct 1836   PP

"The Pickwick Club. Sketches. By Boz"   Morning Advertiser
    no 14,214 25 Oct 1836   PP

"St. James's Theatre" The Times no 16,246 28 Oct 1836 SG

"Notices of New Works"   Metropolitan Magazine 17 no 67
    Nov 1836: 84   PP

"Monthly Review of Literature"   Monthly Magazine   22   no 5
        Nov 1836: 522-24   PP

"Magazine Day"   Sun no 13,770   1 Nov 1836   PP

"Literary Extracts: A Quiet Tenant"   True Sun ns 87   2 Nov
        1836   PP

"Pickwickian Philosophy - Poverty and Oysters"   Morning Herald
        no 16,911   2 Nov 1836   PP

"Literary Examiner"   Examiner no 1501   6 Nov 1836: 710-11   PP

"Review of New Books: Pickwickiana"   Literary Gazette   20
        no 1034   12 Nov 1836: 727-28   PP

"Literary Extract: Paternal Advice"   True Sun ns 97   14 Nov
        1836   PP

"Facts and Scraps: A Bit of Parental Advice"   Weekly Dispatch
        no 1831   20 Nov 1836: 452   PP

"The First of September"   Sporting Magazine   2s 14   no 80
        Dec 1836: 141-47   PP

"Magazines"   Sun no 13,796   3 Dec 1836   PP

"Reviews"   Athenaeum no 475   3 Dec 1836: 841-43   PP

"Literary Examiner"   Examiner no 1505   4 Dec 1836: 775-76   PP

"Pickwick on Proposing"   Morning Post no 20,590   5 Dec 1836 PP

"St. James's Theatre"   Sun no 13,799   7 Dec 1836   VC

"Theatres: St. James's"   True Sun ns 117   7 Dec 1836   VC

"St. James's Theatre"   The Times no 16,280   7 Dec 1836   VC

"St. James's Theatre"   Morning Chronicle no 20,937   7 Dec 1836
        VC

"St. James's Theatre"   Morning Herald no 16,939   7 Dec 1836 VC

"The Stage: St. James's Theatre"   Constitutional and Public
        Ledger 1 no 72   7 Dec 1836   VC

"Fashion and Table-Talk" Globe no 10,634 7 Dec 1836   VC

"St. James's Theatre" Morning Advertiser no 14,251   7 Dec
    1836   VC

"The Theatres" Spectator 9 no 441 10 Dec 1836: 1183   VC

"Theatricals" Figaro in London no 262 10 Dec 1836: 204 VC

"Drama" Literary Gazette 20 no 1038 10 Dec 1836: 795-96 VC

"The Theatres" Carlton Chronicle no 23 10 Dec 1836: 365-66
    VC

"Theatrical Examiner" Examiner no 1506 11 Dec 1836: 791-92
    VC   [John Forster]

"Reviewer: 'Boz'"   Bell's New Weekly Messenger 5 no 259
    11 Dec 1836: 794   PP

"The Drama" Bell's New Weekly Messenger 5 no 259 11 Dec
    1836: 795   VC

"The Theatres" Observer 11 Dec 1836 VC (see BNWM 11.12.1836)

"Theatricals" Champion no 13 11 Dec 1836: 99   VC

"Amusements: St. James's Theatre" Bell's Weekly Messenger
    no 2121 11 Dec 1836: 398   VC

"Theatricals" Age 11 Dec 1836: 406   VC

"The Drama" Bell's Life in London 11 Dec 1836 VC (see
    BNWM 11.12.1836)

"Theatricals" Sunday Times no 738 11 Dec 1836   VC

"Theatricals" Mark Lane Express 4 no 259 12 Dec 1836   VC

"Music and the Drama" Athenaeum no 477 17 Dec 1836: 891
    VC

"Review of New Books" Literary Gazette 20 no 1040 24 Dec
    1836: 822-23   SB

"Spectator's Library" <u>Spectator</u> 9 no 443 26 Dec 1836:
1234-35 SB

"The Spirit of Criticism" <u>Constitutional and Public Ledger</u>
1 no 88 26 Dec 1836

"Reviews" <u>Athenaeum</u> no 479 31 Dec 1836: 916-17 SB

1837

"Notices of New Works" <u>Metropolitan Magazine</u> 18 no 69
Jan 1837: 6 PP

"Crichton" <u>Monthly Review</u> 1 no 1 Jan 1837: 53-69 (review –
<u>Crichton</u> by W.H. Ainsworth)

"Magazine Day" <u>Sun</u> no 13,821 2 Jan 1837 BM

"The Pickwick Papers – No. X" <u>Sun</u> no 13,821 2 Jan 1837 PP

"The Magazines" <u>True Sun</u> ns 141 4 Jan 1837 BM

"Bentley's Miscellany" <u>Morning Post</u> no 20,617 6 Jan 1837
PP

"The Magazines" <u>Constitutional and Public Ledger</u> 1 no 98
6 Jan 1837 BM

"Reviews of New Books" <u>Carlton Chronicle</u> no 27 7 Jan 1837:
425-27 PP,BM

"Literature" <u>Globe</u> no 10,661 7 Jan 1837 BM

"The Public Journals: Public Life of Mr. Tulrumble, once Mayor
of Mudfog" <u>Mirror</u> 29 no 815 7 Jan 1837: 13-16 BM

"Reviews" <u>Athenaeum</u> no 480 7 Jan 1837: 4-6 BM

"The Magazines for the Month" <u>Atlas</u> 12 no 556 8 Jan 1837:
28-29 BM

"Edification of Married Men" <u>Bell's New Weekly Messenger</u> 6
no 263 8 Jan 1837: 23 PP

"Progress of Publication" Morning Advertiser no 14,281 11 Jan
    1837 BM

"Reviewer" Bell's New Weekly Messenger 6 no 264 15 Jan 1837:
    38   PP

"Literature and Art" Weekly Dispatch no 1839 15 Jan 1837:
    39   BM

"A Regular Fat Man" Bell's New Weekly Messenger 6 no 264
    15 Jan 1837: 39   PP

"Miscellaneous: A Roadside Public House" Mark Lane Express
    6 no 264 16 Jan 1837   PP

"Literature" Morning Chronicle no 20,970 19 Jan 1837 BM

"Bentley's Miscellany, No. I. For January" St. James's
    Chronicle no 12,365 24 Jan 1837 BM

"Oliver Twist" Morning Post no 20,637 30 Jan 1837 BM

"Advantage of Being Born in a Workhouse" Globe no 10,680
    30 Jan 1837   BM

"A Board of Guardians of the Poor" The Times no 16,327
    31 Jan 1837   BM

"Literature" St. James's Chronicle no 12,368 31 Jan 1837
    BM

"History of a Foundling" Morning Post no 20,638 31 Jan 1837
    BM

"Notices of New Works" Metropolitan Magazine 18 no 70
    Feb 1837: 46   PP

"The Pickwick Club, &c, by Boz" Monthly Review 1 no 2 Feb
    1837: 153-63   SB,PP,BM

"The Magazines" Constitutional and Public Ledger 1 no 120
    1 Feb 1837   BM

"The Magazines" Sun no 13,848 1 Feb 1837   BM

"Oliver Twist" Morning Post no 20,640 2 Feb 1837   BM

"Magazines" United Services Gazette no 209 4 Feb 1837 PP,BM

"Review of New Books" Carlton Chronicle no 31 4 Feb 1837:
   491   PP,BM

"Literature and Art" Weekly Dispatch no 1842 5 Feb 1837: 70
   PP

"Literature" John Bull 17 no 843 5 Feb 1837: 72   BM

"Review - Literature and Arts: The Magazines" Bell's Weekly
   Messenger no 2129 5 Feb 1837: 47   BM

"Reviewer" Bell's New Weekly Messenger 6 no 268 5 Feb 1837:
   88   PP

"The Public Journals: Oliver Twist" Mirror 29 no 822 25 Feb
   1837: 125-27   BM

"Notices of New Works"   Metropolitan Magazine 18 no 71
   Mar 1837: 77   PP

"Magazines" Sun no 13,873 2 Mar 1837   BM

"Varieties: A Straightforward Witness" Courier no 14,219
   3 Mar 1837   PP

"Reviews of New Books" Carlton Chronicle no 25 4 Mar 1837:
   554-55   PP

"Reviews of New Books" Carlton Chronicle no 25 4 Mar 1837:
   555-56   BM

"Literature" John Bull 17 no 847 5 Mar 1837: 117 (monthly
   magazines)

"Reviewer" Bell's New Weekly Messenger 6 no 271 5 Mar 1837:
   154   PP

"The Periodicals" Morning Advertiser no 14,327 6 Mar 1837
   PP

"Fashion and Table Talk: A Straightforward Witness"   Globe
   no 10,710 6 Mar 1837   PP

"St. James's Theatre" Standard no 3066 7 Mar 1837   ISHW

"The Pickwick Valentine" <u>Morning Herald</u> no 17,019 7 Mar 1837
    PP

"St. James's Theatre" <u>Morning Herald</u> no 17,019 7 Mar 1837
    ISHW

"The Theatres" <u>Morning Post</u> no 20,668 7 Mar 1837 ISHW

"St. James's Theatre" <u>Morning Chronicle</u> no 21,005 7 Mar 1837
    ISHW

"St. James's Theatre" <u>The Times</u> no 16,358 8 Mar 1837
    ISHW

"The Magazines" <u>Morning Post</u> no 20,669 8 Mar 1837 BM

"St. James's" <u>Literary Gazette</u> 21 no 1051 11 Mar 1837: 164
    ISHW

"New Books: The Pickwick Papers. By Boz" <u>Mirror</u> 29 no 824
    11 Mar 1837: 153-55 PP

"Theatricals" <u>Champion</u> no 26 12 Mar 1837: 205 ISHW

"The Literary Examiner" <u>Examiner</u> no 1519 12 Mar 1837:
    165-66 BM [John Forster]

"Literature and Art" <u>Weekly Dispatch</u> no 1847 12 Mar 1837:
    130 BM

"The Drama" <u>Bell's New Weekly Messenger</u> 6 no 272 12 Mar
    1837: 171 ISHW

"Theatricals" <u>Sunday Times</u> no 751 12 Mar 1837 ISHW

"The Theatres: St. James's" <u>Observer</u> 12 Mar 1837 ISHW

"The Drama: St. James's" <u>Bell's Life in London</u> 12 Mar 1837
    ISHW

"Theatricals" <u>Mark Lane Express</u> 6 no 272 13 Mar 1837 ISHW

"Theatres" <u>Magnet</u> 1 no 1 13 Mar 1837 ISHW

"The Public Journals: The Pantomime of Life - By Boz" <u>Mirror</u>
    29 no 825 18 Mar 1837: 170-71 BM

"Theatricals" <u>Figaro in London</u> no 276   18 Mar 1837: 44
    ISHW

"The Theatres" <u>Carlton Chronicle</u> 37   18 Mar 1837: 589
    ISHW

"Literary Extracts: A Straightforward Witness" <u>True Sun</u>
    ns 206 24 Mar 1837   PP

"Posthumous Papers of the Pickwick Club" <u>Eclectic Review</u> 1
    Apr 1837: 339-55   PP

"Recent English Romances" <u>Edinburgh Review</u> 65   no 131
    Apr 1837: 180-204 (review - <u>Attila</u> by G.P.R. James;
    <u>Rookwood</u>, <u>Crichton</u> by W.H. Ainsworth)

"Notices of New Works" <u>Metropolitan Magazine</u> 18 no 72
    Apr 1837: 106-07   PP

"Some Thoughts on Arch-Waggery, and, In Especial, on the
    Genius of 'Boz'" <u>Court Magazine</u> 10 no 4   Apr 1837:
    185-87

"Magazine Day" <u>Sun</u> no 13,900 1 Apr 1837   PP,BM

"Progress of Publication" <u>Morning Advertiser</u> no 14,350 1 Apr
    1837   PP

"A Footman's Resignation" <u>Morning Herald</u> no 17,031 1 Apr
    1837   PP

"Reviews of New Books" <u>Carlton Chronicle</u> no 39 1 Apr 1837:
    615-17   PP

"Reviewer" <u>Bell's New Weekly Messenger</u> 6 no 275 2 Apr 1837:
    218   PP

"Literary Memoranda" <u>Atlas</u> 12 no 568 2 Apr 1837: 217   SB

"Extracts from New Books: The Consequences of Not Keeping
    Awake. By 'Boz'" <u>Magnet</u> 1 no 4 3 Apr 1837: 26-27   PP

"Literature" <u>St. James's Chronicle</u> no 12,395 4 Apr 1837 BM

"Reviews of New Books" <u>Carlton Chronicle</u> no 40 8 Apr 1837:
    635-36   BM

"The Peregrinations of Pickwick" Literary Gazette 21 no 1055
    8 Apr 1837: 228   PP

"Literature and Art" Weekly Dispatch no 1851   9 Apr 1837: 178
    SB

"Literature" John Bull 17 no 852 9 Apr 1837: 76   BM

"Review - Literature and Arts" Bell's Weekly Messenger no 2138
    9 Apr 1837: 119   PP

"Literature" Sunday Times no 757 23 Apr 1837   SB

"Fashion and Table-Talk: How to Get On. A Young London Thief"
    Globe no 10,756 28 Apr 1837   PP,BM

"The Magazines" Carlton Chronicle no 43 29 Apr 1837: 683-84
    PP

"The Pickwick Papers" Chambers's Edinburgh Journal 6 no 274
    29 Apr 1837: 109-10   PP

"The Public Journals: Oliver Twist an Undertaker's Boy-Mute"
    Mirror 29 no 831   29 Apr 1837: 526 [sic;shd be 265]-
    66   BM

"How to Get On. The Apothecary Method" Observer 30 Apr 1837
    PP

"Literature" Bell's Life in London 30 Apr 1837   PP

"Notices of New Works" Metropolitan Magazine 19 no 73
    May 1837: 16   PP

"Magazine Day" Sun no 13,925 1 May 1837   BM

"Progress of Publication" Morning Advertiser no 14,375 1 May
    1837   PP

"Miscellaneous: How to Get On" Mark Lane Express 6 no 279
    1 May 1837   PP

"The Magazines" True Sun ns 240 4 May 1837   BM

"The Literary Fund" The Times no 16,407 4 May 1837

"Literary Fund Society" <u>Morning Chronicle</u> no 21,054 4 May
      1837

"Reviews of New Books" <u>Carlton Chronicle</u> no 44 6 May 1837:
      698-99   BM

"Literature and Art" <u>Weekly Dispatch</u> no 1855 7 May 1837: 226
      BM

"Literature" <u>John Bull</u> 17 no 856 7 May 1837: 224   PP

"Reviewer" <u>Bell's New Weekly Messenger</u> 6 no 280 7 May 1837:
      297-98   PP

"Fashions Among Footmen" <u>Courier</u> no 14,278 11 May 1837 PP

"Sensibility of a Young Pauper" <u>Constitutional and Public
      Ledger</u> 1 no 206 12 May 1837 BM

"A Footman's Resignation" <u>Constitutional and Public Ledger</u>
      1 no 210 17 May 1837   PP

"The Public Journals: Oliver Twist 'Runs Away'" <u>Mirror</u> 29
      no 834 20 May 1837: 313-15   BM

"Literature" <u>Observer</u> 4 Jne 1837   BM

"The Works of Dickens" <u>London and Westminster Review</u> 5/27
      nos 10 & 53   Jul 1837: 194-215   SB,PP,BM
      [Charles Buller]

"Magazine Day" <u>Sun</u> no 13,978 1 Jul 1837   BM

"The Pickwick Papers" <u>Sun</u> no 13,978 1 Jul 1837   PP

"A Scene in the Fleet" <u>Courier</u> no 14,322 1 Jul 1837   PP

"The Literary Examiner" <u>Examiner</u> no 1535 2 Jul 1837: 421-22
      PP   [John Forster]

"Literature: The Magazines" <u>Observer</u> 2 Jul 1837   BM

"Reviewer" <u>Bell's New Weekly Messenger</u> 6 no 288 2 Jul 1837:
      426   PP

"Literature" <u>Bell's Life in London</u> 2 Jul 1837   BM

"Scraps by Boz" <u>Magnet</u> 1 no 17   3 Jul 1837: 133   PP

"The Public Journals: The Prisoner at Large" <u>Mirror</u> 30 no 843
      8 Jul 1837: 27-28   PP

"Literature and Art" <u>Weekly Dispatch</u> no 1864 9 Jul 1837: 334
      BM

"Literary Memoranda" <u>Atlas</u> 12 no 582   9 Jul 1837: 441   BM

"Review - Literature and Arts" <u>Bell's Weekly Messenger</u> no 2151
      9 Jul 1837: 222   BM

"Bentley's Miscellany for June" <u>Mark Lane Express</u> 6 no 289
      10 Jul 1837   BM

"Literature and Art" <u>Weekly Dispatch</u> no 1865   16 Jul 1837:
      346   BM

"Modern Justice - A Sketch from Life" <u>Sunday Times</u> no 769
      16 Jul 1837   BM

"The Public Journals: The Insolvent Debtors' Court" <u>Mirror</u>
      30 no 845   22 Jul 1837: 62-63   PP

"Fashion and Table-Talk: A Street Sketch by Boz"   <u>Globe</u>
      no 10,829   22 Jul 1837   BM

"Facts and Scraps: Imprisonment for Debt"   <u>Weekly Dispatch</u>
      no 1866 23 Jul 1837: 356   PP

"The Public Journals. Oliver Twist and the Pickpockets"
      <u>Mirror</u> 30 no 846   29 Jul 1837: 74-76   BM

"Magazine Day" <u>Sun</u> no 14,004 1 Aug 1837   BM

"Magazines" <u>Sun</u> no 14,005 2 Aug 1837   PP

"Fashion and Table-Talk: The Doctor and the Patient" <u>Globe</u>
      no 10,891 5 Aug 1837   BM

"Literature and Art" <u>Weekly Dispatch</u> no 1868 6 Aug 1837: 382
      (re <u>New Monthly Magazine</u> on practice of continuations)

"Literary Memoranda" <u>Atlas</u> 12 no 586 6 Aug 1837: 505   BM

"Review - Literature and Arts: The Magazines of the Month"
    Bell's Weekly Messenger no 2155 6 Aug 1837: 251   BM

"Reviewer" Bell's New Weekly Messenger 7 no 293 6 Aug 1837:
    35   PP

"Sketches by Boz" Magnet 1 no 22 7 Aug 1837: 171   PP

"The Doctor and the Patient" Observer 7 Aug 1837   BM

"Literature - The Magazines" Observer 13 Aug 1837   BM

"Literature and Art" Weekly Dispatch no 1869 13 Aug 1837:
    394   BM

"Miscellaneous" Mark Lane Express 6 no 294 14 Aug 1837 PP

"New Books: Pickwickiana" Mirror 30 no 850   26 Aug 1837:
    143-44   PP

"Magazine Day" Sun no 14,031 1 Sep 1837   BM

"A Sam Wellerism" Morning Advertiser no 14,480 1 Sep 1837
    PP

"Fashion and Varieties" Courier no 14,375 1 Sep 1837   PP

"Fashion and Varieties: Oliver Twist Again with Thieves"
    Courier no 14,375 1 Sep 1837   BM

"A Glance at the Magazines" Spectator 10 no 479 2 Sep 1837:
    835   BM

"Literature - The Magazines" Morning Chronicle no 21,156
    2 Sep 1837   BM

"Notes of a Reader: Pickwickiana" Mirror 30 no 851   2 Sep
    1837: 156-58 PP

"Literature and Art" Weekly Dispatch no 1872 3 Sep 1837: 430
    BM

"Literary Memoranda" Atlas 12 no 590 3 Sep 1837: 569   BM

"Literature - The Magazines" Observer 3 Sep 1837   PP,BM

"Reviewer" Bell's New Weekly Messenger 7 no 297 3 Sep 1837:
      67   PP

"Literature" Bell's Life in London 3 Sep 1837   PP

"Illustrations: Old Weller" Figaro in London 6 no 301 9 Sep
      1837: 141-42   PP

"The Literary Examiner"   Examiner no 1545   10 Sep 1837:
      581-82   BM   [John Forster]

"Fashion and Table-Talk: Eating in Scotland" Globe no 10,922
      12 Sep 1837   PP

"Literature" St. James's Chronicle no 12,934   12 Sep 1837

"The Gatherer: A Sketch" Mirror 30 no 853   16 Sep 1837: 192
      PP

"Miscellaneous" Mark Lane Express 6 no 299   18 Sep 1837 PP

"The Pickwick Papers" Quarterly Review 59 no 118   Oct 1837:
      484-518   SB,PP   [Abraham Hayward]

"Works of Theodore Hook" London and Westminster Review 6/28
      nos 11 & 54   Oct 1837: 169-98   (comparison to Dickens)
      [John Robertson]

"The Mudfog Association" Morning Herald no 17,185 2 Oct 1837
      BM

"Magazine Day" Sun no 14,057 2 Oct 1837   BM

"Mudfog Association" Morning Post no 20,837 3 Oct 1837   BM

"Literature - The Magazines" Morning Chronicle no 21,181
      3 Oct 1837   PP

"Literature - The Magazines" Morning Chronicle no 21,183
      5 Oct 1837   BM

"Popularity of Coachmen" The Times no 16,539 5 Oct 1837 PP

"Mudfog Statistics" The Times no 16,539 5 Oct 1837   BM

"The Mud-Fog Association" The Times no 16,541 7 Oct 1837 BM

"The Gatherer: Old Weller's Letter (from Pickwick)"   Mirror
    30 no 856   7 Oct 1837: 240   PP

"Mudfog Association"   Sunday Times no 781   8 Oct 1837   BM

"The Widower"   Observer   8 Oct 1837   PP

"Review - Literature and Arts: The Magazines"   Bell's Weekly
    Messenger no 2164   8 Oct 1837: 326   BM

"Facts and Scraps: A Hint for the Poor Law Commissioners"
    Weekly Dispatch no 1877   8 Oct 1837: 488   BM

"Post Boys and Donkies"   Bell's Life in London   8 Oct 1837 PP

"Reviewer"   Bell's New Weekly Messenger 7 no 302   8 Oct 1837:
    107   PP

"Miscellaneous: Mudfog Statistics"   Mark Lane Express 6 no 302
    9 Oct 1837   BM

"Fashion and Varieties: The Critics of Eatanswill"   Courier
    no 14,408   10 Oct 1837   PP

"The Public Journals: The Mudfog Association" Mirror 30 no 857
    14 Oct 1837: 254-55   BM

"The Public Journals: The Mudfog Association" Mirror 30 no 858
    21 Oct 1837: 270-71   BM

"Notes of a Reader: Pickwickiana by Boz"   Mirror 30 no 859
    28 Oct 1837: 285-87   PP

"Fashion and Table-Talk: Removing Paupers"   Globe no 10,962
    28 Oct 1837   BM

"Literature"   Observer   29 Oct 1837   (re Quarterly Review
    59 no 118, and London and Westminster Review 6/28 nos
    11 & 54)

"Literature"   Sun   no 14,081   30 Oct 1837   (re Quarterly
    Review 59 no 118)

"The Periodicals: The Quarterly Review on Boz"   Morning Post
    no 20,860   31 Oct 1837 (re Quarterly Review 59 no 118)

"Varieties: Bull's Eye" Globe no 10,964 31 Oct 1837   BM

"Magazine Day" Sun no 14,083 1 Nov 1837   BM

"Varieties: Beadleism" Globe no 10,966 2 Nov 1837   BM

"The Dignity of a Beadle" The Times no 16,564 3 Nov 1837 BM

"Progress of Publication" Morning Advertiser no 14,534 3 Nov
     1837   SB,PP

"Fashion and Table-Talk: The Wretched Female" Globe no 10,968
     4 Nov 1837 BM

"Literature" John Bull 17 no 882 5 Nov 1837: 537   BM

"Reviewer" Bell's New Weekly Messenger 7 no 306 5 Nov 1837:
     138-39   PP

"Literary Memoranda" Atlas 12 no 598 5 Nov 1837: 713   BM

"Review - Literature and Art: The Magazines for November"
     Bell's Weekly Messenger no 2168 5 Nov 1837: 355   BM

"The Literary Examiner" Examiner no 1553 5 Nov 1837: 708-09
     PP

"Notices of New Publications" Railway Times no 2 5 Nov 1837:
     10   PP

"Magazines of the Month" Railway Times no 2 5 Nov 1837: 10
     BM

"Humourous Sketches by 'Boz'" Magnet 1 no 35 6 Nov 1837: 283
     PP

"Miscellaneous: Mr. Weller's Visit to the Bank" Mark Lane
     Express 6 no 306 6 Nov 1837   PP

"Literature and Art" Weekly Dispatch no 1882 12 Nov 1837:
     550   BM

"The Literary Examiner" Examiner no 1555 19 Nov 1837:
     740-41   BM   [John Forster]

"Magazine Day" Sun no 14,109 1 Dec 1837   BM

"Periodicals" <u>Observer</u> 3 Dec 1837   BM

"Literature" <u>St. James's Chronicle</u> no 12,500   5 Dec 1837
    BM

"Fashion and Table-Talk: Mr. Chitling" <u>Globe</u> no 11,003
    15 Dec 1837   BM

"Notes of a Reader: Pickwickiana" <u>Mirror</u> 30 no 868   16 Dec
    1837: 407-08   PP

"Notes of a Reader: Pickwickiana" <u>Mirror</u> 30 no 870   23 Dec
    1837: 437-38   PP

"Fashion and Table-Talk: Newgate – The Night before an
    Execution" <u>Globe</u> no 11,013   27 Dec 1837   BM

"Fashion and Table-Talk: Smithfield" <u>Globe</u> no 11,015   29 Dec
    1837   BM

1838

"Magazine Day" <u>Sun</u> no 14,135   1 Jan 1838   BM

"Mr. Weller's Opinion of the Ladies" <u>Morning Advertiser</u>
    no 14,586   3 Jan 1838   PP

"Illustrations: The Political Fat Boy" <u>Figaro in London</u> 7
    no 318   6 Jan 1838: 1   PP

"Miscellaneous: Smithfield. Mr. Weller's Opinion of the
    Ladies" <u>Mark Lane Express</u> 7 no 315   8 Jan 1838 PP,BM

"Review – Literature and Arts: The Magazines for January"
    <u>Bell's Weekly Messenger</u> no 2177   8 Jan 1838: 14   PP

"The Public Journals: Oliver Twist" <u>Mirror</u> 31 no 874   13 Jan
    1838: 25-27   BM

"The Drama" <u>Bell's Life in London</u> 28 Jan 1838   ISHW

"Reviewer" <u>Bell's New Weekly Messenger</u> 8 no 320   4 Feb 1838
    BM

"Literature: Magazine Day" Sunday Times no 798   4 Feb 1838 BM

"The Literary Examiner" Examiner no 1566   4 Feb 1838: 68-69
      SYG

"New Books" Magnet 2 no 48   5 Feb 1838   BM

"The Periodicals" Morning Advertiser no 14,614   5 Feb 1838
      BM

"Literature" Courier no 14,508   5 Feb 1838   BM

"The Magazines" Sun no 14,167   7 Feb 1838   BM

"Sketches of Young Gentlemen. By Phiz" Morning Post no 20,948
      10 Feb 1838   SYG

"Literature and Arts: Sketches of Young Gentlemen" Weekly
      Dispatch no 1895   11 Feb 1838: 70   SYG

"Review - Literature and Arts"   Bell's Weekly Messenger
      no 182   11 Feb 1838: 46   BM

"Miscellaneous: Prosperity in Perspective. Election Broils"
      Mark Lane Express 7 no 320   12 Feb 1838   PP

"Review of New Books" Literary Gazette 22 no 1100   17 Feb
      1838: 97-99   MJG

"Spectator's Library"   Spectator 11   no 504   24 Feb 1838:
      184-86   MJG

"Memoirs of Professional and Literary Characters: Mr. Harley"
      Town no 39   24 Feb 1838: 306

"Review of New Books" Literary Gazette 22 no 1101   24 Feb
      1838: 118-19   MJG

"Oliver Twist. By 'Boz'" Sunday Times no 801   25 Feb 1838
      BM

"Reviewer" Bell's New Weekly Messenger 8 no 323   25 Feb 1838
      BM,MJG

"New Books" Magnet 2 no 51   26 Feb 1838   MJG

"Half-a-Crown's Worth of Cheap Knowledge" Fraser's Magazine
   17 no 99 Mar 1838: 279-90 (the lower classes and cheap
   periodicals) [William Makepeace Thackeray]

"Literary Register" Tait's Edinburgh Magazine 5 no 51   Mar
   1838: 196   SYG

"Magazine Day" Sun no 14,186 1 Mar 1838   BM

"The Periodicals" Courier no 14,530 2 Mar 1838   BM

"The Periodicals" Morning Advertiser no 14,638   5 Mar 1838
   BM

"Fashion and Table-Talk: Strange Anecdote of Grimaldi's
   Brother" Globe no 11,070 5 Mar 1838   MJG

"New Books" Magnet 2 no 52 5 Mar 1838   MJG

"Literature" St. James's Chronicle no 12,539 6 Mar 1838
   BM

"The Public Journals: Popping the Question" Mirror 31 no 882
   10 Mar 1838: 155-57   BM

"Literature and Art" Weekly Dispatch no 1899 11 Mar 1838:
   118   MJG

"Reviewer" Bell's New Weekly Messenger 8 no 325 11 Mar 1838
   SYG

"New Books" Mirror 31 no 883 17 Mar 1838: 169-71   MJG

"The Literary Examiner" Examiner no 1572 18 Mar 1838: 164
   MJG

"Literature" Sun no 14,201 19 Mar 1838   MJG

"Literature" Morning Post no 20,980 20 Mar 1838   MJG

"Fashion and Table-Talk" Globe no 11,083 20 Mar 1838   MJG

"Literature: Review of New Books"   Atlas 13 no 619   24 Mar
   1838: 185-86   MJG

"Fashion and Varieties: Oliver Twist at St. James's" <u>Courier</u>
    no 14,553   29 Mar 1838   (dramatisation of OT)

"Literature" <u>Courier</u> no 14,554   30 Mar 1838   NN

"Literary Quacks and Imposters" <u>Town</u> no 44   31 Mar 1838: 349
    (re imitations of Boz)

"Boz's New Periodical" <u>Morning Post</u> no 20,990   31 Mar 1838
    NN

"New Books: Memoirs of Joseph Grimaldi" <u>Mirror</u> 31   no 885
    31 Mar 1838: 202-04   MJG

"Spectator's Library" <u>Spectator</u> 11   no 509   31 Mar 1838:
    304-05   NN

"Reviews" <u>Athenaeum</u> no 544   31 Mar 1838: 227-29   NN

"Monthly Review of Literature: Biography" <u>Monthly Magazine</u>
    25 no 148   Apr 1838: 434-35   MJG

"Memoirs of Joseph Grimaldi" <u>Monthly Review</u> 1 no 4   Apr 1838:
    499-507   MJG

"Literature" <u>Observer</u> 1 Apr 1838   NN

"The Literary Examiner" <u>Examiner</u> no 1574   1 Apr 1838: 195-96
    NN

"Literature" <u>Bell's Life in London</u> 1 Apr 1838   NN

"The New Work by 'Boz'" <u>Bell's New Weekly Messenger</u> 8 no 328
    1 Apr 1838 NN   [Early Edition only]

"Theatricals: St. James's" <u>Sunday Times</u> no 806   1 Apr 1838
    (dramatisation of OT)

"Magazine Day" <u>Sun</u> no 14,215   2 Apr 1838   BM,NN

"Miscellaneous: Gentlemen. A Resolution Passed" <u>Mark Lane
    Express</u> 7 no 327   2 Apr 1838   PP,NN

"The Literary Log-Book" <u>Shipping and Mercantile Gazette</u> no 19
    2 Apr 1838   NN

"The Literary Log-Book" <u>Shipping and Mercantile Gazette</u> no 21
4 Apr 1838 BM

"Literature" <u>Morning Advertiser</u> no 14,666 6 Apr 1838 NN

"The Public Journals: The Life and Adventures of Nicholas
Nickleby" <u>Mirror</u> 31 no 886 7 Apr 1838: 222-23 NN

"Periodicals" <u>United Services Gazette</u> no 272 7 Apr 1838
PP,BM

"Review of New Books" <u>Literary Gazette</u> 22 no 1107 7 Apr
1838: 214 NN

"Review" <u>Athenaeum</u> no 545 7 Apr 1838: 255-56 (review -
<u>Jorrock's Jaunts and Jollities</u> by Robert Surtees)

"Literature and Art" <u>Weekly Dispatch</u> no 1903 8 Apr 1838: 166
NN

"Reviewer" <u>Bell's New Weekly Messenger</u> 8 no 329 8 Apr 1838
NN

"Literature and Arts" <u>Bell's Weekly Messenger</u> no 2190 8 Apr
1838: 110 BM

"Literature: Magazine Day" <u>Sunday Times</u> no 807 8 Apr 1838
BM,NN

"Miscellaneous: Principle" <u>Mark Lane Express</u> 7 no 328 9 Apr
1838 PP

"New Books" <u>Magnet</u> 2 no 56 9 Apr 1838 NN

"Literature" <u>Morning Advertiser</u> no 14,673 14 Apr 1838 BM

"The Public Journals: Nicholas Nickleby" <u>Mirror</u> 31 no 887
14 Apr 1838: 238-39 NN

"Authors and Literary Property" <u>Morning Advertiser</u> no 14,677
19 Apr 1838

"Hood, Boz, and Jorrocks" <u>Monthly Review</u> 2 no 1 May 1838:
98-109 (comic writers)

"Magazine Day" <u>Sun</u> no 14,238 1 May 1838 BM

"Literature" Courier no 14,581   1 May 1838   NN

"Magazines" Sun no 14,239 2 May 1838   NN

"Literature: The Magazines" Shipping and Mercantile Gazette
    no 47 4 May 1838 BM

"Literature: The Magazines" Shipping and Mercantile Gazette
    no 48 5 May 1838 NN

"The Public Journals: Oliver Twist out of Trouble and in the
    Country" Mirror 31 no 891 5 May 1838: 302-03   BM

"Literature and Arts" Bell's Life in London 6 May 1838
    NN

"Reviewer" Bell's New Weekly Messenger 8 no 333 6 May 1838
    NN

"The Literary Examiner" Examiner no 1579 6 May 1838: 278
    NN

"Literature" Observer 6 May 1838   BM

"Reviews - Literature and Arts: The Magazines for May" Bell's
    Weekly Messenger no 2194 6 May 1838: 142   BM

"Magazine Day" Sunday Times no 811 6 May 1838   BM,NN

"Literature" Morning Advertiser no 14,692 7 May 1838 BM

"New Books" Magnet 2 no 60 7 May 1838   NN

"The Magazines" United Services Gazette no 277 12 May 1838
    BM

"Literature and Art" Weekly Dispatch no 1908 13 May 1838:
    226   NN

"Fashion and Table-Talk: Oliver Twist in the Country" Globe
    no 11,133 18 May 1838   BM

"Fashion and Varieties: School Examinations" Courier no
    14,068 [sic; shd be 14,608] 1 Jne 1838 NN

"Magazines" Sun no 14,267 2 Jne 1838   BM

"Literary Notices" Age 3 Jne 1838: 175   BM,NN

"Literature and Art" John Bull 18 no 912 3 Jne 1838: 261 NN

"Reviewer" Bell's New Weekly Messenger 8 no 337 3 Jne 1838
     NN

"Literary Notices: The Magazines" Shipping and Mercantile
     Gazette no 73 4 Jne 1838   BM

"New Books" Magnet 2 no 64 4 Jne 1838   NN

"School-Room at Dotheboys Hall" Morning Chronicle no 21,391
     5 Jne 1838 NN

"Literature" Sun no 14,270 6 Jne 1838   NN

"Literature" Morning Advertiser no 14,718 6 Jne 1838   BM

"Reviewer" Bell's New Weekly Messenger 8 no 338 10 Jne 1838
     BM

"Engravings: Boz" Sunday Times no 816   10 Jne 1838
     (comments on engraving by S. Lawrence)

"New Books" Magnet 2 no 65 11 Jne 1838   BM

"The Public Journals: Oliver Twist" Mirror 31 no 897 16 Jne
     1838: 394-95 BM

"Literature and Art" Weekly Dispatch no 1913 17 Jne 1838: 286
     NN

"Miscellaneous: A Schoolmaster's Assistant and His Son" Mark
     Lane Express 7 no 338 18 Jne 1838   NN

"The Yorkshire Schoolmaster" Shipping and Mercantile Gazette
     no 90 23 Jne 1838   NN

"Literature" Morning Advertiser no 14,737 28 Jne 1838 NN

"Nickleby's Rebellion" Courier no 14,631 28 Jne 1838   NN

"Literature: Magazine Day" Sunday Times no 819 1 Jul 1838
     NN

"Literary Notices" Age 1 Jul 1838: 207 BM

"Magazine Day" Sun no 14,293 2 Jul 1838 BM

"Literary Notices: Boz's Miscellany" Shipping and Mercantile
    Gazette no 98 3 Jul 1838 BM,NN

"Miss Fanny Squeers and Her Femme de Chambre" Morning Post
    no 21,063 6 Jul 1838 NN

"Literature" Morning Advertiser no 14,744 6 Jul 1838 BM

"Literature and Art: Miscellaneous Literature" Weekly Dispatch
    no 1916 8 Jul 1838: 322 NN

"Literature" Sunday Times no 820 8 Jul 1838 NN

"Literary Notices" Age 8 Jul 1838: 212 NN

"New Books" Bell's New Weekly Messenger 8 no 342 8 Jul 1838
    NN

"Reviews - Literature and Arts: The Magazines for July"
    Bell's Weekly Messenger no 2203 8 Jul 1838: 214 BM

"The Literary Examiner" Examiner no 1588 8 Jul 1838: 420 NN

"New Books" Magnet 2 no 69 9 Jul 1838 NN

"Miscellaneous: Touching Dress" Mark Lane Express 7 no 341
    9 Jul 1838 BM

"Vulgar Genteels" Shipping and Mercantile Gazette no 112
    19 Jul 1838 NN

"The Public Journals: Nicholas Nickleby" Mirror 32 no 904
    21 Jul 1838: 60-63 NN

"Magazine Day" Sun no 14,319 1 Aug 1838 BM

"A Member of the Reformed House of Commons" Morning Post
    no 21,086 2 Aug 1838 NN

"The M.P. and His Constituents" Morning Chronicle no 21,441
    2 Aug 1838 NN

"The Periodicals" Courier no 14,658 2 Aug 1838   BM

"Literature" Morning Advertiser no 14,768   3 Aug 1838
      BM,NN

"The Periodicals" Shipping and Mercantile Gazette   no 126
      4 Aug 1838   NN

"Literature" Sun no 14,323 5 Aug 1838   NN

"Literature" Observer 5 Aug 1838   NN

"Literary Notices" Age 5 Aug 1838: 243   BM,NN

"Literature" Bell's Life in London 5 Aug 1838   NN

"New Books" Bell's New Weekly Messenger 8 no 346 5 Aug 1838
      NN

"Literature" Sunday Times no 824 5 Aug 1838   BM,NN

"Reviews – Literature and Arts: Magazines for August" Bell's
      Weekly Messenger no 2207 5 Aug 1838: 246   BM

"New Books" Magnet 2 no 73 6 Aug 1838   NN

"Fashion and Table-Talk: Delicacies" Globe no 11,202 7 Aug
      1838   BM

"Literary Notices" Shipping and Mercantile Gazette no 129
      8 Aug 1838   BM

"Fashion and Table-Talk: Illustration of the 'Aristocratic'"
      Globe no 11,203 8 Aug 1838   NN

"The Decline of Fashionable Novels" Atlas 13 no 639 11 Aug
      1838: 504

"The Public Journals: Nicholas Nickleby" Mirror 32 no 907
      11 Aug 1838: 109-10   NN

"Oliver Twist" Sunday Times no 825 12 Aug 1838   BM

"Notabilia" Examiner no 1593 12 Aug 1838: 507   SYG

"Miscellaneous: Delicacies"   Mark Lane Express   7   no 347
     20 Aug 1838   BM

"Beauties from Boz"   Shipping and Mercantile Gazette   no 148
     30 Aug 1838   NN

"Magazine Day"   Sun   no 14,347   1 Sep 1838   BM

"Literary Notices"   Age   2 Sep 1838: 275   NN

"The Literary Examiner: The Second Meeting of the Mudfog
     Association for the Advancement of Everything" Examiner
     no 1596   2 Sep 1838: 548-49   BM

"Literature"   Morning Advertiser   no 14,795   4 Sep 1838
     BM,NN

"Miss La Creevy and Nickleby"   Globe   no 11,226   4 Sep 1838 NN

"Spectator's Library"   Spectator   11   no 532   8 Sep 1838:
     854-55   BM

"Literary Notices"   Age   9 Sep 1838: 282   BM

"Magazine Day"   Sunday Times   no 829   9 Sep 1838   BM

"Periodicals"   Observer   9 Sep 1838   BM

"New Books"   Bell's New Weekly Messenger   8 no 351   9 Sep 1838
     NN

"New Books"   Magnet   2 no 78   10 Sep 1838   NN

"Literary Memoranda"   Atlas   13 no 644   15 Sep 1838: 587   BM

"Literature"   Sunday Times   no 830   16 Sep 1838   BM,NN

"Meeting of the Mudfog Association"   Shipping and Mercantile
     Gazette   no 166   20 Sep 1838   BM

"Varieties: Illustration of Homeopathy"   Globe   no 11,241
     21 Sep 1838   BM

"New Books"   Bell's New Weekly Messenger   8 no 353   23 Sep 1838
     BM

"The Literary Examiner" <u>Examiner</u> no 1599 23 Sep 1838:
        595-96   NN

"New Books" <u>Magnet</u> 2 no 80   24 Sep 1838   BM

"Miscellanea: A Gem out of 'Nicholas Nickleby'" <u>Athenaeum</u>
        no 570   29 Sep 1838: 716   NN

"Genius and the Public" <u>Fraser's Magazine</u> 18 no 106   Oct
        1838: 379-96

"Dickens's Tales" <u>Edinburgh Review</u> 68 no 137   Oct 1838:
        75-97   SB,PP,BM,NN   [Thomas Henry Lister]

"Sporting Literature" <u>Fraser's Magazine</u> 18 no 106 Oct 1838:
        481-88   PP

"Varieties: A Foggy Morning in London" <u>Globe</u> no 11,249 1 Oct
        1838   NN

"Rehearsal of a Combat" <u>Courier</u> no 14,708 1 Oct 1838   NN

"Magazines" <u>Sun</u> no 14,373 2 Oct 1838   BM

"The Periodicals" <u>Morning Advertiser</u> no 14,820 3 Oct 1838
        NN

"Literature" <u>Sun</u> no 14,375 4 Oct 1838   (review – <u>Edinburgh
        Review</u> 68 no 137)

"Literature" <u>Courier</u> no 14,711 4 Oct 1838   (review –
        <u>Edinburgh Review</u> 68 no 137)

"Literature: Magazine Day" <u>Sunday Times</u> no 833 7 Oct 1838
        BM

"Nicholas Nickleby for October" <u>Sunday Times</u> no 833 7 Oct
        1838   NN

"Seeking a Situation as a Companion to a Lady" <u>Observer</u> 7 Oct
        1838   NN

"Literary Notices" <u>Age</u> 7 Oct 1838: 315   NN

"Literature" <u>Bell's Life in London</u> 7 Oct 1838   NN

"New Books" Bell's New Weekly Messenger 8 no 355 7 Oct 1838
        NN

"Reviews - Literature and Arts" Bell's Weekly Messenger no 216
        7 Oct 1838: 315   BM

"New Books" Magnet 2 no 82 8 Oct 1838   NN

"Nicholas Nickleby in Quest of Employment" Morning Herald
        no 17,505   11 Oct 1838   NN

"Magazines and Other Periodicals"   Morning Advertiser   no
        14,827 11 Oct 1838   BM

"The Public Journals: Nicholas Nickleby" Mirror 32 no 916
        13 Oct 1838: 251   NN

"Periodical Publications"   United Services Gazette   no 300
        13 Oct 1838   NN

"Notabilia" Examiner no 1602 14 Oct 1838: 650-51   NN

"Miscellaneous: Theatrical Horses" Mark Lane Express 7 no 356
        22 Oct 1838 NN

"Nicholas Nickleby in Quest of Employment"   Shipping and
        Mercantile Gazette no 197   31 Oct 1838   NN

"Magazine Day" Sun no 14,399 1 Nov 1838   BM

"The Periodicals" Courier no 14,735 1 Nov 1838   NN

"New Books" Bell's New Weekly Messenger 8 no 359 4 Nov 1838
        NN

"Magazine Day" Sunday Times no 837 4 Nov 1838   BM,NN

"Literature" Morning Advertiser no 14,848 5 Nov 1838
        NN

"Boz" Figaro in London 7 no 360   5 Nov 1838: 168 [sic;
        shd be 174]   NN

"New Books" Magnet 2 no 86 5 Nov 1838   NN

"Literature" Morning Advertiser no 14,849 6 Nov 1838   BM

"Periodical Works" <u>United Services Gazette</u> no 304   10 Nov
    1838   NN

"Literature and Art" <u>Era</u> 1 no 7 11 Nov 1838: 80   BM

"Literary Notices" <u>Age</u> 11 Nov 1838: 355   BM

"Reviews - Literature and Arts"   <u>Bell's Weekly Messenger</u>
    no 2221 11 Nov 1838: 355   BM

"Misplaced Attachment of Mr. John Dounce"   <u>Shipping and
    Mercantile Gazette</u> no 209 14 Nov 1838   SB

"Reviews" <u>Athenaeum</u> no 577   17 Nov 1838: 824-25   OT

"Literature - Review of New Books"   <u>Atlas</u> 13 no 653   17 Nov
    1838: 729-31   OT

"Literature and Art" <u>Weekly Dispatch</u> no 1935   18 Nov 1838:
    550   NN

"The Literary Examiner" <u>Examiner</u> no 1607   18 Nov 1838:
    723-25   OT

"The Dramatic Author and His Clients" <u>Examiner</u> no 1607 18 Nov
    1838: 731 NN

"Literature and Art" <u>Era</u> 1 no 8 18 Nov 1838: 92   OT

"Surrey Theatre" <u>Morning Chronicle</u> no 21,533   20 Nov 1838
    (dramatisation of OT)

"Adelphi Theatre" <u>The Times</u> no 16,891   20 Nov 1838   NN

"Adelphi Theatre. Surrey Theatre"   <u>Morning Advertiser</u> no
    14,861   20 Nov 1838 (dramatisations of OT,NN)

"Literature" <u>Sun</u> no 14,415   20 Nov 1838   OT

"Surrey Theatre"   <u>The Times</u> no 16,892   21 Nov 1838
    (dramatisation of OT)

"Adelphi Theatre. Surrey Theatre" <u>Morning Herald</u> no 17,540
    21 Nov 1838   (dramatisations of OT,NN)

"Spectator's Library"   Spectator   11   no 543   24 Nov 1838:
        1114-16   OT

"Review of New Books"   Literary Gazette 22 no 1140   24 Nov
        1838: 741   OT

"Drama"   Literary Gazette 22 no 1140   24 Nov 1838: 748
        (dramatisations of OT,NN)

"Music and the Drama"   Athenaeum   no 578   24 Nov 1838: 844
        (dramatisations of OT,NN)

"Literature and Art"   Weekly Dispatch no 1936   25 Nov 1838:
        562   OT

"Literature"   Observer   25 Nov 1838   OT

"The Literary Examiner"   Examiner   no 1608   25 Nov 1838:
        740-41   OT

"Oliver Twist. By 'Boz'"   Dublin University Magazine 12 no 72
        Dec 1838: 699-723

"Magazine Day"   Sun no 14,425   1 Dec 1838   BM,OT

"Magazines for December"   Courier no 14,761   1 Dec 1838   BM

"Literature"   Sunday Times no 841   2 Dec 1838   OT

"Literature"   Courier no 14,762   3 Dec 1838   OT

"Literature"   Morning Advertiser no 14,873   4 Dec 1838   NN

"Magazine Day"   Sunday Times no 842   9 Dec 1838   BM,NN

"Literary Notices"   Age   9 Dec 1838: 386   BM,NN

"The Drama"   Bell's Life in London   9 Dec 1838
        (dramatisations of OT,NN)

"New Books"   Bell's New Weekly Messenger 8 no 364   9 Dec 1838
        NN

"New Books"   Magnet 2 no 91   10 Dec 1838   NN

"Literature"   Morning Advertiser no 14,881   13 Dec 1838
        BM

"French Criticism on the Pickwick"   Examiner no 1611   16 Dec
        1838: 790   PP

"Oliver Twist,   By 'Boz'"   Shipping and Mercantile Gazette
        no 238   18 Dec 1838   OT

"Oliver Twist"   Shipping and Mercantile Gazette no 245   26 Dec
        1838   OT

1839

"Boz's Oliver Twist"   Monthly Review 1 no 1   Jan 1839: 29-41
        OT

"Nicholas Nickleby's Return to London"   Courier no 14,795
        1 Jan 1839   NN

"Fashion and Varieties: Miss La Creevy's Visit"   Courier no
        14,796   2 Jan 1839   NN

"Theatrical Last Appearances"   The Times no 16,929   3 Jan 1839
        NN

"Magazines Concluded"   Sun no 14,454   4 Jan 1839   BM

"Literature, &c: Magazines"   United Services Gazette no 312
        5 Jan 1839   BM

"Literature, &c: Serial Works"   United Services Gazette no 312
        5 Jan 1839   NN

"The Literature of 1838"   Atlas 14 no 660   5 Jan 1839: 9

"Literature: Magazine Day"   Sunday Times no 846   6 Jan 1839
        BM,NN

"The Literary Examiner"   Examiner no 1614   6 Jan 1839: 4   NN

"The Magazines for January"   Bell's Weekly Messenger no 2229
        6 Jan 1839   BM,NN

"Literature and Art" <u>Weekly Dispatch</u> no 1942   6 Jan 1839:
     10   NN

"New Books"   <u>Bell's New Weekly Messenger</u> 9 no 368   6 Jan 1839
     NN

"The Magazines"   <u>Observer</u> 6 Jan 1839   NN

"Literature"   <u>Morning Advertiser</u> no 14,902   7 Jan 1839   BM

"New Books"   <u>Magnet</u> 3 no 94   7 Jan 1839   NN

"Varieties: Interior of Bow-Street Police-Office"   <u>Globe</u> no
     11,335 8 Jan 1839   BM

"The Public Journals: London" <u>Mirror</u> 33 no 931   12 Jan 1839:
     31   NN

"A London Manager at a Country Theatre. A Professional
     Display" <u>Observer</u> 13 Jan 1839   NN

"Literature" <u>Bell's Life in London</u> 13 Jan 1839   NN

"Literary Notices" <u>Age</u> 13 Jan 1839: 10   NN

"New Books" <u>Bell's New Weekly Messenger</u> 9 no 369   13 Jan 1839
     BM

"Bentley's Miscellany" <u>Morning Post</u> no 21,226   14 Jan 1839
     BM

"Nicholas Nickleby. Chapters 30,31,32,33"   <u>Morning Post</u> no
     21,226 14 Jan 1839   NN

"New Books" <u>Magnet</u> 3 no 95 14 Jan 1839   BM

"Our Weekly Gossip" <u>Athenaeum</u> no 586   19 Jan 1839: 51-52
     (decline of the novel)

"Miss La Creevy's Visit"   <u>Shipping and Mercantile Gazette</u>
     no 270 24 Jan 1839   NN

"Nicholas Nickleby's Return to London"   <u>Shipping and
     Mercantile Gazette</u> no 271   25 Jan 1839   NN

"From the Magazines for February: The Invaluable Mrs. Squeers"
    Courier no 14,821   31 Jan 1839   NN

"Magazine Day" Sun no 14,479 1 Feb 1839   BM

"From the Magazines for February: A Happy Countenance.
    Mantalini's Endearments. Medical Attendance at Schools"
    Courier no 14,822 1 Feb 1839   NN

"The Magazines of the Month" United Services Gazette no 316
    2 Feb 1839   BM

"Magazine Day" Sunday Times no 850 3 Feb 1839   NN

"The Magazines" Observer 3 Feb 1839   BM,NN

"The Periodicals for February" Morning Post no 21,247 7 Feb
    1839   BM

"Literature:Nicholas Nickleby for February" Morning Advertiser
    no 14,931   9 Feb 1839   BM,NN

"Nicholas Nickleby" United Services Gazette no 317 9 Feb
    1839   NN

"New Books" Bell's New Weekly Messenger 9 no 373 10 Feb 1839
    NN

"New Books" Magnet 3 no 99 11 Feb 1839   NN

"A Family Event" Shipping and Mercantile Gazette no 289
    15 Feb 1839   NN

"Literary Notices" Age 17 Feb 1839: 50   NN

"The Theatres: Adelphi" Morning Post no 21,263 26 Feb 1839
    (dramatisation of OT)

"Mr. Sergeant Talfourd's Copyright Bill" The Times no 16,977
    28 Feb 1839

"The Periodicals" Courier no 14,845 1 Mar 1839   BM

"Theatricals" Atlas 14 no 668 2 Mar 1839: 136
    (dramatisation of OT)

"Magazine Day" Sunday Times no 854   3 Mar 1839   BM,NN

"Varieties: A City Square" Sunday Times no 854   3 Mar 1839
     NN

"The Literary Examiner" Examiner no 1611   3 Mar 1839: 133-34
     BM   [John Forster]

"New Books" Bell's New Weekly Messenger 9 no 376 3 Mar 1839
     NN

"Literature and Art" Era 1 no 23   3 Mar 1839:   272   BM

"The Magazines" Observer   3 Mar 1839   BM

"New Books" Magnet 3 no 102   4 Mar 1839   NN

"The Magazines" Morning Post no 21,269   5 Mar 1839   BM

"Bentley's Miscellany" Morning Herald no 17,630   6 Mar 1839
     BM

"Bentley's Miscellany" Morning Chronicle no 21,621   6 Mar
     1839   BM

"Literature" Morning Advertiser   no 14,962   7 Mar 1839

"Literature, &c: A Parthian Glance at the Magazines" United
     Services Gazette no 322   9 Mar 1839   BM

"Literature and Art" Weekly Dispatch no 1951   10 Mar 1839:
     118   BM

"Literary Notices" Age 10 Mar 1839: 74   NN

"Literature" John Bull 19   no 952   10 Mar 1839: 116
     (popularity of novels in illustrated numbers)

"Bentley's Miscellany" Globe no 11,393   16 Mar 1839   BM

"A Disagreeable Encounter of the Two Old Friends" Shipping
     and Mercantile Gazette no 320   23 Mar 1839   NN

"Literature, &c" United Services Gazette no 324   23 Mar 1839
     NN

"Literature and Art" <u>Weekly Dispatch</u> no 1954 31 Mar 1839:
      154   BM

"Literary Notices" <u>Age</u> 31 Mar 1839: 98 BM (the "Boz" style)

"Magazine-Day" <u>Sun</u> no 14,529 1 Apr 1839   BM

"The Periodicals for April" <u>Morning Post</u> no 21,292   1 Apr
      1839   BM

"Extracts from the Periodicals: The Escape of Smike" <u>Courier</u>
      no 14,871   1 Apr 1839   NN

"A Scene from Nicholas Nickleby" <u>Sun</u> no 14,530 2 Apr 1839 NN

"Fashion and Varieties: Curious Association of Ideas"
      <u>Courier</u> no 14,873   3 Apr 1839   NN

"London Flowers" <u>Courier</u> no 14,873   3 Apr 1839   NN

"Nicholas's Clandestine Visit to his First Love" <u>Courier</u> no
      14,874   4 Apr 1839   NN

"The Public Journals: Nicholas Nickleby. No. 13" <u>Mirror</u> 33
      no 943   6 Apr 1839: 220-23   NN

"Literature, &c: A Parthian Glance at the Periodicals" <u>United
      Services Gazette</u> no 326   6 Apr 1839   BM,NN

"Periodical Literature" <u>Atlas</u> 14 no 673 6 Apr 1839: 216-18
      BM

"Serial Fictions"   <u>Atlas</u> 14 no 673   6 Apr 1839: 219
      (review - <u>Michael Armstrong</u> by Mrs. Trollope)

"Literary Notices" <u>Age</u> 7 Apr 1839: 106   BM,NN

"Literature" <u>Sunday Times</u> no 859 7 Apr 1839   NN

"Curious Association of Ideas" <u>Sunday Times</u> no 859   7 Apr
      1839   NN

"Popular Periodicals" <u>Bell's New Weekly Messenger</u>, <u>Supplement</u>
      no 1   7 Apr 1839   NN

"The Breakfast Table" <u>Era</u> 1 no 28 7 Apr 1839: 332   BM

"Literature" Morning Advertiser no 14,991 10 Apr 1839 NN

"Our Weekly Gossip" Athenaeum no 598 13 Apr 1839: 278-79
        (re "Literary Lionism" London and Westminster Review
        32 no 2)

"Literature and Arts" Bell's Life in London 14 Apr 1839 BM,NN

"Literature" Sunday Times no 861   21 Apr 1839   (shilling
        numbers)

"Association of Ideas" Morning Chronicle no 21,664   27 Apr
        1839   NN

"Fashion and Table-Talk: The Memory of the Dead" Globe no
        11,433   2 May 1839   NN

"Nicholas Nickleby" Bell's New Weekly Messenger 9 no 385
        5 May 1839   NN

"Nicholas Nickleby" Magnet 3 no 111   6 May 1839   NN

"Literature" Morning Advertiser no 15,016   9 May 1839
        BM,NN

"Nicholas Nickleby" Courier no 14,904 9 May 1839   NN

"Varieties: Selfishness of Love" Globe no 11,440   10 May 1839
        NN

"Literature, &c" United Services Gazette no 331 11 May 1839
        NN

"Literature" Sunday Times no 864 12 May 1839   NN

"The Literary Examiner" Examiner no 1632   12 May 1839:
        292-93   (on Romance)

"Literary Notices" Age 12 May 1839: 146   NN

"Notabilia: The Actress's Lodgings" Examiner no 1632 12 May
        1839: 299-300 NN

"Chit-Chat: Boz" Art Union 1 no 4 15 May 1839: 74

"A Scene in the Nickleby Family"   Shipping and Mercantile
    Gazette no 368   18 May 1839   NN

"Literature and Art"   Era 1 no 34   19 May 1839: 404   OT

"Familiar Associations" Shipping and Mercantile Gazette no 372
    23 May 1839   NN

"Beauties of Boz"   Shipping and Mercantile Gazette   no 378
    30 May 1839

"Oliver Twist; or, the Parish Boy's Progress" Quarterly Review
    64 no 127   Jne 1839: 83-102   OT   [Richard Ford]

"Magazine Day"   Sun no 14,582   1 Jne 1839   BM

"Literature"   Bell's Life in London   2 Jne 1839   BM,NN

"Literature"   Observer   2 Jne 1839   BM,NN

"The Literary Examiner: The Last New Number of Nicholas
    Nickleby"   Examiner no 1635   2 Jne 1839: 342   NN

"New Books"   Bell's New Weekly Messenger 9 no 389   2 Jne 1839
    NN

"New Books"   Magnet 3 no 115   3 Jne 1839   NN

"The Periodicals for June"   Morning Post no 21,346   3 Jne 1839
    (imitations of Dickens)

"Beauties of Boz"   Shipping and Mercantile Gazette   no 384
    6 Jne 1839

"Literature, &c"   United Services Gazette no 335   8 Jne 1839
    NN

"The Magazines"   Sunday Times no 868   9 Jne 1839   NN

"Literature and Art"   Weekly Dispatch no 1964   9 Jne 1839: 274
    (imitations of Dickens)

"Literary Notices" Age 9 Jne 1839: 178   NN

"Miscellaneous: The Rules of the King's Bench"   Mark Lane
    Express 8 no 389   10 Jne 1839   NN

"Our Weekly Gossip" Athenaeum no 609 29 Jne 1839: 485-86
      (re - Quarterly Review 64 no 127 on OT)

"Literature" Observer 30 Jne 1839   BM,NN

"Literature" Observer 1 Jul 1839   BM,NN

"Magazines - Continued" Sun no 14,610 4 Jul 1839   NN

"Literature, &c: The Magazines" United Services Gazette no 339
      6 Jul 1839   NN

"Nicholas Nickleby" Bell's New Weekly Messenger, Supplement
      1 no 4 7 Jul 1839   NN

"The Magazines" Sunday Times no 872 7 Jul 1839   NN

"Literature" John Bull 19 no 969 7 Jul 1839: 320-21   BM

"Literary Notices" Age 7 Jul 1839: 210   NN

"Varieties: Remembrance of Pleasant Scenes" Globe no 11,492
      12 Jul 1839   NN

"Specimens of the Periodicals for August" Courier no 14,974
      1 Aug 1839   NN

"Literature, &c" United Services Gazette no 343 3 Aug 1839
      NN

"Literature" Sunday Times no 876 4 Aug 1839   NN

"Literary Notices" Age 4 Aug 1839: 242   NN

"The Magazines" Observer 4 Aug 1839   NN

"New Books" Bell's New Weekly Messenger 9 no 398 4 Aug 1839
      NN

"New Books" Magnet 3 no 124 5 Aug 1839   NN

"The Periodicals for August" Morning Post no 21,385 8 Aug
      1839   BM

"Literature" Bell's Life in London 11 Aug 1839   BM,NN

"The Literary Examiner: The Seventeenth Number of Nicholas
    Nickleby" Examiner no 1645 11 Aug 1839: 501   NN

"The Genteel Hair-Dresser" Sun no 14,644 13 Aug 1839   NN

"Literature" Globe no 11,524 19 Aug 1839

"The Literary Examiner" Examiner no 1647 25 Aug 1839: 532-
    33   (review - The Crayon Papers by Washington Irving;
    periodical writing)

"Literature" Shipping and Mercantile Gazette no 454 27 Aug
    1839   (imitations of Dickens)

"The Magazines" Observer 1 Sep 1839   NN

"Arthur Gride's Return Home. Smike's Death" Courier no 15,000
    3 Sep 1839 NN

"Mr. Lillyvick Re-Appears among the Kenwigses" Sun no 14,665
    6 Sep 1839 NN

"Literature, &c: A Parthian Glance at the Periodicals" United
    Services Gazette no 348   7 Sep 1839   NN

"Literary Notices" Age 8 Sep 1839: 282   NN

"Literature" Sunday Times no 881 8 Sep 1839   NN

"Nicholas Nickleby" Bell's New Weekly Messenger, Supplement
    1 no 6 8 Sep 1839   NN

"The Periodicals" Morning Post no 21,413 10 Sep 1839   NN

"Fashion and Table-Talk: Architecture of Noses" Globe no
    11,544   11 Sep 1839   NN

"Varieties: Leaving Lovers Alone" Globe no 11,545 12 Sep
    1839   NN

"Breaking Up of Dotheboys Hall" Observer 29 Sep 1839 NN

"Yorkshire Schools (From the Preface to Nicholas Nickleby)"
    Courier no 15,025   3 Oct 1839   NN

"Literature" Sun no 14,689 4 Oct 1839   NN

"Table-Talk No. 97" Morning Post no 21,434 4 Oct 1839
    (speech of the lower classes)

"Literature" Morning Advertiser no 15,143 4 Oct 1839   NN

"Ralph Nickleby's Last Moments" Courier no 15,026 4 Oct 1839
    NN

"Literature" United Services Gazette no 352 5 Oct 1839   NN

"Reviews" Town no 123 5 Oct 1839: 983   NN

"Literary Notices" Age 6 Oct 1839: 314   NN

"Literature" Observer 6 Oct 1839   BM,NN

"The Literary Examiner: The Conclusion of Nicholas Nickleby"
    Examiner no 1653 6 Oct 1839: 629-30   NN

"Nicholas Nickleby" Bell's New Weekly Messenger 9 no 406
    6 Oct 1839   NN

"Nicholas Nickleby" Magnet 3 no 133 7 Oct 1839   NN

"Literature" Morning Advertiser no 15,146 8 Oct 1839   BM

"Varieties: All Up with Squeers" Globe no 11,566 8 Oct 1839
    NN

"Fashion and Table-Talk: The Brothers Cheeryble" Globe no
    11,570 12 Oct 1839   NN

"Breakfast Table" Era 2 no 55 13 Oct 1839: 32   NN

"Literature" Sunday Times no 886 13 Oct 1839   NN

"Literature" United Services Gazette no 354 19 Oct 1839
    (imitations of Dickens)

"Literature" Sun no 14,707 25 Oct 1839 (review - Jack
    Sheppard by W.H. Ainsworth)

"Reviews" Athenaeum no 626 26 Oct 1839: 803-05 (review -
    Jack Sheppard by W.H. Ainsworth)

"Spectator's Library" Spectator no 591 26 Oct 1839: 1020-21
    (review - Jack Sheppard by W.H. Ainsworth)

"The Literary Examiner" Examiner no 1656 27 Oct 1839: 677-
    78 NN [Leigh Hunt]

"From the Examiner. The Life and Adventures of Nicholas
    Nickleby" Courier no 15,045 28 Oct 1839   NN

"Table-Talk No. 103" Morning Post no 21,458 1 Nov 1839
    (literary criticism and Jack Sheppard)

"The Literary Examiner" Examiner no 1657 3 Nov 1839: 691-93
    (review - Jack Sheppard by W.H. Ainsworth) [John
Forster]

"Our Literature, and the Housebreakers and Thieves of the Last
    Century" Town no 129 16 Nov 1839: 1028 (review - Jack
    Sheppard by W.H. Ainsworth)

"Review of New Books" Atlas 14 no 706 23 Nov 1839: 751
    (review - Jack Sheppard by W.H. Ainsworth)

"The Jack Sheppard Mania" Atlas 14 no 708 7 Dec 1839: 780

"Bentley's Miscellany for December, 1839" Bell's New Weekly
    Messenger, Supplement [no vol. number] 8 Dec 1839 BM

"Literature" Morning Advertiser no 15,200 10 Dec 1839 BM

"New Books: The Present State of Literature" Bell's New
    Weekly Messenger 9 no 505 15 Dec 1839

"News of Literature and Fine Arts: A New Mode of Puffing"
    United Services Gazette no 364 28 Dec 1839

"The Literary Examiner" Examiner no 1665 29 Dec 1839: 822
    (review - Poor Jack by Captain Marryat, and imitations
    of Dickens)

1840

"Popular Literature of the Day"   British and Foreign Review
10 no 19   Jan 1840: 223-46 (review - Jack Sheppard by
W.H. Ainsworth; Michael Armstrong by Mrs. Trollope)

"William Ainsworth and Jack Sheppard"   Fraser's Magazine 21
no 122   Feb 1840: 227-45   (comparison to OT)
[William Makepeace Thackeray]

"German Translation of the Pickwick Papers"   Dublin Review 8
no 15   Feb 1840: 160-88   PP

"Magazine Day"   Sun   no 14,789   3 Feb 1840   (BM;   W.H.
Ainsworth, comparison to Dickens)

"Books"   Spectator 13 no 606   8 Feb 1840: 137   SYC

"The Magazines"   Sunday Times no 851   10 Feb 1840   SYC

"Review of New Books"   Literary Gazette 24 no 1204   15 Feb
1840: 98-100   SYC

"The Literary Examiner"   Examiner no 1672   16 Feb 1840: 100-
01   SYC

"Boz and His Booksellers"   United Services Gazette no 373   23
Feb 1840

"Table-Talk   No.128"   Morning Post no 21,553   24 Feb 1840
(Boz and contemporary literary taste)

"Literary Memoranda"   Atlas 15 no 720   29 Feb 1840: 139
SYC

"The Age of Jack Sheppardism"   Monthly Magazine 3 no 15
Mar 1840:   229-33

"Recent Novels"   Monthly Chronicle 5   Mar 1840: 219-32
(Jack Sheppardism)

"A Parthian Glance at the the Periodicals"   United Services
Gazette no 374   7 Mar 1840   BM

"New Books"   Mirror 35 no 995   7 Mar 1840: 166-68   SYC

"Jack Sheppard and Pickwick" United Services Gazette no 377
28 Mar 1840

"Varieties: Elderly Gentlemen" Globe no 11,716 31 Mar 1840
SYC

"Charles Dickens and His Works" Fraser's Magazine 21 no 124
Apr 1840: 381-400

"Magazine Day" Sun no 14,839 1 Apr 1840 (re Fraser's
Magazine 21 no 124 on Dickens)

"Periodicals for April" Morning Herald no 17,965 3 Apr 1840
(re Fraser's Magazine 21 no 124 on Dickens)

"The Magazines for April" Bell's Weekly Messenger no 2294
4 Apr 1840: 110 (re Fraser's Magazine 21 no 124 on
Dickens) BM

"Publications Received: Serials, Pictorial Illustrations, and
Prints" Spectator no 614 4 Apr 1840: 331 MHC

"Reviews of New Books: 'Boz'" Literary Gazette 24 no 1211
4 Apr 1840: 211 MHC

"Miscellaneous" Examiner no 1679 5 Apr 1840: 219 MHC

"Boz's New Work" Bell's New Weekly Messenger 10 no 521
5 Apr 1840 [London Edition only] MHC

"Literature" Observer 5 Apr 1840 MHC

"Literature" Sunday Times no 911 5 Apr 1840 (re Fraser's
Magazine 21 no 124 on Dickens)

"Literature and Art" Weekly Dispatch no 2007 5 Apr 1840: 166
(re Fraser's Magazine 21 no 124 on Dickens)

"Literature" Bell's Life in London 5 Apr 1840 MHC

"Fraser's Magazine" Era 2 no 79 5 Apr 1840: 333 (re
Fraser's Magazine 21 no 124 on Dickens)

"Literary Notices" Age 5 Apr 1840: 106 (re Fraser's
Magazine 21 no 124 on Dickens)

"Literature" <u>Bell's Life in London</u> 10 Apr 1840   MHC

"Literature and Art" <u>Weekly Dispatch</u> no 2008   12 Apr 1840:
    178   MHC

"The Literary Examiner. A Gentlemanly Correspondent" <u>Examiner</u>
    no 1680   12 Apr 1840: 230   MHC

"Literary Notices" <u>Age</u>   12 Apr 1840: 114   MHC

"Literature" <u>Sun</u> no 14,850   14 Apr 1840   MHC

"Literature" <u>Morning Advertiser</u>   no 15,312   18 Apr 1840
    BM,MHC

"Serials" <u>Spectator</u> 18 no 616   18 Apr 1840: 380   MHC

"Our Library Table" <u>Athenaeum</u> no 651   18 Apr 1840: 313   SYC

"Literature and Art" <u>John Bull</u>   20 no 1010   19 Apr 1840: 188
    MHC

"Literature" <u>Sun</u> no 14,853   20 Apr 1840   MHC

"Literature" <u>Morning Advertiser</u> no 15,313   20 Apr 1840
    (re <u>Fraser's Magazine</u> 21 no 124   on Dickens)

"Fashion and Table-Talk: Supernatural Visitants"   <u>Globe</u> no
    11,735   22   Apr 1840   MHC

"Master Humphrey's Turnip. A Chimney-Corner Crochet"   <u>Town</u>
    no 52   25 Apr 1840: 1213   (MHC satire)

"The Literary Fund"   <u>Morning Herald</u> no 17,986   30 Apr 1840
    (re the status of literary men)

"Progress of Dramatic Reform"   <u>Monthly Magazine</u> 3 no 17   May
    1840: 498-506   (re the state of contemporary drama)

"Master Humphrey's Clock. By 'Boz'"   <u>Monthly Review</u> 2 no 1
    May 1840: 35-43   MHC

"Master Humphrey's Turnip. A Chimney-Corner Crochet"   <u>Town</u>
    no 153   2 May 1840: 1221   (MHC satire)

"Literature and Art" <u>Weekly Dispatch</u> no 2063 2 May 1840: 214
        (re the practice of serial continuations)

"Literature" <u>Sunday Times</u> no 914 3 May 1840 MHC

"Literary Examiner: Mr Pickwick's Introduction to Master
        Humphrey's Clock" <u>Examiner</u> no 1683 3 May 1840: 276
        MHC

"Literature and Art" <u>Era</u> 2 no 84 3 May 1840: 386   MHC

"Master Humphrey's Turnip. A Chimney-Corner Crochet"   <u>Town</u>
        no 54   9 May 1840: 1229-30   (MHC satire)

"Varieties: Mr. Weller, Sen. on Railways" <u>Globe</u> no 11,754
        14 May 1840   MHC

"Old Weller and the Widow on the Railroad" <u>Courier</u> no 15,212
        14 May 1840   MHC

"Master Humphrey's Turnip. A Chimney-Corner Crochet"   <u>Town</u>
        no 155   16 May 1840: 1237   (MHC satire)

"Mr Weller on Railways" <u>Examiner</u> no 1685   17 May 1840: 309
        MHC

"Literature and Art" <u>Era</u> 2 no 86 17 May 1840: 410   MHC

"Miscellaneous: Mr. Weller, Sen. on Railways"   <u>Mark Lane</u>
        <u>Express</u> 9 no 438 18 May 1840   MHC

"Master Humphrey's Turnip. A Chimney-corner Crochet"   <u>Town</u>
        no 156   23 May 1840: 1245   (MHC satire)

"Varieties: Old Weller and the Widow on the Railroad" <u>Bell's</u>
        <u>New Weekly Messenger</u> 10 no 528   24 May 1840   MHC

"Varieties" <u>Magnet</u> 3 no 166   25 May 1840   MHC

"Mr. Weller, Sen., on Railways"   <u>Morning Herald</u> no 18,007
        25 May 1840   MHC

"Varieties: A Brute of a Husband" <u>Globe</u> no 11,764   26 May
        1840   MHC

"Mr. Weller, Sen., on Railways" Courier no 15,223 27 May
    1840   MHC

"An Enthusiastic Barber" Examiner no 1687 31 May 1840: 340
    MHC

"Notices of New Works" Metropolitan Magazine 28 no 110
    Jne 1840: 51-52   MHC

"Progress of Dramatic Reform" Monthly Magazine 3 no 18 Jne
    1840: 665-71   (re the state of contemporary drama)

"George Cruikshank" London and Westminster Review 34 no 1
    Jne 1840: 1-61   [William Makepeace Thackeray]

"Miscellaneous: An Enthusiastic Barber" Mark Lane Express 9
    no 442 15 Jne 1840   MHC

"Literature" Sunday Times no 922 28 Jne 1840   MHC

"Charles O'Malley" Monthly Review 2 no 3 Jul 1840: 398-411
    (the Dickens school of writing)

"Literature" Morning Advertiser no 15,382 9 Jul 1840   MHC

"The Literary Examiner" Examiner no 1693 12 Jul 1840: 435
    MHC

"Boz's Sketches" New Moral World 1 no 3 18 Jul 1840: 34-35

"Fashion and Table-Talk: A Grave-Yard Incident" Globe no
    11,900 18 Jul 1840   MHC

"Notices of New Works" Metropolitan Magazine 28 no 112
    Aug 1840: 101-02   MHC

"Literature" Observer 9 Aug 1840   (re literary fashions
    and the republication of Henry Fielding's works)

"Literary Notices" Age 9 Aug 1840: 250 (uncommissioned MHC
    illus. by T. Sibson)

"New Publications" Morning Herald no 18,073 11 Aug 1840
    (uncommissioned MHC illus. by T. Sibson)

"Literary Examiner: The Village School" <u>Examiner</u> no 1698
    16 Aug 1840: 517   MHC

"Literature" <u>Courier</u> no 15,295   19 Aug 1840   (moral
    tendencies of works by Fielding, Ainsworth, and Bulwer;
    MHC)

"Varieties: A Village School" <u>Bell's New Weekly Messenger</u> 10
    no 541   23 Aug 1840   MHC

"Varieties" <u>Magnet</u> 4 no 179   24 Aug 1840   MHC

"Fashion and Table-Talk: Jarley's Wax-Work Show"   <u>Globe</u> no
    11,941   4 Sep 1840   MHC

"The Periodicals" <u>Morning Post</u> no 21,719 4 Sep 1840   BM

"Notabilia" <u>Examiner</u> no 1701 6 Sep 1840: 567   MHC

"Varieties: Ingenious Contrivances at a Wax Work Show" <u>Bell's
    New Weekly Messenger</u> 10 no 543 6 Sep 1840   MHC

"Literature and Art" <u>Era</u> 2 no 102 6 Sep 1840: 610 (re tales
    in instalments, particularly in <u>Bentley's Miscellany</u>)

"Varieties" <u>Magnet</u> 4 no 181   7 Sep 1840 MHC

"Varieties: Lady Whips" <u>Globe</u> no 11,945 9 Sep 1840   MHC

"Literature" <u>St. James's Chronicle</u> no 12,934   12 Sep 1840
    (novels in magazines)

"Varieties: A Young Ladies' Boarding School"   <u>Bell's New
    Weekly Messenger</u> 10   no 544   13 Sep 1840   MHC

"Literature" <u>Bell's Life in London</u> 13 Sep 1840   MHC

"Varieties" <u>Magnet</u> 4 no 182   14 Sep 1840   MHC

"Mr. Brass's Kitchen" <u>Tablet</u> no 19   19 Sep 1840: 308   MHC

"Varieties: Lodging-House Mysteries" <u>Bell's New Weekly
    Messenger</u> 10 no 545   20 Sep 1840   MHC

"Varieties" <u>Magnet</u> 4 no 183   21 Sep 1840   MHC

"Varieties: The Office of Mr. Sampson Brass - A Bevis Marks
    Attorney" Globe no 11,956 22 Sep 1840   MHC

"Varieties: A Dinner in the Kitchen. Female Education
    Extraordinary" Bell's New Weekly Messenger 10 no 546
    27 Sep 1840   MHC

"Varieties" Magnet 4 no 183 [sic; shd be 184] 28 Sep 1840
    MHC

"The Magazines" Atlas 15 no 751 3 Oct 1840: 648-49
    (tendencies of contemporary magazines)

"Literature" Bell's Life in London 4 Oct 1840   MHC

"Varieties: Home Affections of the Poor" Globe no 11,970
    8 Oct 1840; rpt in no 11,971 9 Oct 1840   MHC

"The Magazines" Atlas 15 no 752   10 Oct 1840: 664-65
    (continued from 3 Oct 1840)

"Literature" Sunday Times no 938 11 Oct 1840   MHC

"Varieties: 'Boz' at Astley's. Mr. Charles Dickens (Boz)"
    Bell's New Weekly Messenger 10 no 548   11 Oct 1840
    MHC

"Periodicals and Brochures" Morning Post no 21,751 12 Oct
    1840 (the French system of monthly publication)

"Varieties" Magnet 4 no 185 12 Oct 1840   MHC

"New Publications" Morning Herald no 18,127   13 Oct 1840
    (uncommissioned MHC illus. by T. Sibson)

"Literature and Art" Era 3 no 108 18 Oct 1840   (review -
    Nickleby Married by J.Stirling Coyne: the Dickens style
    of writing)

"Varieties: Small Talk" Bell's New Weekly Messenger 10 no 549
    18 Oct 1840 MHC

"Varieties" Magnet 4 no 186 19 Oct 1840   MHC

"Miscellaneous: Churchyard Scene" Mark Lane Express 9 no 460
    19 Oct 1840   MHC

"Literature"   Morning Advertiser no 15,472   22 Oct 1840
   (uncommissioned MHC illus. by T. Sibson)

"Serial Publications" United Services Gazette no 408   24 Oct
   1840   MHC

"Varieties: Beauty in the Moonlight. A Starry Night" Bell's
   New Weekly Messenger 10 no 550   25 Oct 1840   MHC

"Varieties" Magnet 4 no 187   26 Oct 1840   MHC

"Literature and Art" Era 3   no 110   1 Nov 1840
   (imitations of Dickens)

"Magazine Day: A Column for November. An Ancient Country
   Church, England" Globe no 11,991 2 Nov 1840   MHC

"Master Humphrey's Clock. By 'Boz.' Vol. I" Athenaeum no 680
   7 Nov 1840: 887-88   MHC

"Varieties: Travelling by Waggon" Bell's New Weekly Messenger
   10 no 552   8 Nov 1840   MHC

"Varieties" Magnet 4 no 189 9 Nov 1840   MHC

"Adelphi Theatre" Standard   no   5115   10 Nov 1840
   (dramatisation of OCS)

"New Publications" Morning Herald no 18,152 11 Nov 1840
   (uncommissioned MHC illus. by T. Sibson)

"Serials" United Services Gazette no 411 14 Nov 1840   MHC

"Theatricals" Atlas 15 no   757   14 Nov 1840: 743
   (dramatisation of OCS)

"Literature" Sunday Times no 943 15 Nov 1840   MHC

"Varieties: Moistening the Clay" Bell's New Weekly Messenger
   10 no 554 15 Nov 1840   MHC

"Varieties" Magnet 4 no 189 [sic; shd be 190] 16 Nov 1840
   MHC

"Notices of New Works" Metropolitan Magazine 29 no 116
   Dec 1840: 111   MHC

"Literature"   Observer   6 Dec 1840   MHC

"Varieties: Churchyard Reflections"   Bell's New Weekly
     Messenger 10 no 557   6 Dec 1840   MHC

"Literature"   Bell's Life in London   6 Dec 1840   MHC

"Varieties" Magnet 4 no 192   7 Dec 1840   MHC

"A Parthian Glance at the Serials for December"   United
     Services Gazette no 415   12 Dec 1840   MHC

"Varieties: Byron Improved"   Bell's New Weekly Messenger 10
     no 558   13 Dec 1840   MHC

"Varieties" Magnet 4 no 193   14 Dec 1840   MHC

"Popular Prejudice"   Bell's New Weekly Messenger 10 no 559
     20 Dec 1840   MHC

"Varieties" Magnet 4 no 194   21 Dec 1840   MHC

"Varieties: Twelve Pounds Gentlemen"   Bell's New Weekly
     Messenger 10 no 560 27 Dec 1840   MHC

"Varieties" Magnet 4 no 195   28 Dec 1840   MHC

1841

"Literature" Bell's Life in London   3 Jan 1841   MHC

"Varieties: Prisoners at the Bar. The Way of Counsel" Bell's
     New Weekly Messenger 11 no 561   3 Jan 1841   MHC

"Varieties" Magnet 5 no 196   4 Jan 1841   MHC

"Literature and Art" Weekly Dispatch no 2047   10 Jan 1841:
     22 (contemporary newspaper criticism)

"Varieties: Always Suspect Everybody"   Bell's New Weekly
     Messenger 11 no 562   17 Jan 1841   MHC

"Varieties" Magnet 5 no 198   18 Jan 1841   MHC

"Varieties: Love Making. The Death of Quilp"   Bell's New
      Weekly Messenger 11 no 563 24 Jan 1841   MHC

"To the Public" Town no 192 27 Jan 1841: 1521 (satire on
      "Familiar Epistle")

"Varieties: A Striking Attitude" Bell's New Weekly Messenger
      11 no 564   31 Jan 1841   MHC

"Varieties" Magnet 5 no 200 1 Feb 1841   MHC

"Literature" Morning Advertiser no 15,562   4 Feb 1841
      (uncommissioned MHC illus. by T. Sibson)

"Literature, &c" John Bull 21 no 1052 6 Feb 1841: 69   BM

"Miscellaneous: Waggon Travelling"   Mark Lane Express   10
      no 476 8 Feb 1841 MHC

"The Literary World. I"   Mirror 37 no 1046   13 Feb 1841:
      99-101 [Although there are thirteen instalments of this
      feature in Mirror v. 37, most of them on contemporary
      magazines, neither MHC nor Dickens is commented upon
      after this first article]

"Literature" Bell's Life in London 14 Feb 1841   MHC

"Varieties: Boz in St. Paul's Clock. Morning in London"
      Bell's New Weekly Messenger 11 no 567 21 Feb 1841
      MHC

"Varieties" Magnet 5 no 203 22 Feb 1841   MHC

"Reviews" Town no 196 24 Feb 1841: 1554   OCS

"Varieties: The State of Muzziness"   Bell's New Weekly
      Messenger 1 no 568 28 Feb 1841   MHC

"Notices of New Works"   Metropolitan Magazine 30 no 119
      Mar 1841: 78-79 MHC

"Varieties" Magnet 5 no 204 1 Mar 1841   MHC

"Varieties: Hints to Father. Clerkenwell, Sixty Years Ago"
      Bell's New Weekly Messenger 11 no 569 7 Mar 1841 MHC

"Varieties" Magnet 5 no 205   8 Mar 1841   MHC

"Varieties: London at Night" Bell's New Weekly Messenger 11
    no 570   14 Mar 1841   MHC

"Varieties" Magnet 5 no 206   15 Mar 1841   MHC

"Varieties: Muzziness" Globe no 12,109   19 Mar 1841   MHC

"Literature" Era 3 no 132   4 Apr 1841   (general criticism)

"Varieties: The World" Bell's New Weekly Messenger 11 no 573
    4 Apr 1841   MHC

"Reviewer" Bell's New Weekly Messenger 11 no 573   4 Apr 1841
    (review - Charles O'Malley by Harry Lorrequer; the
    Dickens school of writing)

"Varieties" Magnet 5 no 209   5 Apr 1841   MHC

"Varieties: Barnaby's Raven" Globe no 12,125   7 Apr 1841
    MHC

"Varieties"   Bell's New Weekly Messenger 11 no 574   11 Apr
    1841   MHC

"Literature" Bell's Life in London 11 Apr 1841   MHC

"Varieties" Magnet 5 no 210   12 Apr 1841   MHC

"Literature" Era 3 no 134   18 Apr 1841   (re weeklies)

"Varieties: Fortune Hunters" Bell's New Weekly Messenger 11
    no 575   18 Apr 1841   MHC

"Varieties" Magnet 5 no 211   19 Apr 1841   MHC

"Miscellaneous: Sharp Ears"   Mark Lane Express 10   no 486
    19 Apr 1841   MHC

"Literature and Art" Weekly Dispatch no 2063 2 May 1841: 214
    (the practice of publishing magazine stories in parts)

"Literature" Era 3 no 136 2 May 1841 (review - Colin Clink
    by Charles Hooton, and the use of serialisation in
    Bentley's Miscellany)

"Varieties: An Amorous 'Prentice" <u>Bell's New Weekly Messenger</u>
     11   no 577   2 May 1841   MHC

"Varieties" <u>Magnet</u> 5 no 213 3 May 1841   MHC

"Literature, &c" <u>United Services Gazette</u> no 436   8 May 1841
     MHC

"Varieties: Woman's Whimsies" <u>Bell's New Weekly Messenger</u> 11
     no 578 9 May 1841 MHC

"Varieties" <u>Bell's Life in London</u> 9 May 1841   MHC

"Varieties" <u>Magnet</u> 5 no 214 10 May 1841   MHC

"Varieties: Time" <u>Bell's New Weekly Messenger</u> 11 no 180
     [sic; shd be 580]   23 May 1841   MHC

"Varieties" <u>Magnet</u> 5 no 216 24 May 1841   MHC

"Varieties: The Way of the World" <u>Bell's New Weekly Messenger</u>
     11 no 581   30 May 1841   MHC

"Varieties" <u>Magnet</u> 5 no 217 31 May 1841   MHC

"Notices of New Works" <u>Metropolitan Magazine</u> 31 no 123
     Jne 1841: 55-56 MHC

"Varieties: A Spring Morning" <u>Bell's New Weekly Messenger</u> 11
     no 582 6 Jne 1841   MHC

"Varieties" <u>Magnet</u> 5 no 218 7 Jne 1841   MHC

"Varieties: Bells" <u>Bell's New Weekly Messenger</u> 11   no 583
     13 Jne 1841   MHC

"Varieties" <u>Magnet</u> 5 no 219 14 Jne 1841   MHC

"Varieties: A Stormy Night" <u>Bell's New Weekly Messenger</u> 11
     no 584   20 Jne 1841   MHC

"Varieties" <u>Magnet</u> 5 no 220 21 Jne 1841   MHC

"Literature and Art" <u>Era</u> 3 no 144   27 Jne 1841 (remarks
     on novel-writing)

"Varieties: A Parasite. A Lady of an Uncertain Temper" <u>Bell's</u>
<u>New Weekly Messenger</u> 11 no 585 27 Jne 1841   MHC

"Varieties" <u>Magnet</u> 5 no 221 28 Jne 1841   MHC

"Public Dinner to Mr. Dickens" <u>Sun</u> no 15,230 1 Jul 1841

"Literature" <u>Bell's Life in London</u> 4 Jul 1841   MHC

"English Opera House" <u>Morning Post</u> no 21,994   14 Jul 1841
    (dramatisation of BR)

"The Theatres: English Opera House"   <u>Courier</u>   no 15,572
    14 Jul 1841 (dramatisation of BR)

"Literary Melange: Periodical Literature"   <u>Era</u> 3   no 147
    18 Jul 1841

"Theatres"   <u>John Bull</u> no 1076   24 Jul 1841: 357
    (dramatisation of BR)

"Varieties: An Idiot's Happiness" <u>Bell's New Weekly Messenger</u>
    11 no 589 1 Aug 1841   MHC

"Varieties" <u>Magnet</u> 5 no 226 2 Aug 1841   MHC

"Varieties: A Character. By 'Boz'"   <u>Bell's New Weekly</u>
    <u>Messenger</u> 11 no 590 8 Aug 1841   MHC

"Varieties: An Idiot's Happiness" <u>Globe</u> no 12,232   10 Aug
    1841   MHC

"Varieties: A Fine Old English Tory, All of the Olden Time"
    <u>Globe</u> no 12,234   12 Aug 1841   MHC

"Literature and Art" <u>Weekly Dispatch</u> no 2077 15 Aug 1841:
    394   (review - <u>Guy Fawkes</u> by W.H. Ainsworth)

"Theatricals and Music: Strand" <u>Sunday Times</u> no 982   15 Aug
    1841   (dramatisation of BR)

"Reviews of New Books" <u>Literary Gazette</u> 25 no 1283   21 Aug
    1841: 540-41 PNP

"Varieties: Sleepiness" <u>Bell's New Weekly Messenger</u> 11 no 592
    22 Aug 1841   MHC

"Varieties" Magnet 5 no 229   23 Aug 1841   MHC

"Reviews" Tablet no 63 28 Aug 1841: 565-66   PNP

"Reviews: Literature and Art" Bell's Weekly Messenger no 2366
      28 Aug 1841: 282   PNP

"Theodore Hook is dead!" Age 29 Aug 1841: 278

"Notices of New Works"   Metropolitan Magazine 32 no 125
      Sep 1841: 25   MHC

"Literature of the Month" New Monthly Magazine 63 no 249
      Sep 1841: 129-30 PNP

"Literature, &c" United Services Gazette no 454 11 Sep 1841
      PNP (re John Macrone, Dickens's first publisher)

"Literature" Bell's Life in London 19 Sep 1841   MHC

"Literary Examiner" Examiner no 1756 25 Sep 1841: 614 OT

"Literature" Bell's Life in London 3 Oct 1841   MHC

"Varieties: Picture of London" Globe no 12,281 6 Oct 1841
      MHC

"Charles Chesterfield. By Mrs. Trollope" The Times no 17,796
      8 Oct 1841 (imitations of Dickens)

"Table-Talk No. 223" Morning Post no 22,072 13 Oct 1841
      (the merchandising of literature)

"Reviews" Tablet no 76 23 Oct 1841: 693-94   (re Dickens's
      mechanical production of literature)

"Varieties: Rivalry in Love" Bell's New Weekly Messenger 11
      no 600 24 Oct 1841 MHC

"Varieties" Magnet 5 no 236   25 Oct 1841   MHC

"Master Humphrey's Clock" Town no 233 10 Nov 1841: 1852
      (MHC satire)

"Literature" John Bull 21 no 1092 13 Nov 1841: 549   MHC

"Master Humphrey's Clock"   <u>Town</u> no 234   17 Nov 1841: 1861
   (MHC satire)

"Master Humphrey's Clock"   <u>Town</u> no 235   24 Nov 1841: 1869
   (MHC satire)

"Notices of New Works"   <u>Metropolitan Magazine</u>   32   no 128
   Dec 1841: 111-12   MHC

"Master Humphrey's Clock"   <u>Town</u> no 236   1 Dec 1841: 1877
   (MHC satire)

"The Literary Examiner"   <u>Examiner</u> no 1766   4 Dec 1841: 772-74
   MHC   [John Forster]

"Serials"   <u>Spectator</u> 14 no 701   4 Dec 1841: 1170   MHC

"Master Humphrey's Clock"   <u>Town</u> no 237   8 Dec 1841: 1885-86
   (MHC satire)

"A Parthian Glance at the Serials of the Month"   <u>United
Services Gazette</u> no 465   11 Dec 1841   MHC

"Reviews"   <u>Athenaeum</u>   no 738   18 Dec 1841: 970 (review –
   novels by G.P.R. James; <u>Old Saint Paul's</u> by W.H.
   Ainsworth)

"Adelphi Theatre"   <u>The Times</u> no 17,859   21 Dec 1841
   (dramatisation of BR)

"Adelphi Theatre"   <u>Morning Herald</u> no 18,502   21 Dec 1841
   (dramatisation of BR)

"Master Humphrey's Clock"   <u>Town</u> no 239   22 Dec 1841: 1901
   (MHC satire)

"Literature"   <u>Era</u> 4 no 170   26 Dec 1841 (review – <u>Old Saint
Paul's</u> by W.H. Ainsworth and the practice of publishing
   novels in newspaper instalments)

"Theatricals and Music: Adelphi"   <u>Sunday Times</u> no 1001
   26 Dec 1841   (dramatisation of BR)

"The Theatre" <u>Observer</u>   26 Dec 1841 (dramatisation of BR)

"Public Amusements: The Adelphi" <u>Weekly Dispatch</u>   no 2096
        26 Dec 1841: 620   (dramatisation of BR)

"The Theatres: Adelphi"   <u>Sun</u> no 15,385   28 Dec 1841
        (dramatisation of BR)

"Master Humphrey's Clock" <u>Town</u> no 240   29 Dec 1841: 1909
        (MHC satire)

"Master Humphrey's Clock" <u>Town</u> no 241   5 Jan 1842: 1917
        (MHC satire)

"Master Humphrey's Clock" <u>Town</u> no 242   12 Jan 1842: 1925
        (MHC satire)

"Master Humphrey's Clock" <u>Town</u> no 243   19 Jan 1842: 1934
        (MHC satire)

"Master Humphrey's Clock" <u>Town</u> no 244   26 Jan 1842: 1939
        (MHC satire)

II. REVIEWS: LISTED BY WORKS OF DICKENS

Sketches by Boz (MM,SB)

"Magazine Day" <u>Sun</u> no 12,863 2 Dec 1833   MM

"The Monthly" <u>Bell's New Weekly Messenger</u> (<u>Reviewer</u>) 2 no 102
    8 Dec 1833: 98   MM

"Magazine Day" <u>Sun</u> no 12,889 1 Jan 1834   MM

"The Magazines" <u>Morning Advertiser</u> no 13,344 3 Jan 1834 MM

"The Monthly" <u>Bell's New Weekly Messenger</u> (<u>Reviewer</u>) 3 no 106
    5 Jan 1834: 2   MM

"True Sun Daily Review" <u>True Sun</u> no 585 15 Jan 1834   MM

"Magazine Day" <u>Sun</u> no 2,915 [<u>sic</u>; shd be 12, 915] 1 Feb 1834
    MM

"Review - Literature and Arts" <u>Bell's Weekly Messenger</u> no 1975
    10 Feb 1834: 46   MM

"The Magazines" <u>Morning Advertiser</u> no 13,379 13 Feb 1834
    MM

"Magazine Day" <u>Sun</u> no 12,966 1 Apr 1834   MM

"The Magazines" <u>Morning Advertiser</u> no 13,421 3 Apr 1834
    MM

"The Monthly" <u>Bell's New Weekly Messenger</u> (<u>Reviewer</u>) 2 no 119
    6 Apr 1834: 28   MM

"Literature and Art" <u>Weekly Dispatch</u> no 1696 6 Apr 1834: 106
    MM

"The Magazines" <u>Morning Advertiser</u> no 13,446 2 May 1834
    MM

"The Monthly" <u>Bell's New Weekly Messenger</u> (<u>Reviewer</u>) 3 no 123
    4 May 1834: 36   MM

"Literature and Art" <u>Weekly Dispatch</u> no 1700 4 May 1834: 142
  MM

"Literature and Art" <u>Weekly Dispatch</u> no 1713 3 Aug 1834: 252
  MM

"Review - Literature and Arts" <u>Bell's Weekly Messenger</u> no 2000
  3 Aug 1834: 245-46   MM

"Literature" <u>Observer</u> no 2185 10 Aug 1834   MM

"The Magazines" <u>True Sun</u> no 827 1 Oct 1834   MM

"The Magazines" <u>Morning Advertiser</u> no 13,576 1 Oct 1834
  MM

"Magazines" <u>Sun</u> no 13,126 4 Oct 1834   MM

"The Magazines" <u>Morning Herald</u> no 16,266 4 Oct 1834   MM

"Literature" <u>Observer</u> no 2198 5 Oct 1834   MM

"The Magazines" <u>Sunday Times</u> no 624 5 Oct 1834   MM

"Review - Literature and Arts" <u>Bell's Weekly Messenger</u> no 2010
  12 Oct 1834: 323   MM

"Magazine Day" <u>Sun</u> no 13,202 1 Jan 1835   MM

"Literature and Art" <u>Weekly Dispatch</u> no 1735 4 Jan 1835: 8
  MM

"Review - Literature and Art" <u>Bell's Weekly Messenger</u> no 2022
  11 Jan 1835: 10   MM

"The Magazines" <u>Sun</u> no 13,230 4 Feb 1835   MM

"Reviewer" <u>Bell's New Weekly Messenger</u> 4 no 163 8 Feb 1835:
  85-86   MM

"Literature and Art" <u>Weekly Dispatch</u> no 1740 8 Feb 1835: 54
  MM

"Review - Literature and Art" <u>Bell's Weekly Messenger</u> no 2027
  15 Feb 1835: 50   MM

"Literature" Observer 3 May 1835   MM

"Magazine Day" Sun no 13,460 2 Nov 1835   MM

"Progress of Publication" Morning Advertiser no 14,003
    11 Feb 1836   SB

"Literature" Morning Chronicle no 20,696 11 Feb 1836   SB
    [George Hogarth]

"Review of New Books" Literary Gazette 20 no 995 13 Feb
    1836: 102   SB

"Literature" Bell's Life in London 14 Feb 1836 (see MC
    11.2.1836)   SB

"Literature" Sun no 13,550 15 Feb 1836   SB

"The Sketches of Boz" Spectator 9 no 399 20 Feb 1836:
    182-83   SB

"Our Library Table" Athenaeum no 434 20 Feb 1836: 145 SB

"Literature" Sunday Times no 696 21 Feb 1836   SB

"Literary Memoranda" Atlas 11 no 510 21 Feb 1836: 123
    SB

"Literature" True Sun no 1258 25 Feb 1836   SB

"The Literary Examiner" Examiner no 1456   28 Feb 1836:
    132-33   SB

"Literature and Art" Weekly Dispatch no 1793 28 Feb 1836:
    78   SB

"Notices of New Works" Metropolitan Magazine 15 no 59
    Mar 1836: 77   SB

"Sketches by 'Boz'" Monthly Review 1 no 3 Mar 1836: 350-57
    SB

"Magazines" Morning Advertiser no 14,022 4 Mar 1836   MM

"Literature" Morning Post no 20,363 12 Mar 1836   SB

"Miscellaneous" <u>Literary Gazette</u> 20 no 1003 9 Apr 1836: 233
     PP,LF

"Literature" <u>Bell's Life in London</u> 10 Apr 1836 PP,LF

"Notabilia: Shabby-Genteel People" <u>Examiner</u> no 1471 10 Apr
     1836: 234-35   SB

"New Books" <u>Mirror</u> 27 no 772 16 Apr 1836: 249-51   SB

"Critical Notices" <u>New Monthly Magazine</u> 47 no 185 May 1836:
     105   SB

"Literature of the Month" <u>Court Magazine</u> 8 no 5 May 1836:
     227 LF

"The Magazines" <u>True Sun</u> no 1316 3 May 1836   MM

"Literature" <u>Morning Post</u> no 20,413 11 May 1836   PP,LF

"The Magazines" <u>Sun</u> no 13,642 2 Jne 1836   PP,LF

"Review of New Books" <u>Literary Gazette</u> 20 no 1040 24 Dec
     1836: 822-23   SB

"Spectator's Library" <u>Spectator</u> 9 no 443 26 Dec 1836:
     1234-35   SB

"Reviews" <u>Athenaeum</u> no 479 31 Dec 1836: 916-17   SB

"The Pickwick Club, &c, by Boz" <u>Monthly Review</u> 1 no 2 Feb
     1837: 153-63   SB,PP,BM

"Literary Memoranda" <u>Atlas</u> 12 no 568 2 Apr 1837: 217   SB

"Literature and Art" <u>Weekly Dispatch</u> no 1851 9 Apr 1837: 178
     SB

"Literature" <u>Sunday Times</u> no 757 23 Apr 1837   SB

"The Works of Dickens" <u>London and Westminster Review</u> 5/27 nos
     10 & 53 Jul 1837: 194-215 SB,PP,BM   [Charles Buller]

"The Pickwick Papers" <u>Quarterly Review</u> 59 no 118 Oct 1837:
     484-518 SB,PP [Abraham Hayward]

"Progress of Publication" Morning Advertiser no 14,534 3 Nov
    1837   SB,PP

"Dickens's Tales" Edinburgh Review 68 no 137   Oct 1838:
    75-97   SB,PP,BM,NN   [T.H. Lister]

"Misplaced Attachment of Mr. John Dounce"   Shipping and
    Mercantile Gazette no 209 14 Nov 1838   SB

Pickwick Papers (PP)

"Literary Memoranda" Atlas 11 no 516 3 Apr 1836: 220   PP

"A Cabman's Description of His Horse" The Times no 16,071
    7 Apr 1836 PP

"A Cabman's Description of His Horse" Morning Advertiser no
    14,052 8 Apr 1836   PP

"A Cabman's Description of His Horse" Morning Post no 20,386
    8 Apr 1836   PP

"A Cabman's Description of His Horse" Morning Herald no 16,735
    9 Apr 1836 PP

"Miscellaneous" Literary Gazette 20 no 1003 9 Apr 1836: 233
    PP,LF

"Fact and Scraps - Original and Select: A Cabman's Description
    of His Horse" Weekly Dispatch no 1799 10 Apr 1836: 134
    PP

"A Cabman's Description of His Horse" Sunday Times no 703
    10 Apr 1836   PP

"Literature" Bell's Life in London 10 Apr 1836   PP, LF

"Progress of Publication" Spectator 9 no 407 16 Apr 1836:
    373   PP

"Miscellaneous: A Cabman's Description of His Horse" Mark
    Lane Express 4 no 225   18 Apr 1836: 126   PP

"Notices of New Books"   Metropolitan Magazine 16 no 61
     May 1836: 15   PP,LF

"Magazine Day" Sun no 13,615 2 May 1836   PP

"Literature" Morning Post no 20,413 11 May 1836   PP,LF

"Notices of New Works"   Metropolitan Magazine 16 no 62
     Jne 1836: 46-47   PP

"The Magazines" Sun no 13,642 2 Jne 1836   PP,LF

"Literature" Morning Chronicle no 20,791 7 Jne 1836   PP

"Literature and Fine Arts" Globe no 10,478 8 Jne 1836   PP

"Reviews of New Books" Carlton Chronicle 1 11 Jne 1836: 10
     PP

"Literature" John Bull 16 no 809 13 Jne 1836: 190   PP

"Notices of New Works"   Metropolitan Magazine 16 no 63
     Jul 1836: 76   PP

"Reviews of New Books" Carlton Chronicle no 4 2 Jul 1836:
     57-58   PP

"The Magazines" Sun no 13,669 4 Jul 1836   PP

"Miscellaneous" Literary Gazette 20 no 1016 . 9 Jul 1836: 442
     PP

"Notices of New Works"   Metropolitan Magazine 16 no 64
     Aug 1836: 110-11   PP,LF

"Miscellany: A Contested Election" Carlton Chronicle no 9
     6 Aug 1836: 131   PP

"Original Papers: The Literary Men of Town" Carlton Chronicle
     no 9 6 Aug 1836: 141   PP

"Literature" Bell's Life in London 7 Aug 1836   PP

"A Contested Election" The Times no 16,178 10 Aug 1836 PP

"A Contested Election" True Sun ns 15 10 Aug 1836   PP

"A Contested Election"   Public Ledger 78 no 24,312   13 Aug
      1836   PP

"Miscellaneous"   Literary Gazette 20 no 1021   13 Aug 1836: 520
      PP

"Miscellaneous: A Contested Election"   Mark Lane Express 4
      no 242   15 Aug 1836: 262   PP

"Literature"   Morning Post no 20,496   16 Aug 1836   PP

"A Contested Election"   Morning Chronicle   no 20,843   18 Aug
      1836   PP

"Progress of Publication"   Spectator 9 no 425   20 Aug 1836:
      805   PP

"Facts and Scraps, Original and Select: An Election Manoeuvre"
      Weekly Dispatch no 1818   21 Aug 1836: 310   PP

"Notices of New Works"   Metropolitan Magazine   17   no 65
      Sep 1836: 13   PP

"Critical Notices"   New Monthly Magazine 48 no 189   Sep 1836:
      102-04   PP

"Magazines"   Sun   no 13,719   2 Sep 1836   PP

"Literary Examiner"   Examiner no 1492   4 Sep 1836: 563-65   PP

"Literature"   Bell's Life in London   4 Sep 1836   PP

"Miscellaneous"   Literary Gazette 20 no 1025   10 Sep 1836: 584
      PP

"Literature"   John Bull 16 no 822   12 Sep 1836: 295   PP

"Particulars of Pie-Making"   True Sun ns 60   1 Oct 1836   PP

"Cockney Sportsmen"   St. James's Chronicle no 21,316   1 Oct
      1836   PP

"Particulars of Pie-Making"   The Times no 16,223   1 Oct 1836
      PP

"Particulars of Pie-Making" Morning Post no 20,537 3 Oct
      1836   PP

"Magazines" Morning Chronicle no 20,884 5 Oct 1836   PP

"A Shooting Party" True Sun ns 65 7 Oct 1836   PP

"Particulars of Pie-Making" Morning Advertiser no 14,209
      8 Oct 1836   PP

"Literary Examiner" Examiner no 1497 9 Oct 1836: 647-48
      PP

"Miscellaneous: Cure for the Gout. Twopenny Rope" Mark Lane
      Express 4 no 250 10 Oct 1836   PP

"The Law" True Sun ns 72 15 Oct 1836   PP

"Varieties" Bell's New Weekly Messenger 5 no 251 16 Oct
      1836: 667   PP

"Miscellaneous: Particulars of Pie-Making" Mark Lane Express
      4 no 251 17 Oct 1836   PP

"The Pickwick Club. Sketches. By Boz" Morning Advertiser
      no 14,214 25 Oct 1836   PP

"Notices of New Works" Metropolitan Magazine 17 no 67
      Nov 1836. 84   PP

"Monthly Review of Literature" Monthly Magazine 22 no 5 Nov
      1836: 522-24 PP

"Magazine Day" Sun no 13,770 1 Nov 1836   PP

"Literary Extracts: A Quiet Tenant" True Sun ns 87 2 Nov
      1836   PP

"Pickwickian Philosophy - Poverty and Oysters" Morning Herald
      no 16,911 2 Nov 1836   PP

"Literary Examiner" Examiner no 1501 6 Nov 1836: 710-11 PP

"Review of New Books: Pickwickiana" Literary Gazette 20 no
      1034 12 Nov 1836: 727-28   PP

"Literary Extract: Paternal Advice" True Sun ns 97 14 Nov
     1836   PP

"Facts and Scraps: A Bit of Parental Advice" Weekly Dispatch
     no 1831   20 Nov 1836: 452   PP

"The First of September" Sporting Magazine 2s 14 no 80
     Dec 1836: 141-47 PP

"Magazines" Sun no 13,796 3 Dec 1836   PP

"Reviews" Athenaeum no 475 3 Dec 1836: 841-43   PP

"Literary Examiner" Examiner no 1505 4 Dec 1836: 775-76
     PP

"Pickwick on Proposing" Morning Post no 20,590 5 Dec 1836
     PP

"Reviewer: 'Boz'" Bell's New Weekly Messenger 5 no 259
     11 Dec 1836: 794 PP

"Notices of New Works" Metropolitan Magazine 18 no 69
     Jan 1837: 6   PP

"The Pickwick Papers - No. X" Sun no 13,821 2 Jan 1837 PP

"Bentley's Miscellany" Morning Post no 20,617 6 Jan 1837
     PP

"Edification of Married Men" Bell's New Weekly Messenger 6
     no 263 8 Jan 1837: 23   PP

"Reviewer" Bell's New Weekly Messenger 6 no 264 15 Jan 1837:
     38   PP

"A Regular Fat Man" Bell's New Weekly Messenger 6 no 264
     15 Jan 1837: 39   PP

"Miscellaneous: A Roadside Public House" Mark Lane Express
     6 no 264   16 Jan 1837 PP

"Notices of New Works" Metropolitan Magazine 18 no 70
     Feb 1837: 46   PP

"The Pickwick Club, &c, by Boz"   Monthly Review 1 no 2
    Feb 1837: 153-63   SB,PP,BM

"Literature and Art" Weekly Dispatch no 1842 5 Feb 1837: 70
    PP

"Reviewer" Bell's New Weekly Messenger 6 no 268 5 Feb 1837:
    88   PP

"Notices of New Works"   Metropolitan Magazine 18   no 71
    Mar 1837: 77   PP

"Varieties: A Straightforward Witness"   Courier   no 14,219
    3 Mar 1837   PP

"Reviews of New Books" Carlton Chronicle no 25 4 Mar 1837:
    554-55   PP

"Reviewer" Bell's New Weekly Messenger 6 no 271 5 Mar 1837:
    154   PP

"The Periodicals" Morning Advertiser no 14,327 6 Mar 1837
    PP

"Fashion and Table Talk: A Straightforward Witness"   Globe
    no 10,710   6 Mar 1837   PP

"The Pickwick Valentine" Morning Herald no 17,019 7 Mar 1837
    PP

"New Books: The Pickwick Papers. By Boz"   Mirror 29 no 824
    11 Mar 1837: 153-55   PP

"Literary Extracts: A Straightforward Witness"   True Sun ns
    206   24 Mar 1837   ГР

"Some Thoughts on Arch-Waggery, and, In Especial, on the
    Genius of 'Boz'" Court Magazine 10 no 4 Apr 1837:
    185-87

"Notices of New Works"   Metropolitan Magazine 18   no 72
    Apr 1837: 106-07   PP

"Posthumous Papers of the Pickwick Club" Eclectic Review 1
    Apr 1837: 339-55   PP

"Magazine Day" Sun no 13,900 1 Apr 1837   PP,BM

"Progress of Publication" Morning Advertiser no 14,350 1 Apr
    1837   PP

"A Footman's Resignation" Morning Herald no 17,031 1 Apr
    1837   PP

"Reviews of New Books" Carlton Chronicle no 39 1 Apr 1837:
    615-17   PP

"Reviewer" Bell's New Weekly Messenger 6 no 275 2 Apr 1837:
    218   PP

"Extracts from New Books: The Consequences of Not Keeping
    Awake. By 'Boz'"   Magnet 1 no 4 3 Apr 1837: 26-27
    PP

"The Peregrinations of Pickwick" Literary Gazette 21 no 1055
    8 Apr 1837: 228   PP

"Review - Literature and Arts" Bell's Weekly Messenger no 2138
    9 Apr 1837: 119   PP

"Fashion and Table-Talk: How to Get On. A Young London Thief"
    Globe no 10,756 28 Apr 1837   PP,BM

"The Magazines" Carlton Chronicle no 43 29 Apr 1837: 683-84
    PP

"The Pickwick Papers" Chambers's Edinburgh Journal 6 no 274
    29 Apr 1837: 109-10   PP

"How to Get On. The Apothecary Method" Observer 30 Apr 1837
    PP

"Literature" Bell's Life in London 30 Apr 1837   PP

"Notices of New Works" Metropolitan Magazine 19 no 73
    May 1837: 16   PP

"Progress of Publication" Morning Advertiser no 14,375 1 May
    1837   PP

"Miscellaneous: How to Get On" Mark Lane Express 6 no 279
    1 May 1837   PP

"Literature" John Bull 17 no 856 7 May 1837: 224   PP

"Reviewer" Bell's New Weekly Messenger 6 no 280 7 May 1837:
    297-98   PP

"Fashions Among Footmen" Courier no 14,278 11 May 1837 PP

"A Footman's Resignation" Constitutional and Public Ledger
    1 no 210 17 May 1837   PP

"The Works of Dickens" London and Westminster Review 5/27 nos
    10 & 53 Jul 1837: 194-215 SB,PP,BM [Charles Buller]

"The Pickwick Papers" Sun no 13,978 1 Jul 1837   PP

"A Scene in the Fleet" Courier no 14,322 1 Jul 1837   PP

"Reviewer" Bell's New Weekly Messenger 6 no 288 2 Jul 1837:
    426   PP

"The Literary Examiner" Examiner no 1535 2 Jul 1837: 421-22
    PP [John Forster]

"Scraps by Boz" Magnet 1 no 17 3 Jul 1837: 133   PP

"The Public Journals: The Prisoner at Large" Mirror 30 no 843
    8 Jul 1837: 27-28   PP

"The Public Journals: The Insolvent Debtors' Court" Mirror
    30 no 845 22 Jul 1837: 62-63   PP

"Facts and Scraps: Imprisonment for Debt" Weekly Dispatch
    no 1866 23 Jul 1837: 356   PP

"Magazines" Sun no 14,005 2 Aug 1837   PP

"Reviewer" Bell's New Weekly Messenger 7 no 293 6 Aug 1837:
    35   PP

"Sketches by Boz" Magnet 1 no 22 7 Aug 1837: 171   PP

"Miscellaneous" Mark Lane Express 6 no 294 14 Aug 1837 PP

"New Books: Pickwickiana" Mirror 30 no 850 26 Aug 1837:
    143-44   PP

100

"A Sam Wellerism" Morning Advertiser no 14,480 1 Sep 1837
    PP

"Fashion and Varieties" Courier no 14,375 1 Sep 1837   PP

"Notes of a Reader: Pickwickiana" Mirror 30 no 851   2 Sep
    1837: 156-58 PP

"Reviewer" Bell's New Weekly Messenger 7 no 297   3 Sep 1837:
    67   PP

"Literature" Bell's Life in London 3 Sep 1837   PP

"Illustrations: Old Weller" Figaro in London 6 no 301 9 Sep
    1837: 141-42 PP

"Fashion and Table-Talk: Eating in Scotland" Globe no 10,922
    12 Sep 1837   PP

"Literature" St. James's Chronicle no 12,934   12 Sep 1837

"The Gatherer: A Sketch" Mirror 30 no 853   16 Sep 1837: 192
    PP

"Miscellaneous" Mark Lane Express 6 no 299   18 Sep 1837 PP

"The Pickwick Papers" Quarterly Review 59 no 118   Oct 1837:
    484-518   SB,PP   [Abraham Hayward]

"Literature - The Magazines" Morning Chronicle   no 21,181
    3 Oct 1837 PP

"Popularity of Coachmen" The Times no 16,539   5 Oct 1837
    PP

"The Gatherer: Old Weller's Letter (from Pickwick)"   Mirror
    30 no 856 7 Oct 1837: 240   PP

"The Widower" Observer 8 Oct 1837   PP

"Post Boys and Donkies" Bell's Life in London 8 Oct 1837
    PP

"Reviewer" Bell's New Weekly Messenger 7 no 302 8 Oct 1837:
    107   PP

"Fashion and Varieties: The Critics of Eatanswill" <u>Courier</u> no 14,408   10 Oct 1837   PP

"Notes of a Reader: Pickwickiana by Boz" <u>Mirror</u> 30 no 859 28 Oct 1837: 285-87   PP

"Reviewer" <u>Bell's New Weekly Messenger</u> 7 no 306   5 Nov 1837: 138-39   PP

"Progress of Publication" <u>Morning Advertiser</u> no 14,534   3 Nov 1837   SB,PP

"The Literary Examiner" <u>Examiner</u> no 1553   5 Nov 1837: 708-09 PP

"Notices of New Publications" <u>Railway Times</u> no 2   5 Nov 1837: 10   PP

"Humourous Sketches by 'Boz'" <u>Magnet</u> 1 no 35   6 Nov 1837: 283 PP

"Miscellaneous: Mr. Weller's Visit to the Bank" <u>Mark Lane Express</u> 6 no 306   6 Nov 1837   PP

"Notes of a Reader: Pickwickiana" <u>Mirror</u> 30 no 868   16 Dec 1837: 407-08   PP

"Notes of a Reader: Pickwickiana" <u>Mirror</u> 30 no 870   23 Dec 1837: 437-38   PP

"Mr. Weller's Opinion of the Ladies" <u>Morning Advertiser</u> no 14,586   3 Jan 1838   PP

"Illustrations: The Political Fat Boy" <u>Figaro in London</u> 7 no 318   6 Jan 1838: 1   PP

"Miscellaneous: Smithfield. Mr. Weller's Opinion of the Ladies" <u>Mark Lane Express</u> 7 no 315   8 Jan 1838   PP,BM

"Review – Literature and Arts: The Magazines for January" <u>Bell's Weekly Messenger</u> no 2177   8 Jan 1838: 14   PP

"Miscellaneous: Prosperity in Perspective. Election Broils" <u>Mark Lane Express</u> 7   no 320   12 Feb 1838   PP

"Miscellaneous: Gentlemen. A Resolution Passed"   Mark Lane
        Express 7 no 327   2 Apr 1838   PP,NN

"Periodicals"   United Services Gazette   no 272   7 Apr 1838
        PP,BM

"Miscellaneous: Principle"   Mark Lane Express 7 no 328   9 Apr
        1838   PP

"Dickens's Tales"   Edinburgh Review   68   no 137   Oct 1838:
        75-97   SB,PP,BM,NN   [Thomas Henry Lister]

"Sporting Literature"   Fraser's Magazine 18 no 106   Oct 1838:
        481-88   PP

"French Criticism on the Pickwick"   Examiner no 1611   16 Dec
        1838: 790   PP

"German Translation of the Pickwick Papers"   Dublin Review 8
        no 15   Feb 1840:   160-88   PP

"Charles Dickens and His Works"   Fraser's Magazine 21 no 124
        Apr 1840: 381-400

Sunday Under Three Heads (SUTH)

"Literature"   Bell's Life in London   3 Jul 1836   SUTH

"Literature and Art"   Weekly Dispatch no 1811   3 Jul 1836: 246
        SUTH

"Literary Memoranda"   Atlas 11 no 531   17 Jul 1836: 457   SUTH

"Reviews of New Books"   Carlton Chronicle no 6   23 Jul 1836:
        104-05   SUTH

"Notices of New Works"   Metropolitan Magazine   16   no   64
        Aug 1836: 111   SUTH

"Literature"   Morning Post no 20,491   10 Aug 1836   SUTH

The Strange Gentleman (SG)

"Theatricals, &c" <u>Mark Lane Express</u> 4 no 248   26 Sep 1836
   SG

"Theatres" <u>Morning Chronicle</u> no 20,880   30 Sep 1836   SG

"St. James's Theatre" <u>Morning Herald</u> no 16,883   30 Sep 1836
   SG

"St. James's Theatre" <u>Standard</u> no 2931   30 Sep 1836   SG

"The Theatres" <u>Courier</u> no 14,090   30 Sep 1836   SG

"The Theatres" <u>Globe</u> no 10,576   30 Sep 1836   SG

"St. James's Theatre" <u>Morning Advertiser</u> no 14,202   30 Sep
   1836   SG

"St. James's Theatre" <u>The Times</u> no 16,222   30 Sep 1836   SG

"The Theatres" <u>Morning Post</u> no 20,535   30 Sep 1836   SG

"St. James's Theatre" <u>Constitutional and Public Ledger</u> 1
   no 14   30 Sep 1836   SG

"Music and the Drama" <u>Athenaeum</u> no 466   1 Oct 1836: 708
   SG

"St. James's Theatre" <u>Morning Post</u> no 20,536   1 Oct 1836
   SG

"Theatres" <u>Courier</u> no 14,091   1 Oct 1836   SG

"Drama" <u>Literary Gazette</u> 20 no 1028   1 Oct 1836: 637   SG

"Magazine Day" <u>Sun</u> no 13,744   1 Oct 1836   SG

"The Theatres" <u>Carlton Chronicle</u> no 13   1 Oct 1836: 206
   SG

"The Theatres" <u>United Services Gazette</u> no 191   1 Oct 1836
   SG

"Theatricals" <u>Age</u> 2 Oct 1836: 326   SG

"The Drama" <u>Bell's Life in London</u> 2 Oct 1836   SG

"Amusements: St. James's Theatre" <u>Bell's Weekly Messenger</u>
    no 2111 2 Oct 1836: 314   SG

"The Theatres" <u>Observer</u> 2 Oct 1836   SG

"The Drama" <u>Champion</u> no 3 2 Oct 1836: 22   SG

"Theatricals" <u>Atlas</u> 11 no 542 2 Oct 1836: 631   SG

"The Winter Theatrical Campaign" <u>Weekly Dispatch</u> no 1824
    2 Oct 1836: 368   SG

"Theatricals" <u>Sunday Times</u> no 728 2 Oct 1836   SG

"The Drama" <u>Bell's New Weekly Messenger</u> 5 no 249 2 Oct 1836:
    634   SG

"Theatricals" <u>Figaro in London</u> no 253 8 Oct 1836: 167-68
    SG

"St. James's Theatre" <u>The Times</u> no 16,246 28 Oct 1836
    SG

The Village Coquettes (VC)

"St. James's Theatre" <u>Sun</u> no 13,799 7 Dec 1836   VC

"Theatres: St. James's" <u>True Sun</u> ns 117 7 Dec 1836   VC

"St. James's Theatre" <u>The Times</u> no 16,280 7 Dec 1836   VC

"St. James's Theatre" <u>Morning Chronicle</u> no 20,937 7 Dec 1836
    VC

"St. James's Theatre" <u>Morning Herald</u> no 16,939 7 Dec 1836
    VC

"The Stage: St. James's Theatre" <u>Constitutional and Public
    Ledger</u> 1 no 72 7 Dec 1836   VC

"Fashion and Table-Talk" <u>Globe</u> no 10,634 7 Dec 1836   VC

"St. James's Theatre" <u>Morning Advertiser</u> no 14,251 7 Dec
    1836   VC

"The Theatres" <u>Spectator</u> 9 no 441 10 Dec 1836: 1183   VC

"Theatricals" <u>Figaro in London</u> no 262 10 Dec 1836: 204
    VC

"Drama" <u>Literary Gazette</u> 20 no 1038   10 Dec 1836: 795-96
    VC

"The Theatres" <u>Carlton Chronicle</u> no 23 10 Dec 1836: 365-66
    VC

"Theatrical Examiner" <u>Examiner</u> no 1506 11 Dec 1836: 791-92
    VC   [John Forster]

"The Drama" <u>Bell's New Weekly Messenger</u> 5 no 259   11 Dec
    1836: 795   VC

"The Theatres" <u>Observer</u>   11 Dec 1836   VC   (see BNWM
    11.12.1836)

"Theatricals" <u>Champion</u> no 13 11 Dec 1836: 99   VC

"Amusements: St. James's Theatre"   <u>Bell's Weekly Messenger</u>
    no 2121 11 Dec 1836: 398   VC

"Theatricals" <u>Age</u> 11 Dec 1836: 406   VC

"The Drama" <u>Bell's Life in London</u> 11 Dec 1836   VC   (see
    BNWM 11.12.1836)

"Theatricals" <u>Sunday Times</u> no 738 11 Dec 1836   VC

"Theatricals" <u>Mark Lane Express</u> 4 no 259 12 Dec 1836   VC

"Music and the Drama" <u>Athenaeum</u> no 477 17 Dec 1836: 891
    VC

Is She His Wife? (**ISHW**)

"St. James's Theatre" <u>Standard</u> no 3066   7 Mar 1837   ISHW

"St. James's Theatre" <u>Morning Herald</u> no 17,019   7 Mar 1837
      ISHW

"The Theatres" <u>Morning Post</u> no 20,668   7 Mar 1837   ISHW

"St. James's Theatre" <u>Morning Chronicle</u> no 21,005   7 Mar 1837
      ISHW

"St. James's Theatre"   <u>The Times</u> no 16,358   8 Mar 1837
      ISHW

"St. James's" <u>Literary Gazette</u> 21 no 1051   11 Mar 1837: 164
      ISHW

"Theatricals" <u>Champion</u> no 26   12 Mar 1837: 205   ISHW

"The Drama" <u>Bell's New Weekly Messenger</u> 6 no 272   12 Mar
      1837: 171   ISHW

"Theatricals" <u>Sunday Times</u> no 751   12 Mar 1837   ISHW

"The Theatres: St. James's" <u>Observer</u> 12 Mar 1837   ISHW

"The Drama: St. James's" <u>Bell's Life in London</u> 12 Mar 1837
      ISHW

"Theatricals" <u>Mark Lane Express</u> 6 no 272   13 Mar 1837   ISHW

"Theatres" <u>Magnet</u> 1 no 1   13 Mar 1837   ISHW

"Theatricals" <u>Figaro in London</u> no 276   18 Mar 1837: 44   ISHW

"The Theatres" <u>Carlton Chronicle</u> 37   18 Mar 1837: 589   ISHW

"The Drama" <u>Bell's Life in London</u> 28 Jan 1838   ISHW

Bentley's Miscellany / Oliver Twist (BM, OT)

"Magazine Day" <u>Sun</u> no 13,821 2 Jan 1837   BM

"The Magazines" <u>True Sun</u> ns 141   4 Jan 1837   BM

"The Magazines" <u>Constitutional and Public Ledger</u> 1 no 98
    6 Jan 1837   BM

"Reviews of New Books" <u>Carlton Chronicle</u> no 27 7 Jan 1837:
    425-27   PP,BM

"Literature" <u>Globe</u> no 10,661 7 Jan 1837   BM

"The Public Journals: Public Life of Mr. Tulrumble, once Mayor
    of Mudfog" <u>Mirror</u> 29 no 815 7 Jan 1837: 13-16   BM

"Reviews" <u>Athenaeum</u> no 480 7 Jan 1837: 4-6   BM

"The Magazines for the Month" <u>Atlas</u> 12 no 556 8 Jan 1837:
    28-29   BM

"Progress of Publication"   <u>Morning Advertiser</u>   no   14,281
    11 Jan 1837   BM

"Literature and Art" <u>Weekly Dispatch</u> no 1839 15 Jan 1837:
    34   BM

"Literature" <u>Morning Chronicle</u> no 20,970 19 Jan 1837 BM

"Bentley's Miscellany, No. I. For January"   <u>St. James's
    Chronicle</u> no 12,365 24 Jan 1837   BM

"Oliver Twist" <u>Morning Post</u> no 20,637 30 Jan 1837   BM

"Advantage of Being Born in a Workhouse"   <u>Globe</u> no 10,680
    30 Jan 1837   BM

"A Board of Guardians of the Poor" <u>The Times</u> no 16,327 31 Jan
    1837   BM

"Literature" <u>St. James's Chronicle</u> no 12,368 31 Jan 1837
    BM

"History of a Foundling" <u>Morning Post</u> no 20,638 31 Jan 1837
    BM

"The Pickwick Club, &c, by Boz" Monthly Review 1 no 2
    Feb 1837: 153-63   SB,PP,BM

"The Magazines" Constitutional and Public Ledger 1 no 120
    1 Feb 1837   BM

"The Magazines" Sun no 13,848 1 Feb 1837   BM

"Oliver Twist" Morning Post no 20,640 2 Feb 1837   BM

"Magazines" United Services Gazette no 209 4 Feb 1837 PP,BM

"Review of New Books" Carlton Chronicle no 31 4 Feb 1837:
    491   PP,BM

"Literature" John Bull 17 no 843 5 Feb 1837: 72   BM

"Review - Literature and Arts: The Magazines" Bell's Weekly
    Messenger no 2129   5 Feb 1837: 47   BM

"The Public Journals: Oliver Twist" Mirror 29 no 822 25 Feb
    1837: 125-27 BM

"Magazines" Sun no 13,873 2 Mar 1837   BM

"Reviews of New Books" Carlton Chronicle no 25 4 Mar 1837:
    555-56   BM

"The Magazines" Morning Post no 20,669 8 Mar 1837   BM

"The Literary Examiner" Examiner no 1519 12 Mar 1837:
    165-66   BM   [John Forster]

"Literature and Art" Weekly Dispatch no 1847 12 Mar 1837:
    130   BM

"The Public Journals: The Pantomime of Life - By Boz" Mirror
    29 no 825   18 Mar 1837: 170-71   BM

"Literature" St. James's Chronicle no 12,395 4 Apr 1837 BM

"Reviews of New Books" Carlton Chronicle no 40 8 Apr 1837:
    635-36   BM

"Literature" John Bull 17 no 852 9 Apr 1837: 76   BM

"The Public Journals: Oliver Twist an Undertaker's Boy-Mute"
    <u>Mirror</u> 29 no 831 29 Apr 1837: 526 [<u>sic</u>; shd be 265] –
    66 BM

"Magazine Day" <u>Sun</u> no 13,925 1 May 1837   BM

"The Magazines" <u>True Sun</u> ns 240 4 May 1837   BM

"Reviews of New Books" <u>Carlton Chronicle</u> no 44 6 May 1837:
    698-99 BM

"Literature and Art" <u>Weekly Dispatch</u> no 1855 7 May 1837: 226
    BM

"Sensibility of a Young Pauper" <u>Constitutional and Public</u>
    <u>Ledger</u> 1 no 206 12 May 1837 BM

"The Public Journals: Oliver Twist 'Runs Away'" <u>Mirror</u> 29
    no 834 20 May 1837: 313-15   BM

"Literature" <u>Observer</u> 4 Jne 1837   BM

"The Works of Dickens" <u>London and Westminster Review</u> 5/27
    nos 10 & 53 Jul 1837: 194-215   SB,PP,BM [Charles
    Buller]

"Magazine Day" <u>Sun</u> no 13,978 1 Jul 1837   BM

"Literature: The Magazines" <u>Observer</u> 2 Jul 1837   BM

"Literature" <u>Bell's Life in London</u> 2 Jul 1837   BM

"Literature and Art" <u>Weekly Dispatch</u> no 1864 9 Jul 1837: 334
    BM

"Literary Memoranda" <u>Atlas</u> 12 no 582 9 Jul 1837: 441   BM

"Review – Literature and Arts"   <u>Bell's Weekly Messenger</u> no
    2151 9 Jul 1837: 222   BM

"Bentley's Miscellany for June" <u>Mark Lane Express</u> 6 no 289
    10 Jul 1837 BM

"Literature and Art" <u>Weekly Dispatch</u> no 1865 16 Jul 1837:
    346 BM

"Modern Justice - A Sketch from Life"   Sunday Times no 769
     16 Jul 1837   BM

"Fashion and Table-Talk: A Street Sketch by Boz"   Globe   no
     10,829   22 Jul 1837   BM

"The   Public   Journals.   Oliver   Twist   and   the   Pickpockets"
     Mirror 30 no 846   29 Jul 1837: 74-76   BM

"Magazine Day"   Sun   no 14,004   1 Aug 1837   BM

"Fashion and Table-Talk: The Doctor and the Patient"   Globe
     no 10,891   5 Aug 1837   BM

"Literary Memoranda"   Atlas 12 no 586   6 Aug 1837: 505   BM

"Review - Literature and Arts: The Magazines of the Month"
     Bell's Weekly Messenger no 2155   6 Aug 1837: 251   BM

"The Doctor and the Patient"   Observer   7 Aug 1837   BM

"Literature - The Magazines"   Observer   13 Aug 1837   BM

"Literature and Art"   Weekly Dispatch no 1869   13 Aug 1837:
     394   BM

"Magazine Day"   Sun no 14,031   1 Sep 1837   BM

"Fashion   and   Varieties: Oliver   Twist   Again   with   Thieves"
     Courier no 14,375   1 Sep 1837   BM

"A Glance at the Magazines"   Spectator 10 no 479   2 Sep 1837:
     835   BM

"Literature - The Magazines"   Morning Chronicle   no 21,156
     2 Sep 1837   BM

"Literature and Art"   Weekly Dispatch no 1872   3 Sep 1837: 430
     BM

"Literary Memoranda"   Atlas 12 no 590   3 Sep 1837: 569   BM

"Literature - The Magazines"   Observer   3 Sep 1837   PP,BM

"The Literary Examiner"   Examiner no 1545   10 Sep 1837: 581-
     82   BM   [John Forster]

"The Mudfog Association" <u>Morning Herald</u> no 17,185 2 Oct 1837
    BM

"Magazine Day" <u>Sun</u> no 14,057 2 Oct 1837   BM

"Mudfog Association" <u>Morning Post</u> no 20,837 3 Oct 1837
    BM

"Literature - The Magazines" <u>Morning Chronicle</u> no 21,183
    5 Oct 1837   BM

"Mudfog Statistics" <u>The Times</u> no 16,539 5 Oct 1837   BM

"The Mud-Fog Association" <u>The Times</u> no 16,541 7 Oct 1837
    BM

"Mudfog Association" <u>Sunday Times</u> no 781 8 Oct 1837   BM

"Review - Literature and Arts: The Magazines" <u>Bell's Weekly</u>
    <u>Messenger</u> no 2164   8 Oct 1837: 326   BM

"Facts and Scraps: A Hint for the Poor Law Commissioners"
    <u>Weekly Dispatch</u> no 1877   8 Oct 1837: 488   BM

"Miscellaneous: Mudfog Statistics" <u>Mark Lane Express</u> 6 no 302
    9 Oct 1837 BM

"The Public Journals: The Mudfog Association" <u>Mirror</u> 30
    no 857 14 Oct 1837: 254-55   BM

"The Public Journals: The Mudfog Association" <u>Mirror</u> 30
    no 858 21 Oct 1837: 270-71   BM

"Fashion and Table-Talk: Removing Paupers" <u>Globe</u> no 10,962
    28 Oct 1837   BM

"Literature" <u>Observer</u> 29 Oct 1837 (re <u>Quarterly Review</u> 59
    no 118, and <u>London and Westminster Review</u> 6 nos 11 & 54)

"Literature" <u>Sun</u> no 14,081 30 Oct 1837   (re <u>Quarterly</u>
    <u>Review</u> 59 no 118)

"The Periodicals: The Quarterly Review on Boz" <u>Morning Post</u>
    no 20,860 31 Oct 1837 (re <u>Quarterly Review</u> 59 no 118)

"Varieties: Bull's Eye" <u>Globe</u> no 10,964 31 Oct 1837   BM

"Magazine Day" Sun no 14,083 1 Nov 1837   BM

"Varieties: Beadleism" Globe no 10,966 2 Nov 1837 BM

"The Dignity of a Beadle" The Times no 16,564 3 Nov 1837
    BM

"Fashion and Table-Talk: The Wretched Female" Globe no 10,968
    4 Nov 1837 BM

"Literature" John Bull 17 no 882 5 Nov 1837: 537   BM

"Literary Memoranda" Atlas 12 no 598 5 Nov 1837: 713   BM

"Review - Literature and Art: The Magazines for November"
    Bell's Weekly Messenger no 2168 5 Nov 1837: 355   BM

"Magazines of the Month" Railway Times no 2 5 Nov 1837: 10
    BM

"Literature and Art" Weekly Dispatch no 1882 12 Nov 1837:
    550   BM

"The Literary Examiner" Examiner no 1555 19 Nov 1837: 740-
    41   BM   [John Forster]

"Magazine Day" Sun no 14,109 1 Dec 1837   BM

"Periodicals" Observer 3 Dec 1837   BM

"Literature" St. James's Chronicle no 12,500 5 Dec 1837 BM

"Fashion and Table-Talk: Mr. Chitling" Globe no 11,003
    15 Dec 1837   BM

"Fashion and Table-Talk: Newgate - The Night before an
    Execution" Globe no 11,013 27 Dec 1837   BM

"Fashion and Table-Talk: Smithfield" Globe no 11,015 29 Dec
    1837   BM

"Magazine Day" Sun no 14,135 1 Jan 1838   BM

"Miscellaneous: Smithfield. Mr. Weller's Opinion of the
    Ladies" Mark Lane Express 7 no 315 8 Jan 1838 PP,BM

"The Public Journals: Oliver Twist" <u>Mirror</u> 31 no 874 13 Jan
    1838: 25-27 BM

"Reviewer" <u>Bell's New Weekly Messenger</u> 8 no 320 4 Feb 1838
    BM

"Literature: Magazine Day" <u>Sunday Times</u> no 798 4 Feb 1838
    BM

"New Books" <u>Magnet</u> 2 no 48 5 Feb 1838   BM

"The Periodicals" <u>Morning Advertiser</u> no 14,614 5 Feb 1838
    BM

"Literature" <u>Courier</u> no 14,508 5 Feb 1838   BM

"The Magazines" <u>Sun</u> no 14,167 7 Feb 1838   BM

"Review - Literature and Arts" <u>Bell's Weekly Messenger</u> no 2182
    11 Feb 1838: 46   BM

"Oliver Twist. By 'Boz'" <u>Sunday Times</u> no 801 25 Feb 1838
    BM

"Magazine Day" <u>Sun</u> no 14,186 1 Mar 1838   BM

"The Periodicals" <u>Courier</u> no 14,530 2 Mar 1838   BM

"The Periodicals" <u>Morning Advertiser</u> no 14,638 5 Mar 1838
    BM

"Literature" <u>St. James's Chronicle</u> no 12,539 6 Mar 1838
    BM

"The Public Journals: Popping the Question" <u>Mirror</u> 31 no 882
    10 Mar 1838: 155-57   BM

"Fashion and Varieties: Oliver Twist at St. James's" <u>Courier</u>
    no 14,553 29 Mar 1838   (dramatisation of OT)

"Theatricals: St. James's" <u>Sunday Times</u> no 806 1 Apr 1838
    (dramatisation of OT)

"Magazine Day" <u>Sun</u> no 14,215 2 Apr 1838   BM,NN

"The Literary Log-Book" Shipping and Mercantile Gazette no 21
4 Apr 1838   BM

"Periodicals"   United Services Gazette   no 272   7 Apr 1838
PP,BM

"Literature and Arts"   Bell's Weekly Messenger no 2190   8 Apr
1838: 110   BM

"Literature: Magazine Day"   Sunday Times no 807   8 Apr 1838
BM,NN

"Literature"   Morning Advertiser no 14,673   14 Apr 1838   BM

"Magazine Day"   Sun no 14,238   1 May 1838   BM

"Literature: The Magazines"   Shipping and Mercantile Gazette
no 47   4 May 1838   BM

"The Public Journals: Oliver Twist out of Trouble and in the
Country"   Mirror 31 no 891   5 May 1838: 302-03   BM

"Literature"   Observer   6 May 1838   BM

"Reviews - Literature and Arts: The Magazines for May"   Bell's
Weekly Messenger no 2194   6 May 1838: 142   BM

"Magazine Day"   Sunday Times   no 811   6 May 1838   BM,NN

"Literature"   Morning Advertiser no 14,692   7 May 1838   BM

"The Magazines"   United Services Gazette no 277   12 May 1838
BM

"Fashion and Table-Talk: Oliver Twist in the Country"   Globe
no 11,133   18 May 1838   BM

"Magazines"   Sun no 14,267   2 Jne 1838   BM

"Literary Notices"   Age   3 Jne 1838: 175   BM,NN

"Literary Notices: The Magazines"   Shipping and Mercantile
Gazette no 73   4 Jne 1838   BM

"Literature"   Morning Advertiser no 14,718   6 Jne 1838   BM

"Reviewer" <u>Bell's New Weekly Messenger</u> 8 no 338   10 Jne 1838
     BM

"New Books" <u>Magnet</u> 2 no 65   11 Jne 1838   BM

"The Public Journals: Oliver Twist" <u>Mirror</u> 31 no 897   16 Jne
     1838: 394-95   BM

"Literary Notices" <u>Age</u> 1 Jul 1838: 207   BM

"Magazine Day" <u>Sun</u> no 14,293   2 Jul 1838   BM

"Literary Notices: Boz's Miscellany" <u>Shipping and Mercantile</u>
     <u>Gazette</u> no 98   3 Jul 1838   BM,NN

"Literature" <u>Morning Advertiser</u> no 14,744   6 Jul 1838 BM

"Reviews - Literature and Arts: The Magazines for July"
     <u>Bell's Weekly Messenger</u> no 2203   8 Jul 1838: 214   BM

"Miscellaneous: Touching Dress" <u>Mark Lane Express</u> 7 no 341
     9 Jul 1838   BM

"Magazine Day" <u>Sun</u> no 14,319   1 Aug 1838   BM

"The Periodicals" <u>Courier</u> no 14,658   2 Aug 1838   BM

"Reviews - Literature and Arts: Magazines for August" <u>Bell's</u>
     <u>Weekly Messenger</u> no 2207   5 Aug 1838: 246   BM

"Literature" <u>Morning Advertiser</u> no 14,768   3 Aug 1838 BM,NN

"Literary Notices" <u>Age</u> 5 Aug 1838: 243 BM,NN

"Literature" <u>Sunday Times</u> no 824   5 Aug 1838 BM,NN

"Fashion and Table-Talk: Delicacies" <u>Globe</u> no 11,202   7 Aug
     1838   BM

"Literary Notices" <u>Shipping and Mercantile Gazette</u> no 129
     8 Aug 1838   BM

"Oliver Twist" <u>Sunday Times</u> no 825   12 Aug 1838   BM

"Miscellaneous: Delicacies"   <u>Mark Lane Express</u> 7 no 347
     20 Aug 1838   BM

"Magazine Day" <u>Sun</u> no 14,347 1 Sep 1838   BM

"The Literary Examiner: The Second Meeting of the Mudfog
    Association for the Advancement of Everything" <u>Examiner</u>
    no 1596 2 Sep 1838: 548-49   BM

"Spectator's Library"   <u>Spectator</u> 11 no 532   8 Sep 1838:
    854-55   BM

"Literary Notices" <u>Age</u> 9 Sep 1838: 282   BM

"Magazine Day" <u>Sunday Times</u> no 829 9 Sep 1838   BM

"Periodicals" <u>Observer</u> 9 Sep 1838   BM

"Literary Memoranda" <u>Atlas</u> 13 no 644 15 Sep 1838: 587 BM

"Literature" <u>Sunday Times</u> no 830 16 Sep 1838   BM,NN

"Meeting of the Mudfog Association" <u>Shipping and Mercantile
    Gazette</u> no 166 20 Sep 1838   BM

"Varieties: Illustration of Homeopathy" <u>Globe</u> no 11,241
    21 Sep 1838   BM

"New Books" <u>Bell's New Weekly Messenger</u> 8 no 353 23 Sep 1838
    BM

"New Books" <u>Magnet</u> 2 no 80 24 Sep 1838   BM

"Dickens's Tales"   <u>Edinburgh Review</u> 68 no 137   Oct 1838:
    75-97 SB,PP,BM,NN [Thomas Henry Lister]

"Magazines" <u>Sun</u> no 14,373 2 Oct 1838   BM

"Literature: Magazine Day" <u>Sunday Times</u> no 833   7 Oct 1838
    BM

"Reviews - Literature and Arts"   <u>Bell's Weekly Messenger</u>
    no 2216 7 Oct 1838: 315   BM

"Magazines and Other Periodicals"   <u>Morning Advertiser</u>   no
    14,827 11 Oct 1838   BM

"Magazine Day" <u>Sun</u> no 14,399 1 Nov 1838   BM

"Literature" <u>Morning Advertiser</u> no 14,849 6 Nov 1838 BM

"Literature and Art" <u>Era</u> 1 no 7 11 Nov 1838: 80 BM

"Literary Notices" <u>Age</u> 11 Nov 1838: 355 BM

"Reviews - Literature and Arts" <u>Bell's Weekly Messenger</u> no
2221 11 Nov 1838: 355 BM

"Reviews" <u>Athenaeum</u> no 577 17 Nov 1838: 824-25 OT

"Literature - Review of New Books" <u>Atlas</u> 13 no 653 17 Nov
1838: 729-31 OT

"The Literary Examiner" <u>Examiner</u> no 1607 18 Nov 1838:
723-25 OT

"Literature and Art" <u>Era</u> 1 no 8 18 Nov 1838: 92 OT

"Adelphi Theatre. Surrey Theatre" <u>Morning Advertiser</u> no
14,861 20 Nov 1838 (dramatisations of OT,NN)

"Surrey Theatre" <u>Morning Chronicle</u> no 21,533 20 Nov 1838
(dramatisation of OT)

"Literature" <u>Sun</u> no 14,415 20 Nov 1838 OT

"Adelphi Theatre. Surrey Theatre" <u>Morning</u> Herald no 17,540
21 Nov 1838 (dramatisations of OT,NN)

"Surrey Theatre" <u>The Times</u> no 16,892 21 Nov 1838
(dramatisation of OT)

"Spectator's Library" <u>Spectator</u> 11 no 543 24 Nov 1838:
1114-16 OT

"Review of New Books" <u>Literary Gazette</u> 22 no 1140 24 Nov
1838: 741 OT

"Drama" <u>Literary Gazette</u> 22 no 1140 24 Nov 1838: 748
(dramatisations of OT,NN)

"Music and the Drama" <u>Athenaeum</u> no 578 24 Nov 1838: 844
(dramatisations of OT,NN)

"Literature and Art" Weekly Dispatch no 1936 25 Nov 1838:
562 OT

"Literature" Observer 25 Nov 1838 OT

"The Literary Examiner" Examiner no 1608 25 Nov 1838:
740-41 OT

"Oliver Twist. By 'Boz'" Dublin University Magazine 12 no 72
Dec 1838: 699-723

"Magazine Day" Sun no 14,425 1 Dec 1838 BM,OT

"Magazines for December" Courier no 14,761 1 Dec 1838 BM

"Literature" Sunday Times no 841 2 Dec 1838 OT

"Literature" Courier no 14,762 3 Dec 1838 OT

"Magazine Day" Sunday Times no 842 9 Dec 1838 BM,NN

"Literary Notices" Age 9 Dec 1838: 386 BM,NN

"The Drama" Bell's Life in London 9 Dec 1838
(dramatisations of OT,NN)

"Literature" Morning Advertiser no 14,881 13 Dec 1838 BM

"Oliver Twist, By 'Boz'" Shipping and Mercantile Gazette
no 238 18 Dec 1838 OT

"Oliver Twist" Shipping and Mercantile Gazette no 245 26 Dec
1838 OT

"Boz's Oliver Twist" Monthly Review 1 no 1 Jan 1839: 29-41
OT

"Magazines Concluded" Sun no 14,454 4 Jan 1839 BM

"Literature, &c: Magazines" United Services Gazette no 312
5 Jan 1839 BM

"Literature: Magazine Day" Sunday Times no 846 6 Jan 1839
BM,NN

"The Magazines for January" Bell's Weekly Messenger no 2229
      6 Jan 1839   BM,NN

"Literature" Morning Advertiser no 14,902 7 Jan 1839   BM

"Varieties: Interior of Bow-Street Police-Office" Globe no
      11,335 8 Jan 1839   BM

"New Books" Bell's New Weekly Messenger 9 no 369 13 Jan 1839
      BM

"New Books" Magnet 3 no 95 14 Jan 1839   BM

"Bentley's Miscellany" Morning Post no 21,226 14 Jan 1839
      BM

"Magazine Day" Sun no 14,479 1 Feb 1839   BM

"The Magazines of the Month" United Services Gazette no 316
      2 Feb 1839   BM

"The Magazines" Observer 3 Feb 1839   BM,NN

"The Periodicals for February" Morning Post no 21,247 7 Feb
      1839   BM

"The Theatres: Adelphi" Morning Post no 21,263 26 Feb 1839
      (dramatisation of OT)

"The Periodicals" Courier no 14,845 1 Mar 1839   BM

"Theatricals"   Atlas 14 no 668   2 Mar 1839: 136
      (dramatisation of OT)

"The Literary Examiner" Examiner no 1611 3 Mar 1839: 133-34
      BM   [John Forster]

"Magazine Day" Sunday Times no 854 3 Mar 1839   BM,NN

"Literature and Art" Era 1 no 23 3 Mar 1839: 272 BM

"The Magazines" Observer 3 Mar 1839   BM

"The Magazines" Morning Post no 21,269 5 Mar 1839   BM

"Bentley's Miscellany"   Morning Herald no 17,630   6 Mar 1839
BM

"Bentley's Miscellany"   Morning Chronicle no 21,621   6 Mar
1839   BM

"Literature, &c: A Parthian Glance at the Magazines"   United
Services Gazette no 322   9 Mar 1839   BM

"Literature and Art"   Weekly Dispatch no 1951   10 Mar 1839:
118   BM

"Bentley's Miscellany"   Globe no 11,393   16 Mar 1839   BM

"Literature and Art"   Weekly Dispatch no 1954   31 Mar 1839:
154   BM

"Literary Notices"   Age 31 Mar 1839: 98   BM (the "Boz" style)

"Magazine-Day"   Sun no 14,529   1 Apr 1839   BM

"The Periodicals for April"   Morning Post no 21,292   1 Apr
1839   BM

"Periodical Literature"   Atlas 14 no 673   6 Apr 1839: 216-18
BM

"Literature, &c: A Parthian Glance at the Periodicals"   United
Services Gazette   no 316   6 Apr 1839   BM,NN

"Literary Notices"   Age   7 Apr 1839: 106 BM,NN

"The Breakfast Table"   Era 1 no 28   7 Apr 1839: 332   BM

"Literature and Arts"   Bell's Life in London   14 Apr 1839
BM,NN

"Literature"   Morning Advertiser   no 15,016   9 May 1839
BM,NN

"Literature and Art"   Era 1 no 34   19 May 1839: 404   OT

"Oliver Twist; or, the Parish Boy's Progress"   Quarterly
Review 64 no 127   Jne 1839: 83-102   OT   [Richard Ford]

"Magazine Day"   Sun no 14,582   1 Jne 1839   BM

"Literature" Bell's Life in London 2 Jne 1839 BM,NN

"Our Weekly Gossip" Athenaeum no 609 29 Jne 1839: 485-86
    (re - Quarterly Review 64 no 127 on OT)

"Literature" Observer 30 Jne 1839 BM,NN

"Literature" Observer 1 Jul 1839 BM,NN

"Literature" Bell's Life in London 11 Aug 1839 BM,NN

"Literature" Morning Advertiser no 15,200 10 Dec 1839 BM

"The Literary Examiner" Examiner no 1665 29 Dec 1839: 822
    (review - Poor Jack by Captain Marryat, and imitations
    of Dickens)

"Popular Literature of the Day" British and Foreign Review
    10 no 19 Jan 1840: 223-46 (review - Jack Sheppard by
    W.H. Ainsworth; Michael Armstrong by Mrs. Trollope;
    comparison to Dickens)

"William Ainsworth and Jack Sheppard" Fraser's Magazine 21
    no 122   Feb 1840: 227-45   (comparison to OT)
    [William Makepeace Thackeray]

"Magazine Day" Sun no 14,789 3 Feb 1840   (BM; W.H.
    Ainsworth, comparison to Dickens)

"A Parthian Glance at the the Periodicals" United Services
    Gazette no 374 7 Mar 1840   BM

"Charles Dickens and His Works" Fraser's Magazine 21 no 124
    Apr 1840: 381-400

"The Magazines for April" Bell's Weekly Messenger no 2294
    4 Apr 1840: 110 (re Fraser's Magazine 21 no 124 on
    Dickens)   BM

"To the Public" Town no 192 27 Jan 1841: 1521 (satire on
    "Familiar Epistle")

"Literature, &c" John Bull 21 no 1052 6 Feb 1841: 69   BM

Sketches of Young Gentlemen (SYG)

"The Literary Examiner" Examiner no 1566   4 Feb 1838: 68-69
        SYG

"Sketches of Young Gentlemen / by Phiz"   Morning Post   no
        20,948   10 Feb 1838   SYG

"Literature and Arts: Sketches of Young Gentlemen"   Weekly
        Dispatch no 1895   11 Feb 1838: 70   SYG

"Literary Register"   Tait's Edinburgh Magazine   5   no   51
        Mar 1838: 196   SYG

"Reviewer"   Bell's New Weekly Messenger 8 no 325   11 Mar 1838
        SYG

"Notabilia"   Examiner no 1593   12 Aug 1838: 507   SYG

Memoirs of Joseph Grimaldi (MJG)

"Review of New Books"   Literary Gazette 22 no 1100   17 Feb
        1838: 97-99   MJG

"Spectator's Library"   Spectator   11   no   504   24 Feb 1838:
        184-86   MJG

"Review of New Books"   Literary Gazette 22 no 1101   24 Feb
        1838: 118-19   MJG

"Reviewer"   Bell's New Weekly Messenger 8 no 323   25 Feb 1838
        BM,MJG

"New Books"   Magnet 2 no 51   26 Feb 1838   MJG

"Fashion and Table-Talk: Strange Anecdote   of   Grimaldi's
        Brother"   Globe no 11,070   5 Mar 1838   MJG

"New Books"   Magnet 2 no 52   5 Mar 1838   MJG

"Literature and Art"   Weekly Dispatch no 1899   11 Mar 1838:
        118   MJG

"New Books" <u>Mirror</u> 31 no 883 17 Mar 1838: 169-71   MJG

"The Literary Examiner" <u>Examiner</u> no 1572 18 Mar 1838: 164
    MJG

"Literature" <u>Sun</u> no 14,201 19 Mar 1838   MJG

"Literature" <u>Morning Post</u> no 20,980 20 Mar 1838   MJG

"Fashion and Table-Talk" <u>Globe</u> no 11,083 20 Mar 1838   MJG

"Literature: Review of New Books" <u>Atlas</u> 13 no 619   24 Mar
    1838: 185-86   MJG

"New Books: Memoirs of Joseph Grimaldi" <u>Mirror</u> 31 no 885
    31 Mar 1838: 202-04   MJG

"Monthly Review of Literature: Biography" <u>Monthly Magazine</u>
    25 no 148 Apr 1838: 434-35   MJG

"Memoirs of Joseph Grimaldi" <u>Monthly Review</u> 1 no 4 Apr 1838:
    499-507   MJG

<u>Nicholas Nickleby</u> (NN)

"Literature" <u>Courier</u> no 14,554 30 Mar 1838   NN

"Literary Quacks and Imposters" <u>Town</u> no 44 31 Mar 1838: 349
    (imitations of Boz)

"Boz's New Periodical" <u>Morning Post</u> no 20,990 31 Mar 1838
    NN

"Spectator's Library" <u>Spectator</u> 11 no 509 31 Mar 1838:
    304-05   NN

"Reviews" <u>Athenaeum</u> no 544 31 Mar 1838: 227-29   NN

"Literature" <u>Observer</u> 1 Apr 1838   NN

"The Literary Examiner" <u>Examiner</u> no 1574 1 Apr 1838: 195-96
    NN

"Literature" Bell's Life in London 1 Apr 1838   NN

"The New Work by 'Boz'" Bell's New Weekly Messenger 8 no 328
     1 Apr 1838   NN   [Early Edition only]

"Miscellaneous: Gentlemen. A Resolution Passed" Mark Lane
     Express 7 no 327   2 Apr 1838   PP,NN

"The Literary Log-Book" Shipping and Mercantile Gazette no 19
     2 Apr 1838 NN

"Magazine Day" Sun no 14,215 2 Apr 1838   BM,NN

"Literature" Morning Advertiser no 14,666 6 Apr 1838   NN

"The Public Journals: The Life and Adventures of Nicholas
     Nickleby" Mirror 31 no 886   7 Apr 1838: 222-23   NN

"Review of New Books" Literary Gazette 22 no 1107   7 Apr
     1838: 214 NN

"Literature and Art" Weekly Dispatch no 1903 8 Apr 1838: 166
     NN

"Reviewer" Bell's New Weekly Messenger 8 no 329 8 Apr 1838
     NN

"Literature" Sunday Times no 807 8 Apr 1838   BM,NN

"New Books" Magnet 2 no 56 9 Apr 1838   NN

"The Public Journals: Nicholas Nickleby"   Mirror 31 no 887
     14 Apr 1838: 238-39   NN

"Literature" Courier no 14,581   1 May 1838   NN

"Magazines" Sun no 14,239 2 May 1838   NN

"Literature: The Magazines" Shipping and Mercantile Gazette
     no 48 5 May 1838 NN

"Literature and Arts" Bell's Life in London 6 May 1838 NN

"Reviewer" Bell's New Weekly Messenger 8 no 333 6 May 1838
     NN

"The Literary Examiner" Examiner no 1579 6 May 1838: 278
    NN

"Magazine Day" Sunday Times no 811 6 May 1838   BM,NN

"New Books" Magnet 2 no 60 7 May 1838   NN

"Literature and Art" Weekly Dispatch no 1908 13 May 1838:
    226   NN

"Fashion and Varieties: School Examinations" Courier no
    14,068 [sic; shd be 14,608] 1 Jne 1838 NN

"Literature and Art" John Bull 18 no 912 3 Jne 1838: 261
    NN

"Reviewer" Bell's New Weekly Messenger 8 no 337 3 Jne 1838
    NN

"New Books" Magnet 2 no 64 4 Jne 1838   NN

"School-Room at Dotheboys Hall" Morning Chronicle no 21,391
    5 Jne 1838 NN

"Literature" Sun no 14,270 6 Jne 1838   NN

"Literature and Art" Weekly Dispatch no 1913 17 Jne 1838:
    286   NN

"Miscellaneous: A Schoolmaster's Assistant and His Son" Mark
    Lane Express 7 no 338 18 Jne 1838   NN

"The Yorkshire Schoolmaster" Shipping and Mercantile Gazette
    no 90 23 Jne 1838   NN

"Literature" Morning Advertiser no 14,737 28 Jne 1838   NN

"Nickleby's Rebellion" Courier no 14,631 28 Jne 1838   NN

"Literature: Magazine Day" Sunday Times no 819 1 Jul 1838
    NN

"Literary Notices: Boz's Miscellany" Shipping and Mercantile
    Gazette no 98 3 Jul 1838   BM,NN

"Miss Fanny Squeers and Her Femme de Chambre"   Morning Post
        no 21,063   6 Jul 1838   NN

"Literature and Art: Miscellaneous Literature" Weekly Dispatch
        no 1916   8 Jul 1838: 322   NN

"Literature"   Sunday Times no 820   8 Jul 1838   NN

"Literary Notices"   Age   8 Jul 1838: 212   NN

"New Books"   Bell's New Weekly Messenger 8 no 342   8 Jul 1838
        NN

"The Literary Examiner"   Examiner no 1588   8 Jul 1838: 420
        NN

"New Books"   Magnet 2 no 69   9 Jul 1838   NN

"Vulgar Genteels"   Shipping and Mercantile Gazette   no 112
        19 Jul 1838   NN

"The Public Journals: Nicholas Nickleby"   Mirror 32 no 904
        21 Jul 1838: 60-63   NN

"A Member of the Reformed House of Commons"   Morning Post
        no 21,086   2 Aug 1838   NN

"The M.P. and His Constituents"   Morning Chronicle   no 21,441
        2 Aug 1838   NN

"Literature"   Morning Advertiser   no 14,768   3 Aug 1838 BM,NN

"The Periodicals"   Shipping and Mercantile Gazette   no   126
        4 Aug 1838   NN

"Literature"   Sun no 14,323   5 Aug 1838   NN

"Literature"   Observer   5 Aug 1838   NN

"Literary Notices"   Age   5 Aug 1838: 243   BM,NN

"Literature"   Bell's Life in London   5 Aug 1838   NN

"New Books"   Bell's New Weekly Messenger 8 no 346   5 Aug 1838
        NN

"Literature" Sunday Times no 824 5 Aug 1838   BM,NN

"New Books" Magnet 2 no 73   6 Aug 1838   NN

"Fashion and Table-Talk: Illustration of the 'Aristocratic'"
     Globe no 11,203 8 Aug 1838   NN

"The Public Journals: Nicholas Nickleby" Mirror 32 no 907
     11 Aug 1838: 109-10   NN

"Beauties from Boz" Shipping and Mercantile Gazette no 148
     30 Aug 1838   NN

"Literary Notices" Age 2 Sep 1838: 275   NN

"Literature" Morning Advertiser no 14,795 4 Sep 1838 BM,NN

"Miss La Creevy and Nickleby" Globe no 11,226   4 Sep 1838
     NN

"New Books" Bell's New Weekly Messenger 8 no 351 9 Sep 1838
     NN

"New Books" Magnet 2 no 78   10 Sep 1838   NN

"Literature" Sunday Times no 830 16 Sep 1838   BM,NN

"The Literary Examiner" Examiner no 1599   23 Sep 1838:
     595-50   NN

"Miscellanea: A Gem out of 'Nicholas Nickleby'" Athenaeum
     no 570   29 Sep 1838: 716   NN

"Genius and the Public" Fraser's Magazine 18 no 106   Oct
     1838: 379-96

"Dickens's Tales" Edinburgh Review 68 no 137   Oct 1838:
     75-97   SB,PP,BM,NN   [Thomas Henry Lister]

"Varieties: A Foggy Morning in London" Globe no 11,249 1 Oct
     1838   NN

"Rehearsal of a Combat" Courier no 14,708 1 Oct 1838   NN

"The Periodicals" Morning Advertiser no 14,820   3 Oct 1838
     NN

"Literature" Sun no 14,375   4 Oct 1838   (review - Edinburgh Review 68 no 137)

"Literature" Courier   no 14,711   4 Oct 1838   (review - Edinburgh Review 68   no 137)

"Nicholas Nickleby for October" Sunday Times no 833   7 Oct 1838   NN

"Seeking a Situation as a Companion to a Lady" Observer 7 Oct 1838   NN

"Literary Notices" Age 7 Oct 1838: 315   NN

"Literature" Bell's Life in London 7 Oct 1838   NN

"New Books" Bell's New Weekly Messenger 8 no 355   7 Oct 1838 NN

"New Books" Magnet 2 no 82   8 Oct 1838 NN

"Nicholas Nickleby in Quest of Employment"   Morning Herald no 17,505   11 Oct 1838   NN

"The Public Journals: Nicholas Nickleby"   Mirror 32 no 916 13 Oct 1838: 251   NN

"Periodical Publications" United Services Gazette no   300 13 Oct 1838   NN

"Notabilia" Examiner no 1602 14 Oct 1838:   650-51   NN

"Miscellaneous: Theatrical Horses" Mark Lane Express 7 no 356 22 Oct 1838 NN

"Nicholas Nickleby in Quest of Employment"   Shipping and Mercantile Gazette no 197 31 Oct 1838   NN

"The Periodicals" Courier no 14,735 1 Nov 1838   NN

"New Books" Bell's New Weekly Messenger 8 no 359   4 Nov 1838 NN

"Magazine Day" Sunday Times no 837 4 Nov 1838   BM,NN

"Literature"   Morning Advertiser   no 14,848   5 Nov 1838
     NN

"Boz"   Figaro in London 7 no 360   5 Nov 1838: 168   [sic;
     shd be 174]   NN

"New Books"   Magnet 2 no 86   5 Nov 1838   NN

"Periodical Works"   United Services Gazette no 304   10 Nov
     1838   NN

"Literature and Art"   Weekly Dispatch no 1935   18 Nov 1838:
     550   NN

"The Dramatic Author and His Clients" Examiner no 1607 18 Nov
     1838: 731 NN

"Adelphi Theatre"   The Times no 16,891   20 Nov 1838   NN

"Adelphi Theatre. Surrey Theatre"   Morning Advertiser   no
     14,861   20 Nov 1838   (dramatisations of OT,NN)

"Adelphi Theatre. Surrey Theatre"   Morning Herald no 17,540
     21 Nov 1838   (dramatisations of OT,NN)

"Drama"   Literary Gazette 22 no 1140   24 Nov 1838: 748
     (dramatisations of OT,NN)

"Music and the Drama"   Athenaeum   no 578   24 Nov 1838: 844
     (dramatisations of OT,NN)

"Literature" Morning Advertiser no 14,873 4 Dec 1838   NN

"Magazine Day"   Sunday Times no 842   9 Dec 1838   BM,NN

"Literary Notices"   Age   9 Dec 1838: 386   BM,NN

"The   Drama"   Bell's Life in London   9   Dec   1838
     (dramatisations of OT,NN)

"New Books"   Bell's New Weekly Messenger 8 no 364   9 Dec 1838
     NN

"New Books"   Magnet 2 no 91   10 Dec 1838   NN

"Nicholas Nickleby's Return to London"   Courier   no 14,795
    1 Jan 1839   NN

"Fashion and Varieties: Miss La Creevy's Visit"   Courier no
    14,796   2 Jan 1839   NN

"Theatrical Last Appearances"   The Times no 16,929   3 Jan 1839
    NN

"Literature, &c: Serial Works"   United Services Gazette no 312
    5 Jan 1839   NN

"Literature: Magazine Day"   Sunday Times no 846   6 Jan 1839
    BM,NN

"The Literary Examiner"   Examiner no 1614   6 Jan 1839: 4   NN

"The Magazines for January"   Bell's Weekly Messenger no 2229
    6 Jan 1839   BM,NN

"Literature and Art"   Weekly Dispatch no 1942   6 Jan 1839: 10
    NN

"New Books"   Bell's New Weekly Messenger 9 no 368   6 Jan 1839
    NN

"The Magazines"   Observer 6 Jan 1839   NN

"New Books"   Magnet 3 no 94   7 Jan 1839   NN

"The Public Journals: London"   Mirror 33 no 931   12 Jan 1839:
    31   NN

"A London Manager at a Country Theatre. A Professional
    Display"   Observer 13 Jan 1839   NN

"Literature"   Bell's Life in London   13 Jan 1839   NN

"Literary Notices"   Age   13 Jan 1839: 10   NN

"Nicholas Nickleby. Chapters 30, 31, 32, 33"   Morning Post
    no 21,226   14 Jan 1839   NN

"Miss La Creevy's Visit"   Shipping and Mercantile Gazette no
    270   24 Jan 1839   NN

"Nicholas Nickleby's Return to London" Shipping and Mercantile Gazette no 271 25 Jan 1839   NN

"From the Magazines for February: The Invaluable Mrs. Squeers" Courier no 14,821 31 Jan 1839   NN

"From the Magazines for February: A Happy Countenance. Mantalini's Endearments. Medical Attendance at Schools" Courier no 14,822 1 Feb 1839   NN

"Magazine Day" Sunday Times no 850 3 Feb 1839   NN

"The Magazines" Observer 3 Feb 1839   BM,NN

"Literature: Nicholas Nickleby for February" Morning Advertiser no 14,931 9 Feb 1839   BM,NN

"Nicholas Nickleby" United Services Gazette no 317 9 Feb 1839   NN

"New Books" Bell's New Weekly Messenger 9 no 373 10 Feb 1839 NN

"New Books" Magnet 3 no 99 11 Feb 1839   NN

"A Family Event" Shipping and Mercantile Gazette no 289 15 Feb 1839   NN

"Literary Notices" Age 17 Feb 1839: 50   NN

"Magazine Day" Sunday Times no 854 3 Mar 1839   BM,NN

"Varieties: A City Square" Sunday Times no 854 3 Mar 1839 NN

"New Books" Bell's New Weekly Messenger 9 no 376 3 Mar 1839 NN

"New Books" Magnet 3 no 102 4 Mar 1839   NN

"Literary Notices" Age 10 Mar 1839: 74   NN

"A Disagreeable Encounter of the Two Old Friends" Shipping and Mercantile Gazette no 320 23 Mar 1839   NN

"Literature, &c" <u>United Services Gazette</u> no 324   23 Mar 1839
    NN

"Extracts from the Periodicals: The Escape of Smike" <u>Courier</u>
    no 14,871   1 Apr 1839   NN

"A Scene from Nicholas Nickleby" <u>Sun</u> no 14,530   2 Apr 1839
    NN

"Fashion and Varieties: Curious Association of Ideas" <u>Courier</u>
    no 14,873 3 Apr 1839   NN

"London Flowers" <u>Courier</u> no 14,873   3 Apr 1839   NN

"Nicholas's Clandestine Visit to his First Love"   <u>Courier</u> no
    14,874   4 Apr 1839   NN

"The Public Journals: Nicholas Nickleby. No. 13"   <u>Mirror</u> 33
    no 943   6 Apr 1839: 220-23   NN

"Literature, &c: A Parthian Glance at the Periodicals" <u>United
    Services Gazette</u> no 326 6 Apr 1839   BM,NN

"Literary Notices" <u>Age</u> 7 Apr 1839: 106   BM,NN

"Literature" <u>Sunday Times</u> no 859 7 Apr 1839   NN

"Curious Association of Ideas"   <u>Sunday Times</u> no 859   7 Apr
    1839   NN

"Popular Periodicals" <u>Bell's New Weekly Messenger</u>, <u>Supplement</u>
    no 1   7 Apr 1839   NN

"Literature" <u>Morning Advertiser</u> no 14,991 10 Apr 1839 NN

"Literature and Arts"   <u>Bell's Life in London</u> 14 Apr 1839
    BM,NN

"Association of Ideas" <u>Morning Chronicle</u> no 21,664   27 Apr
    1839   NN

"Fashion and Table-Talk: The Memory of the Dead" <u>Globe</u> no
    11,433 2 May 1839 NN

"Nicholas Nickleby"   <u>Bell's New Weekly Messenger</u> 9   no 385
    5 May 1839   NN

"Nicholas Nickleby" <u>Magnet</u> 3 no 111 6 May 1839   NN

"Literature" <u>Morning Advertiser</u> no 15,016 9 May 1839
   BM,NN

"Nicholas Nickleby" <u>Courier</u> no 14,904 9 May 1839   NN

"Varieties: Selfishness of Love" <u>Globe</u> no 11,440 10 May 1839
   NN

"Literature, &c" <u>United Services Gazette</u> no 331 11 May 1839
   NN

"Literature" <u>Sunday Times</u> no 864 12 May 1839   NN

"Literary Notices" <u>Age</u> 12 May 1839: 146   NN

"Notabilia: The Actress's Lodgings" <u>Examiner</u> no 1632 12 May
   1839: 299-300   NN

"Chit-Chat: Boz" <u>Art Union</u> 1 no 4 15 May 1839: 74

"A Scene in the Nickleby Family"   <u>Shipping and Mercantile
   Gazette</u> no 368 18 May 1839   NN

"Familiar Associations" <u>Shipping and Mercantile Gazette</u> no
   372 23 May 1839   NN

"Beauties of Boz" <u>Shipping and Mercantile Gazette</u> no 378
   30 May 1839

"Literature" <u>Bell's Life in London</u> 2 Jne 1839   BM,NN

"Literature" <u>Observer</u> 2 Jne 1839   BM,NN

"The Literary Examiner: The Last New Number of Nicholas
   Nickleby" <u>Examiner</u> no 1635 2 Jne 1839: 342   NN

"New Books" <u>Bell's New Weekly Messenger</u> 9 no 389 2 Jne 1839
   NN

"New Books" <u>Magnet</u> 3 no 115 3 Jne 1839   NN

"The Periodicals for June" <u>Morning Post</u> no 21,346 3 Jne 1839
   (imitations of Dickens)

"Beauties of Boz"   Shipping and Mercantile Gazette   no   384
     6 Jne 1839

"Literature, &c"   United Services Gazette no 335   8 Jne 1839
     NN

"The Magazines"   Sunday Times no 868   9 Jne 1839   NN

"Literature and Art"   Weekly Dispatch no 1964   9 Jne 1839: 274
     (imitations of Dickens)

"Literary Notices"   Age   9 Jne 1839: 178   NN

"Miscellaneous: The Rules of the King's Bench"   Mark Lane
     Express 8 no 389   10 Jne 1839   NN

"Literature"   Observer   30 Jne 1839   BM,NN

"Literature"   Observer   1 Jul 1839   BM,NN

"Magazines - Continued"   Sun   no 14,610   4 Jul 1839   NN

"Literature, &c: The Magazines"   United Services Gazette
     no 339   6 Jul 1839   NN

"Nicholas Nickleby"   Bell's New Weekly Messenger, Supplement
     1 no 4   7 Jul 1839   NN

"The Magazines"   Sunday Times no 872   7 Jul 1839   NN

"Literary Notices"   Age   7 Jul 1839: 210   NN

"Varieties: Remembrance of Pleasant Scenes"   Globe no 11,492
     12 Jul 1839   NN

"Specimens of the Periodicals for August"   Courier   no 14,974
     1 Aug 1839   NN

"Literature, &c"   United Services Gazette no 343   3 Aug 1839
     NN

"Literature"   Sunday Times no 876   4 Aug 1839   NN

"Literary Notices"   Age   4 Aug 1839: 242   NN

"The Magazines"   Observer 4 Aug 1839   NN

"New Books" <u>Bell's New Weekly Messenger</u> 9 no 398 4 Aug 1839
      NN

"New Books" <u>Magnet</u> 3 no 124   5 Aug 1839   NN

"Literature" <u>Bell's Life in London</u> 11 Aug 1839   BM,NN

"The Literary Examiner: The Seventeenth Number of Nicholas
      Nickleby" <u>Examiner</u> no 1645 11 Aug 1839: 501   NN

"The Genteel Hair-Dresser" <u>Sun</u> no 14,644 13 Aug 1839   NN

"Literature" <u>Shipping and Mercantile Gazette</u> no 454   27 Aug
      1839   (imitations of Dickens)

"The Magazines" <u>Observer</u> 1 Sep 1839   NN

"Arthur Gride's Return Home. Smike's Death" <u>Courier</u> no 15,000
      3 Sep 1839 NN

"Mr. Lillyvick Re-Appears among the Kenwigses" <u>Sun</u> no 14,665
      6 Sep 1839 NN

"Literature, &c: A Parthian Glance at the Periodicals" <u>United
      Services Gazette</u> no 348   7 Sep 1839   NN

"Literary Notices" <u>Age</u> 8 Sep 1839: 282   NN

"Literature" <u>Sunday Times</u> no 881 8 Sep 1839   NN

"Nicholas Nickleby" <u>Bell's New Weekly Messenger</u>, <u>Supplement</u>
      1 no 6   8 Sep 1839   NN

"The Periodicals" <u>Morning Post</u> no 21,413   10 Sep 1839   NN

"Fashion and Table-Talk: Architecture of Noses" <u>Globe</u> no
      11,544 11 Sep 1839   NN

"Varieties: Leaving Lovers Alone" <u>Globe</u> no 11,545   12 Sep
      1839   NN

"Breaking Up of Dotheboys Hall" <u>Observer</u> 29 Sep 1839   NN

"Yorkshire Schools (From the Preface to Nicholas Nickleby)"
      <u>Courier</u> no 15,025   3 Oct 1839   NN

"Literature"   Sun no 14,689   4 Oct 1839   NN

"Literature"   Morning Advertiser no 15,143   4 Oct 1839   NN

"Ralph Nickleby's Last Moments"   Courier no 15,026   4 Oct 1839
     NN

"Literature"   United Services Gazette no 352   5 Oct 1839
     NN

"Reviews"   Town no 123   5 Oct 1839: 983   NN

"Literary Notices"   Age   6 Oct 1839: 314   NN

"Literature"   Observer   6 Oct 1839   BM,NN

"The Literary Examiner: The Conclusion of Nicholas Nickleby"
     Examiner no 1653   6 Oct 1839: 629-30   NN

"Nicholas Nickleby"   Bell's New Weekly Messenger   9   no 406
     6 Oct 1839   NN

"Nicholas Nickleby"   Magnet 3 no 133   7 Oct 1839   NN

"Varieties: All Up with Squeers"   Globe no 11,566   8 Oct 1839
     NN

"Fashion and Table-Talk: The Brothers Cheeryble"   Globe no
     11,570   12 Oct 1839   NN

"Breakfast Table"   Era 2 no 55   13 Oct 1839: 32   NN

"Literature"   Sunday Times no 886   13 Oct 1839   NN

"Literature"   United Services Gazette no 354   19 Oct 1839
     (imitations of Dickens)

"The Literary Examiner"   Examiner   no 1656   27 Oct 1839:
     677-78   NN   [Leigh   Hunt]

"From the Examiner. The Life and Adventures of Nicholas
     Nickleby"   Courier   no 15,045   28 Oct 1839   NN

"Charles Dickens and His Works"   Fraser's Magazine 21 no 124
     Apr 1840: 381-400

"Magazine Day" <u>Sun</u> no 14,839 1 Apr 1840   (re <u>Fraser's</u>
     <u>Magazine</u> 21 no 124 on Dickens)

"Periodicals for April" <u>Morning Herald</u> no 17,965 3 Apr 1840
     (re <u>Fraser's Magazine</u> 21 no 124 on Dickens)

Sketches of Young Couples (SYC)

"Books" <u>Spectator</u> 13 no 606 8 Feb 1840: 137   SYC

"The Magazines" <u>Sunday Times</u> no 851 10 Feb 1840   SYC

"Review of New Books" <u>Literary Gazette</u> 24 no 1204   15 Feb
     1840: 98-100   SYC

"The Literary Examiner" <u>Examiner</u> no 1672   16 Feb 1840:
     100-01 SYC

"Table-Talk No.128 <u>Morning Post</u> no 21,553   24 Feb 1840
     (Boz and contemporary literary taste)

"Literary Memoranda" <u>Atlas</u> 15 no 720 29 Feb 1840: 139
     SYC

"New Books" <u>Mirror</u> 35 no 995 7 Mar 1840: 166-68   SYC

"Varieties: Elderly Gentlemen" <u>Globe</u> no 11,716   31 Mar 1840
     SYC

"Our Library Table" <u>Athenaeum</u> no 651 18 Apr 1840: 313 SYC

Master Humphrey's Clock (MHC, OCS)

"Publications Received: Serials, Pictorial Illustrations, and Prints" <u>Spectator</u> no 614 4 Apr 1840: 331   MHC

"Reviews of New Books: 'Boz'" <u>Literary Gazette</u> 24 no 1211 4 Apr 1840: 211   MHC

"Miscellaneous" <u>Examiner</u> no 1679 5 Apr 1840: 219   MHC

"Boz's New Work" <u>Bell's New Weekly Messenger</u> 10 no 521 5 Apr 1840 [London Edition only]   MHC

"Literature" <u>Observer</u> 5 Apr 1840   MHC

"Literature" <u>Sunday Times</u> no 911 5 Apr 1840 (re <u>Fraser's Magazine</u> 21 no 124 on Dickens)

"Literature and Art" <u>Weekly Dispatch</u> no 2007 5 Apr 1840: 166 (re <u>Fraser's Magazine</u> 21 no 124 on Dickens)

"Literature" <u>Bell's Life in London</u> 5 Apr 1840   MHC

"Fraser's Magazine" <u>Era</u> 2 no 79 5 Apr 1840: 333 (re <u>Fraser's Magazine</u> 21 no 124 on Dickens)

"Literary Notices" <u>Age</u> 5 Apr 1840: 106 (re <u>Fraser's Magazine</u> 21 no 124 on Dickens)

"Literature" <u>Bell's Life in London</u> 10 Apr 1840   MHC

"Literature and Art" <u>Weekly Dispatch</u> no 2008 12 Apr 1840: 178   MHC

"The Literary Examiner. A Gentlemanly Correspondent" <u>Examiner</u> no 1680 12 Apr 1840: 230   MHC

"Literary Notices" <u>Age</u> 12 Apr 1840: 114   MHC

"Literature" <u>Sun</u> no 14,850 14 Apr 1840   MHC

"Literature" <u>Morning Advertiser</u> no 15,312 18 Apr 1840 BM,MHC

"Serials" <u>Spectator</u> 13 no 616 18 Apr 1840: 380   MHC

"Literature and Art" <u>John Bull</u> 20 no 1010 19 Apr 1840: 188
MHC

"Literature" <u>Sun</u> no 14,853 20 Apr 1840 MHC

"Literature" <u>Morning Advertiser</u> no 15,313 20 Apr 1840
(re <u>Fraser's</u> 21 no 124 on Dickens)

"Fashion and Table-Talk: Supernatural Visitants" <u>Globe</u> no
11,735 22 Apr 1840 MHC

"Master Humphrey's Turnip. A Chimney-Corner Crochet" <u>Town</u>
no 152 25 Apr 1840: 1213 (MHC satire)

"Master Humphrey's Clock. By 'Boz'" <u>Monthly Review</u> 2 no 1
May 1840: 35-43 MHC

"Master Humphrey's Turnip. A Chimney-Corner Crochet" <u>Town</u>
no 153 2 May 1840: 1221 (MHC satire)

"Literature and Art" <u>Weekly Dispatch</u> no 2063 2 May 1840: 214
(re the practice of serial continuations)

"Literature" <u>Sunday Times</u> no 914 3 May 1840 MHC

"Literary Examiner: Mr Pickwick's , Introduction to Master
Humphrey's Clock" <u>Examiner</u> no 1683 3 May 1840: 276
MHC

"Literature and Art" <u>Era</u> 2 no 84 3 May 1840: 386 MHC

"Master Humphrey's Turnip. A Chimney-Corner Crochet" <u>Town</u>
no 154 9 May 1840: 1229-30 (MHC satire)

"Varieties: Mr. Weller, Sen. on Railways" <u>Globe</u> no 11,754
14 May 1840 MHC

"Old Weller and the Widow on the Railroad" <u>Courier</u> no 15,212
14 May 1840 MHC

"Master Humphrey's Turnip. A Chimney-Corner Crochet" <u>Town</u>
no 155 16 May 1840: 1237 (MHC satire)

"Mr Weller on Railways" <u>Examiner</u> no 1685 17 May 1840: 309
MHC

"Literature and Art" Era 2 no 86 17 May 1840: 410   MHC

"Miscellaneous: Mr. Weller, Sen. on Railways" Mark Lane
      Express 9 no 438   18 May 1840   MHC

"Master Humphrey's Turnip. A Chimney-corner Crochet" Town
      no 156 23 May 1840: 1245   (MHC satire)

"Varieties: Old Weller and the Widow on the Railroad" Bell's
      New Weekly Messenger 10 no 528 24 May 1840   MHC

"Varieties" Magnet 3 no 166 25 May 1840   MHC

"Mr. Weller, Sen., on Railways"   Morning Herald no 18,007
      25 May 1840   MHC

"Varieties: A Brute of a Husband" Globe no 11,764   26 May
      1840   MHC

"Mr. Weller, Sen., on Railways" Courier no 15,223   27 May
      1840   MHC

"An Enthusiastic Barber" Examiner no 1687   31 May 1840: 340
      MHC

"Notices of New Works" Metropolitan Magazine 28 no   110
      Jne 1840: 51-52   MHC

"Miscellaneous: An Enthusiastic Barber" Mark Lane Express 9
      no 442 15 Jne 1840   MHC

"Literature" Sunday Times no 922 28 Jne 1840   MHC

"Literature" Morning Advertiser no 15,382 9 Jul 1840   MHC

"The Literary Examiner" Examiner no 1693   12 Jul 1840: 435
      MHC

"Boz's Sketches" New Moral World 1 no 3 18 Jul 1840: 34-35

"Fashion and Table-Talk: A Grave-Yard Incident" Globe no
      11,900   18 Jul 1840   MHC

"Notices of New Works" Metropolitan Magazine 28 no   112
      Aug 1840: 101-02   MHC

"Literary Notices" Age 9 Aug 1840: 250 (uncommissioned
    MHC illus. by T. Sibson)

"New Publications" Morning Herald no 18,073 11 Aug 1840
    (uncommissioned MHC illus. by T. Sibson)

"Literary Examiner: The Village School" Examiner no 1698
    16 Aug 1840: 517 MHC

"Literature" Courier no 15,295 19 Aug 1840 (moral
    tendencies of works by Fielding, Ainsworth, and Bulwer;
    MHC)

"Varieties: A Village School" Bell's New Weekly Messenger 10
    no 541 23 Aug 1840 MHC

"Varieties" Magnet 4 no 179 24 Aug 1840 MHC

"Fashion and Table-Talk: Jarley's Wax-Work Show" Globe no
    11,941 4 Sep 1840 MHC

"Notabilia" Examiner no 1701 6 Sep 1840: 567 MHC

"Varieties: Ingenious Contrivances at a Wax Work Show" Bell's
    New Weekly Messenger 10 no 543 6 Sep 1840 MHC

"Varieties" Magnet 4 no 181 7 Sep 1840 MHC

"Varieties: Lady Whips" Globe no 11,945 9 Sep 1840 MHC

"Varieties: A Young Ladies' Boarding School" Bell's New
    Weekly Messenger 10 no 544 13 Sep 1840 MHC

"Literature" Bell's Life in London 13 Sep 1840 MHC

"Varieties" Magnet 4 no 182 14 Sep 1840 MHC

"Mr. Brass's Kitchen" Tablet no 19 19 Sep 1840: 308 MHC

"Varieties: Lodging-House Mysteries" Bell's New Weekly
    Messenger 10 no 545 20 Sep 1840 MHC

"Varieties" Magnet 4 no 183 21 Sep 1840 MHC

"Varieties: The Office of Mr. Sampson Brass - A Bevis Marks
    Attorney" Globe no 11,956 22 Sep 1840 MHC

"Varieties: A Dinner in the Kitchen. Female Education Extraordinary" <u>Bell's New Weekly Messenger</u> 10 no 546 27 Sep 1840   MHC

"Varieties" <u>Magnet</u> 4 no 183 [<u>sic</u>; shd be 184] 28 Sep 1840 MHC

"Literature" <u>Bell's Life in London</u> 4 Oct 1840   MHC

"Varieties: Home Affections of the Poor" <u>Globe</u> no 11,970 8 Oct 1840; rpt in no 11,971 9 Oct 1840   MHC

"The Magazines" <u>Atlas</u> 15 no 752 10 Oct 1840: 664-65 (continued from 3 Oct 1840)

"Literature" <u>Sunday Times</u> no 938 11 Oct 1840   MHC

"Varieties: 'Boz' at Astley's. Mr. Charles Dickens (Boz)" <u>Bell's New Weekly Messenger</u> 10 no 548 11 Oct 1840 MHC

"Varieties" <u>Magnet</u> 4 no 185 12 Oct 1840   MHC

"New Publications" <u>Morning Herald</u> no 18,127 13 Oct 1840 (uncommissioned MHC illus. by T. Sibson)

"Varieties: Small Talk" <u>Bell's New Weekly Messenger</u> 10 no 549 18 Oct 1840   MHC

"Varieties" <u>Magnet</u> 4 no 186 19 Oct 1840   MHC

"Miscellaneous: Churchyard Scene" <u>Mark Lane Express</u> 9 no 460 19 Oct 1840   MHC

"Literature" <u>Morning Advertiser</u> no 15,472   22 Oct 1840 (uncommissioned MHC illus. by T. Sibson)

"Serial Publications" <u>United Services Gazette</u> no 408 24 Oct 1840   MHC

"Varieties: Beauty in the Moonlight. A Starry Night" <u>Bell's New Weekly Messenger</u> 10 no 550 25 Oct 1840   MHC

"Varieties" <u>Magnet</u> 4 no 187 26 Oct 1840   MHC

"Literature and Art"   Era 3   no 110   1 Nov 1840
     (imitations of Dickens)

"Magazine Day: A Column for November. An Ancient Country
     Church, England" Globe no 11,991 2 Nov 1840   MHC

"Master Humphrey's Clock. By 'Boz.' Vol. I" Athenaeum no 680
     7 Nov 1840: 887-88   MHC

"Varieties: Travelling by Waggon" Bell's New Weekly Messenger
     10 no 552   8 Nov 1840   MHC

"Varieties" Magnet 4 no 189   9 Nov 1840   MHC

"Adelphi Theatre"   Standard   no 5115   10 Nov 1840
     (dramatisation of OCS)

"New Publications" Morning Herald no 18,152   11 Nov 1840
     (uncommissioned MHC illus. by T. Sibson)

"Serials" United Services Gazette no 411   14 Nov 1840   MHC

"Theatricals"   Atlas 15 no 757   14 Nov 1840: 743
     (dramatisation of OCS)

"Literature" Sunday Times no 943 15 Nov 1840   MHC

"Varieties: Moistening the Clay" Bell's New Weekly Messenger
     10 no 554 15 Nov 1840   MHC

"Varieties" Magnet 4 no 189 [sic; shd be 190] 16 Nov 1840
     MHC

"Notices of New Works"   Metropolitan Magazine 29 no 116
     Dec 1840: 111   MHC

"Literature" Observer 6 Dec 1840   MHC

"Varieties: Churchyard Reflections"   Bell's New Weekly
     Messenger 10 no 557   6 Dec 1840   MHC

"Literature" Bell's Life in London 6 Dec 1840   MHC

"Varieties" Magnet 4 no 192 7 Dec 1840   MHC

"A Parthian Glance at the Serials for December" <u>United Services Gazette</u> no 415   12 Dec 1840   MHC

"Varieties: Byron Improved" <u>Bell's New Weekly Messenger</u> 10 no 558   13 Dec 1840   MHC

"Varieties" <u>Magnet</u> 4 no 193   14 Dec 1840   MHC

"Popular Prejudice" <u>Bell's New Weekly Messenger</u> 10 no 559   20 Dec 1840   MHC

"Varieties" <u>Magnet</u> 4 no 194   21 Dec 1840   MHC

"Varieties: Twelve Pounds Gentlemen" <u>Bell's New Weekly Messenger</u> 10 no 560   27 Dec 1840   MHC

"Varieties" <u>Magnet</u> 4 no 195   28 Dec 1840   MHC

"Literature" <u>Bell's Life in London</u>   3 Jan 1841   MHC

"Varieties: Prisoners at the Bar. The Way of Counsel" <u>Bell's New Weekly Messenger</u> 11 no 561   3 Jan 1841   MHC

"Varieties" <u>Magnet</u> 5 no 196   4 Jan 1841   MHC

"Varieties: Always Suspect Everybody" <u>Bell's New Weekly Messenger</u> 11 no 562   17 Jan 1841   MHC

"Varieties" <u>Magnet</u> 5 no 198   18 Jan 1841   MHC

"Varieties: Love Making. The Death of Quilp" <u>Bell's New Weekly Messenger</u> 11 no 563   24 Jan 1841   MHC

"Varieties: A Striking Attitude" <u>Bell's New Weekly Messenger</u> 11 no 564   31 Jan 1841   MHC

"Varieties" <u>Magnet</u> 5 no 200   1 Feb 1841   MHC

"Literature" <u>Morning Advertiser</u> no 15,562   4 Feb 1841 (uncommissioned MHC illus. by T. Sibson)

"Miscellaneous: Waggon Travelling" <u>Mark Lane Express</u> 10 no 476   8 Feb 1841   MHC

"The Literary World. I" <u>Mirror</u> 37 no 1046   13 Feb 1841: 99-101   MHC

"Literature" Bell's Life in London 14 Feb 1841 MHC

"Varieties: Boz in St. Paul's Clock. Morning in London"
   Bell's New Weekly Messenger 11 no 567 21 Feb 1841 MHC

"Varieties" Magnet 5 no 203 22 Feb 1841 MHC

"Reviews" Town no 196 24 Feb 1841: 1554 OCS

"Notices of New Works" Metropolitan Magazine 30 no 119
   Mar 1841: 78-79 MHC

Master Humphrey's Clock (MHC, BR)

"Varieties: The State of Muzziness" Bell's New Weekly
   Messenger 1 no 568 28 Feb 1841 MHC

"Varieties" Magnet 5 no 204 1 Mar 1841 MHC

"Varieties: Hints to Father. Clerkenwell, Sixty Years Ago"
   Bell's New Weekly Messenger 11 no 569 7 Mar 1841 MHC

"Varieties" Magnet 5 no 205 8 Mar 1841 MHC

"Varieties: London at Night" Bell's New Weekly Messenger 11
   no 570 14 Mar 1841 MHC

"Varieties" Magnet 5 no 206 15 Mar 1841 MHC

"Varieties: Muzziness" Globe no 12,109 19 Mar 1841 MHC

"Varieties: The World" Bell's New Weekly Messenger 11 no 573
   4 Apr 1841 MHC

"Varieties" Magnet 5 no 209 5 Apr 1841 MHC

"Varieties: Barnaby's Raven" Globe no 12,125 7 Apr 1841
   MHC

"Varieties" Bell's New Weekly Messenger 11 no 574 11 Apr
   1841 MHC

"Literature"   <u>Bell's Life in London</u>   11 Apr 1841   MHC

"Varieties"   <u>Magnet</u> 5 no 210   12 Apr 1841   MHC

"Varieties: Fortune Hunters"   <u>Bell's New Weekly Messenger</u> 11
      no 575   18 Apr 1841   MHC

"Varieties"   <u>Magnet</u> 5 no 211   19 Apr 1841   MHC

"Miscellaneous: Sharp Ears"   <u>Mark Lane Express</u> 10   no 486
      19 Apr 1841   MHC

"Varieties: An Amorous 'Prentice"   <u>Bell's New Weekly Messenger</u>
      11 no 577   2 May 1841   MHC

"Varieties"   <u>Magnet</u> 5 no 213   3 May 1841   MHC

"Literature, &c"   <u>United Services Gazette</u> no 436   8 May 1841
      MHC

"Varieties: Woman's Whimsies"   <u>Bell's New Weekly Messenger</u> 11
      no 578   9 May 1841   MHC

"Varieties"   <u>Bell's Life in London</u> 9 May 1841   MHC

"Varieties"   <u>Magnet</u> 5 no 214   10 May 1841   MHC

"Varieties: Time"   <u>Bell's New Weekly Messenger</u> 11   no 180
      [<u>sic</u>; shd be 580]   23 May 1841   MHC

"Varieties"   <u>Magnet</u> 5 no 216   24 May 1841   MHC

"Varieties: The Way of the World"   <u>Bell's New Weekly Messenger</u>
      11 no 581   30 May 1841   MHC

"Varieties"   <u>Magnet</u> 5 no 217   31 May 1841   MHC

"Notices of New Works"   <u>Metropolitan Magazine</u>   31   no 123
      Jne 1841: 55-56 MHC

"Varieties: A Spring Morning"   <u>Bell's New Weekly Messenger</u> 11
      no 582   6 Jne 1841   MHC

"Varieties"   <u>Magnet</u> 5 no 218   7 Jne 1841   MHC

"Varieties: Bells"   <u>Bell's New Weekly Messenger</u>   11   no 583
     13 Jne 1841   MHC

"Varieties"   <u>Magnet</u> 5 no 219   14 Jne 1841   MHC

"Varieties: A Stormy Night"   <u>Bell's New Weekly Messenger</u> 11
     no 584   20 Jne 1841   MHC

"Varieties"   <u>Magnet</u> 5 no 220   21 Jne 1841   MHC

"Varieties: A Parasite. A Lady of an Uncertain Temper"   <u>Bell's</u>
     <u>New Weekly Messenger</u> 11 no 585   27 Jne 1841   MHC

"Varieties"   <u>Magnet</u> 5 no 221   28 Jne 1841   MHC

"Public Dinner to Mr. Dickens"   <u>Sun</u> no 15,230   1 Jul 1841

"Literature"   <u>Bell's Life in London</u>   4 Jul 1841   MHC

"English Opera House"   <u>Morning Post</u> no 21,994   14 Jul 1841
     (dramatisation of BR)

"The Theatres: English Opera House"   <u>Courier</u> no 15,572   14 Jul
     1841   (dramatisation of BR)

"Theatres"   <u>John Bull</u> no 1076   24 Jul 1841: 357
     (dramatisation of BR)

"Varieties: An Idiot's Happiness"   <u>Bell's New Weekly Messenger</u>
     11 no 589   1 Aug 1841   MHC

"Varieties"   <u>Magnet</u> 5 no 226   2 Aug 1841   MHC

"Varieties: A Character. By 'Boz'"   <u>Bell's New Weekly</u>
     <u>Messenger</u> 11 no 590   8 Aug 1841   MHC

"Varieties: An Idiot's Happiness"   <u>Globe</u> no 12,232   10 Aug
     1841   MHC

"Varieties: A Fine Old English Tory, All of the Olden Time"
     <u>Globe</u> no 12,234   12 Aug 1841   MHC

"Theatricals and Music: Strand"   <u>Sunday Times</u> no 982   15 Aug
     1841   (dramatisation of BR)

"Varieties: Sleepiness" Bell's New Weekly Messenger 11 no 592
        22 Aug 1841   MHC

"Varieties" Magnet 5 no 229 23 Aug 1841   MHC

"Notices of New Works" Metropolitan Magazine   32   no   125
        Sep 1841: 25   MHC

"Literature" Bell's Life in London 19 Sep 1841   MHC

"Literary Examiner" Examiner no 1756 25 Sep 1841: 614   OT

"Literature" Bell's Life in London 3 Oct 1841   MHC

"Varieties: Picture of London" Globe no 12,281   6 Oct 1841
        MHC

"Reviews" Tablet no 76 23 Oct 1841: 693-94 (re Dickens's
        mechanical production of literature)

"Varieties: Rivalry in Love" Bell's New Weekly Messenger 11
        no 600 24 Oct 1841   MHC

"Varieties" Magnet 5 no 236 25 Oct 1841   MHC

"Master Humphrey's Clock" Town no 233 10 Nov 1841: 1852
        (MHC satire)

"Literature" John Bull 21 no 1092 13 Nov 1841: 549   MHC

"Master Humphrey's Clock" Town no 234 17 Nov 1841: 1861
        (MHC satire)

"Master Humphrey's Clock" Town no 235 24 Nov 1841: 1869
        (MHC satire)

"Notices of New Works" Metropolitan Magazine 32   no   128
        Dec 1841: 111-12 MHC

"Master Humphrey's Clock" Town no 236 1 Dec 1841: 1877
        (MHC satire)

"The Literary Examiner" Examiner no 1766 4 Dec 1841: 772-74
        MHC   [John Forster]

"Serials" Spectator 14 no 701 4 Dec 1841: 1170   MHC

"Master Humphrey's Clock" <u>Town</u> no 237 8 Dec 1841: 1885-86
(MHC satire)

"A Parthian Glance at the Serials of the Month" <u>United</u>
<u>Services Gazette</u> no 465 11 Dec 1841 MHC

"Adelphi Theatre" <u>The Times</u> no 17,859 21 Dec 1841
(dramatisation of BR)

"Adelphi Theatre" <u>Morning Herald</u> no 18,502 21 Dec 1841
(dramatisation of BR)

"Master Humphrey's Clock" <u>Town</u> no 239 22 Dec 1841: 1901
(MHC satire)

"Theatricals and Music: Adelphi" <u>Sunday Times</u> no 1001
26 Dec 1841 (dramatisation of BR)

"The Theatre" <u>Observer</u> 26 Dec 1841 (dramatisation of BR)

"Public Amusements: The Adelphi" <u>Weekly Dispatch</u> no 2096
26 Dec 1841: 620 (dramatisation of BR)

"The Theatres: Adelphi" <u>Sun</u> no 15,385 28 Dec 1841
(dramatisation of BR)

"Master Humphrey's Clock" <u>Town</u> no 240 29 Dec 1841: 1909
(MHC satire)

"Master Humphrey's Clock" <u>Town</u> no 241 5 Jan 1842: 1917
(MHC satire)

"Master Humphrey's Clock" <u>Town</u> no 242 12 Jan 1842: 1925
(MHC satire)

"Master Humphrey's Clock" <u>Town</u> no 243 19 Jan 1842: 1934
(MHC satire)

"Master Humphrey's Clock" <u>Town</u> no 244 26 Jan 1842: 1939
(MHC satire)

150

The Pic Nic Papers (PNP)

"Reviews of New Books"   <u>Literary Gazette</u> 25 no 1283   21 Aug
      1841:   540-41   PNP

"Reviews"   <u>Tablet</u> no 63   28 Aug 1841: 565-66   PNP

"Reviews: Literature and Art"   <u>Bell's Weekly Messenger</u> no 2366
      28 Aug 1841: 282   PNP

"Literature of the Month"   <u>New Monthly Magazine</u>   63   no 249
      Sep 1841: 129-30   PNP

III. REVIEWS: LISTED BY PERIODICAL

THE AGE

"The Very Age and Body of the Time"

1833:	6 Jan - 29 Dec
1834:	5 Jan - 28 Dec
1835:	4 Jan - 27 Dec
1836:	3 Jan - 25 Dec
1837:	1 Jan - 31 Dec
1838:	7 Jan - 30 Dec
1839:	6 Jan - 29 Dec
1840:	5 Jan - 27 Dec
1841:	3 Jan - 26 Dec

2 Oct 1836: 326	SG
11 Dec 1836: 406	VC
3 Jne 1838: 175	BM / NN
1 Jul 1838: 207	BM
8 Jul 1838: 212	NN
5 Aug 1838: 243	BM / NN
2 Sep 1838: 275	NN
9 Sep 1838: 282	BM
7 Oct 1838: 315	BM / NN
11 Nov 1838: 355	BM
9 Dec 1838: 386	BM / NN
13 Jan 1839: 10	NN
17 Feb 1839: 50	NN

10 Mar 1839: 74	NN
31 Mar 1839: 98	BM (the "Boz" style)
7 Apr 1839: 106	BM / NN
12 May 1839: 146	NN
9 Jne 1839: 178	NN
7 Jul 1839: 210	NN
4 Aug 1839: 242	NN
8 Sep 1839: 282	NN
6 Oct 1839: 314	NN
4 Apr 1840: 106	Fraser's Magazine on Dickens
12 Apr 1840: 114	MHC
9 Aug 1840: 250	MHC
29 Aug 1841: 278	Theodore Hook

Notes: Tory. No real literature or magazine departments:
instead, reviews are given under "Table-Talk," "Memorabilia,"
"Theatricals" and other such formulaic headings. Gives more
attention to Pickwick Abroad, a travesty published in the
Monthly Magazine from January to June 1838, than to Pickwick.
Has much praise for Bentley's Miscellany, especially during
run of Jack Sheppard there (January 1839 to February 1840).
Bentley and Colburn advertise in its pages frequently. See
note in Westminster Review 10 no 20 Apr 1829: 471. Price
sixpence.

THE ART-UNION

1839:	1	nos 1 - 11	(15 Feb - 15 Dec)
1840:	2	nos 12 - 23	(15 Jan - 15 Dec)
1841:	3	nos 24 - 35	(15 Jan - 15 Dec)

1   no 4   (15 May 1839): 74   "Boz"

THE ATHENAEUM

1828:	nos 1 - 62	2 Jan - 31 Dec
1829:	nos 63 - 114	7 Jan - 30 Dec
1830:	nos 115 - 165	9 Jan - 25 Dec
1831:	nos 166 - 218	1 Jan - 31 Dec
1832:	nos 219 - 270	7 Jan - 29 Dec
1833:	nos 271 - 322	5 Jan - 28 Dec
1834:	nos 323 - 374	4 Jan - 27 Dec
1835:	nos 375 - 426	3 Jan - 26 Dec
1836:	nos 427 - 479	2 Jan - 31 Dec
1837:	nos 480 - 531	7 Jan - 30 Dec
1838:	nos 532 - 583	6 Jan - 29 Dec
1839:	nos 584 - 635	5 Jan - 28 Dec
1840:	nos 636 - 687	4 Jan - 26 Dec
1841:	nos 688 - 739	2 Jan - 25 Dec

no 1	2 Jan 1828: 1-2; 10-12 12-14	Introductory; Novel-writing; The drama
no 3	16 Jan 1828: 33	Sketches of Contemporary Authors (I)
no 4	23 Jan 1828: 49-50	Sketches:Francis Jeffrey (II)
no 5	29 Jan 1828: 65-66	Sketches: Southey (III)
no 7	12 Feb 1828: 97-99	Sketches: William Cobbett (IV)

no 8	19 Feb 1828: 112–15	Sketches: William Wordsworth (V)
no 9	22 Feb 1828: 129–30	Sketches: Thomas Moore (VI)
no 11	29 Feb 1828: 161–63	Sketches: Henry Brougham(VII)
no 13	7 Mar 1828: 193–94	Sketches: Percy Bysshe Shelley (VIII)
no 14	11 Mar 1828: 217–19	Sketches: Walter Scott (IX)
no 16	18 Mar 1828: 249–50	Sketches: James Mackintosh(X)
no 18	25 Mar 1828: 273–75	Periodical Literature (I)
no 19	28 Mar 1828: 289–91	Sketches: Maria Edgeworth(XI)
no 20	1 Apr 1828: 305–07	Periodical Literature (II)
no 22	8 Apr 1828: 335–37	Periodical Literature (III)
no 23	8 Apr 1828: 351–52	Sketches: Lord Byron (XII)
no 24	15 Apr 1828: 367–69	Periodical Literature (IV)
no 26	23 Apr 1828: 399–400	Periodical Literature (V)
no 28	7 May 1828: 431–32	Periodical Literature (VI)
no 34	18 Jne 1828: 527–29	Sketches: James Mill (XIII)
no 40	30 Jul 1828: 623–24	Sketches: George Crabbe (XIV)
no 42	13 Aug 1828: 655–56	Female authorship
no 44	27 Aug 1828: 695–96	Periodical Press
no 47	17 Sep 1828: 735–36	Colburn's publishing list
no 146	14 Aug 1830: 497	End of literary anonymity
no 149	4 Sep 1830: 552–55	Colburn and Bentley's National Library

no 174	26 Feb 1831: 129	Colburn and Bentley's National Library
no 207	15 Oct 1831: 666-67	Depression in literary affairs
no 208	22 Oct 1831: 692	Depression in literary affairs
no 212	19 Nov 1831: 755	Depression in literary affairs
no 220	14 Jan 1832: 34-35	State of British literature
no 221	21 Jan 1832: 50	Crisis in the book trade
no 223	4 Feb 1832: 82-83	Crisis in the book trade
no 227	3 Mar 1832: 146	The magazines
no 231	31 Mar 1832: 210-11	Useful knowledge publishing
no 235	28 Apr 1832: 274-75	Crisis in the book trade
no 237	12 May 1832: 307	Periodical literature
no 238	19 May 1832: 322	Paucity of imaginative works
no 239	26 May 1832: 338-39	Growth of newspaper reading
no 241	9 Jne 1832: 371	The magazines
no 242	16 Jne 1832: 286	Revival of book trade
no 249	4 Aug 1832: 507	Periodical literature
no 254	8 Sep 1832: 588-89	Ritchie's Library of Romance
no 270	29 Dec 1832: 836-37	Ritchie's Library of Romance
no 275	2 Feb 1833: 74-75	Crisis in the book trade
no 276	9 Feb 1833: 90	Periodical literature
no 278	23 Feb 1833: 122	Contemporary literature
no 283	30 Mar 1833: 202	Crisis in the book trade
no 288	4 May 1833: 281-82	The magazines

no 290	18 May 1833: 315	The publishing of fiction
no 300	27 Jul 1833: 499	New periodicals
no 305	31 Aug 1833: 589	State of publishing
no 307	14 Sep 1833: 618	Defence of the novel
no 313	26 Oct 1833: 713-21	Biographical...History
no 315	9 Nov 1833: 752-53	Novel writing
no 316	16 Nov 1833: 769-77	Biographical...History
no 318	30 Nov 1833: 809-15	Biographical...History
no 320	14 Dec 1833: 849-55	Biographical...History
no 322	28 Dec 1833: 890-94	Biographical...History
no 325	18 Jan 1834: 50	The magazines
no 352	26 Jul 1834: 554	Publishing affairs
no 366	2 Nov 1834: 804-07	Discussion of aesthetics
no 373	20 Dec 1834: 921	State of publishing world
no 383	28 Feb 1835: 169	Literature and politics
no 384	7 Mar 1835: 185	The magazines
no 388	4 Apr 1835: 266	Court Magazine
no 391	25 Apr 1835: 322	Depressed state of book trade
no 418	31 Oct 1835: 817	Utilitarianism
no 423	5 Dec 1835: 913	Flood of novel publishing
no 425	19 Dec 1835: 950-51	Revival in literary affairs
no 426	26 Dec 1835: 968-69	Periodical literature
no 434	20 Feb 1836: 145	SB

no 445   7 May 1836: 329   Monthly magazines

no 455   16 Jul 1836: 497-99   English literature

no 466   1 Oct 1836: 708   SG

no 475   3 Dec 1836: 841-43   PP

no 477   17 Dec 1836: 891   VC

no 479   31 Dec 1836: 916-17   SB

no 480   7 Jan 1837: 4-6   BM

no 519   7 Oct 1837: 741-42   Lockhart, Life of Scott

no 544   31 Mar 1838: 227-29   NN

no 545   7 Apr 1838: 255-56   Surtees, Jorrock's Jaunts and
                                         Jollities

no 570   29 Sep 1838: 716   NN

no 577   17 Nov 1838: 824-25   OT

no 578   24 Nov 1838: 844   OT./ NN (dramatisations)

no 586   19 Jan 1839: 51-52   Decline of the novel

no 594   16 Mar 1839: 195-97   State of the novel

no 598   13 Apr 1839: 278-79   Literary lionism

no 609   29 Jne 1839: 485-86   Quarterly Review on OT

no 626   26 Oct 1839: 803-05   W.H. Ainsworth, Jack Sheppard

no 651   18 Apr 1840: 313   SYC

no 680   7 Nov 1840: 887-88   MHC

no 738   18 Dec 1841: 970   G.P.R. James, W.H. Ainsworth

158

Notes:
Liberal ("independent"). Headings include "Reviews" (always
the leading article), "Our Library Table" (shorter reviews),
and "Original Papers." See also, "Our Weekly Gossip" for news
of the publishing world. See Westminster Review 10 no 20 Apr
1829: 480; Leslie A. Marchand, The Athenaeum: A Mirror of
Victorian Culture (1971); British Literary Magazines, v. 2.

THE ATLAS

"A General Newspaper and Journal of Literature"

1833:	8	nos 347 - 398	6 Jan - 29 Dec
1834:	9	nos 399 - 450	5 Jan - 28 Dec
1835:	9/10	nos 451 - 502	4 Jan - 27 Dec
1836:	11	nos 503 - 554	3 Jan - 25 Dec
1837:	12	nos 555 - 607	1 Jan - 31 Dec
1838:	13	nos 608 - 659	7 Jan - 29 Dec
1839:	14	nos 660 - 711	5 Jan - 28 Dec
1840:	15	nos 712 - 763	4 Jan - 26 Dec
1841:	16	nos 764 - 815	2 Jan - 25 Dec

11	510	21 Feb 1836: 123	SB
11	516	3 Apr 1836: 220	PP
11	531	17 Jul 1836: 457	SUTH
11	542	2 Oct 1836: 631	SG
11	556	8 Jan 1837: 28-29	BM
12	568	2 Apr 1837: 217	SB
12	582	9 Jul 1837: 441	BM
12	586	6 Aug 1837: 505	BM

12	590	3 Sep 1837: 569	BM
12	598	5 Nov 1837: 713	BM
13	619	24 Mar 1838: 185-86	MJG
13	639	11 Aug 1838: 504	Fashionable novels
13	644	15 Sep 1838: 587	BM
13	653	17 Nov 1838: 729-31	OT
13	657	15 Dec 1838: 792-93	Essay-writing
14	660	5 Jan 1839: 9	Literature of 1838
14	668	2 Mar 1839: 136	OT (dramatisation)
14	673	6 Apr 1839: 218;219	BM; Mrs. Trollope Michael Armstrong
14	706	23 Nov 1839: 751	Ainsworth, Jack Sheppard
14	708	7 Dec 1839: 780	Ainsworth, Jack Sheppard
15	720	29 Feb 1840: 139	SYC
15	751	3 Oct 1840: 648-49	The magazines
15	752	10 Oct 1840: 664-65	The magazines
15	757	14 Nov 1840: 743	OCS (dramatisation)

Notes:
Headings include "Literature" (mostly non-fiction), "Review of New Books," and occasionally, "Serial Fictions" and "Periodicals." It is noteworthy that there are no reviews of Nicholas Nickleby in 1839 and 1840, and none at all of Master Humphrey's Clock. In 1841, there are no notices of Dickens, even in the theatricals columns. Price one shilling.

BELL'S LIFE IN LONDON AND SPORTING CHRONICLE

1833:	12	nos 391 - 590	6 Jan - 29 Dec
1834:	13	nos 591 - 640	5 Jan - 28 Dec
1835:	14	nos 641 - *	4 Jan - 27 Dec
1836:			3 Jan - 25 Dec
1837:			1 Jan - 31 Dec
1838:			7 Jan - 30 Dec
1839:			6 Jan - 29 Dec
1840:			5 Jan - 27 Dec
1841:			3 Jan - 26 Dec

*[Numbering ends with no 646 (15 Feb 1835)]

14 Feb 1836	SB
10 Apr 1836	PP / LF
3 Jul 1836	SUTH
7 Aug 1836	PP
4 Sep 1836	PP
2 Oct 1836	SG
11 Dec 1836	VC
12 Mar 1837	ISHW
30 Apr 1837	PP
2 Jul 1837	BM
3 Sep 1837	PP
8 Oct 1837	PP
28 Jan 1838	ISHW
1 Apr 1838	NN

6 May 1838	NN
5 Aug 1838	NN
7 Oct 1838	NN
9 Dec 1838	OT / NN (dramatisations)
13 Jan 1839	NN
14 Apr 1839	BM / NN
2 Jne 1839	BM / NN
11 Aug 1839	BM / NN
5 Apr 1840	MHC
10 Apr 1840	MHC
13 Sep 1840	MHC
4 Oct 1840	MHC
6 Dec 1840	MHC
3 Jan 1841	MHC
14 Feb 1841	MHC
11 Apr 1841	MHC
9 May 1841	MHC
4 Jul 1841	MHC
19 Sep 1841	MHC
3 Oct 1841	MHC

Notes:
A feature called "Literature" begins in 1835 but appears only
sporadically; <u>Pickwick</u> is noticed for its humour, but no
attempt is made to comment on it in a literary way.   The

paper's emphasis is on sporting. It has both "Town" and "Country" editions. Its price is set at fivepence until 1835; it sells for sevenpence from then until 18 Sep 1836, when the price goes back to fivepence. No issue numbers are given after no 646 on 15 Feb 1835. The <u>Westminster Review</u> says of this paper that it has the largest circulation (estimated at 22,000) of all the Sunday papers; like most of the Sunday papers, it was liberal in political sympathies (WR 10 no 20 Apr 1829: 479).

BELL'S NEW WEEKLY MESSENGER

"Advocate and Entertainer of the People"

1832:	1	nos 1 - 53	1 Jan - 30 Dec
1833:	2	nos 54 - 105	6 Jan - 29 Dec
1834:	3	nos 106 - 157	5 Jan - 28 Dec
1835:	4	nos 158 - 209	4 Jan - 27 Dec
1836:	5	nos 210 - 261	3 Jan - 25 Dec
1837:	6	nos 262 - 288	1 Jan - 2 Jul
	7	nos 289 - 314	9 Jul - 31 Dec

"Enlarged Series" begins (4 to 6 cols.)

| 1838: | 8 | nos 315 - 367 | 7 Jan - 30 Dec |
| 1839: | 9 | nos 368 - 507 | 6 Jan - 29 Dec |

Supplement (literary) begins in April

| 1840: | 10 | nos 508 - 560 | 5 Jan - 27 Dec |
| 1841: | 11 | nos 561 - 609 | 3 Jan - 26 Dec |

1	no	1	1 Jan 1832: 1	Modern literature
1	no	7	12 Feb 1832: 28	MM
1	no	8	19 Feb 1832: 29	Novelist's Library
1	no	10	4 Mar 1832: 40	MM
1	no	27	1 Jul 1832: 93	Book reviewing
1	no	32	5 Aug 1832: 104	Metropolitan
2	no	54	6 Jan 1833: 2	MM
2	no	67	7 Apr 1833: 28	MM
2	no	72	12 May 1833: 37	Library of Romance
2	no	102	8 Dec 1833: 98	SB
3	no	106	5 Jan 1834: 2	MM
3	no	119	6 Apr 1834: 28	MM
3	no	123	4 May 1834: 36	MM
3	no	127	1 Jne 1834: 43	Ainsworth, Rookwood
4	no	103	0 Feb 1835: 85 86	MM
5	no	249	2 Oct 1836: 634	SG
5	no	251	16 Oct 1836: 667	PP
6	no	259	11 Dec 1836: 794;795	PP / VC
6	no	263	8 Jan 1837: 23	PP
6	no	264	15 Jan 1837: 38,39	PP (2)
6	no	268	5 Feb 1837: 88	PP
6	no	271	5 Mar 1837: 154	PP
6	no	272	12 Mar 1837: 171	ISHW

6	no 275	2 Apr 1837: 218		PP
6	no 280	7 May 1837: 297-98		PP
6	no 288	2 Jul 1837: 426		PP
6	no 293	6 Aug 1837: 35		PP
7	no 297	3 Sep 1837: 67		PP
7	no 302	8 Oct 1837: 107		PP
7	no 306	5 Nov 1837: 138-39		PP
8	no 320	4 Feb 1838		BM
8	no 325	11 Mar 1838		MJG
8	no 328	1 Apr 1838		NN
8	no 329	8 Apr 1838		NN
8	no 333	6 May 1838		NN
8	no 337	3 Jne 1838		NN
8	no 338	10 Jne 1838		BM
8	no 342	8 Jul 1838		NN
8	no 346	5 Aug 1838		NN
8	no 351	9 Sep 1838		NN
8	no 353	23 Sep 1838		BM
8	no 355	7 Oct 1838		NN
8	no 359	4 Nov 1838		NN
8	no 364	9 Dec 1838		NN
9	no 368	6 Jan 1839		NN
9	no 369	13 Jan 1839		BM

9	no 373	10 Feb 1839	NN
9	no 376	3 Mar 1839	NN
Supplement 1	[no number] 7 Apr 1839		NN
9	no 385	5 May 1839	NN
9	no 389	2 Jne 1839	NN
Supplement 1	no 4 7 Jul 1839		NN
9	no 398	4 Aug 1839	NN
Supplement 1	no 6 8 Sep 1839		NN
9	no 406	6 Oct 1839	NN
Supplement	8 Dec 1839		BM
9	no 505	15 Dec 1839	State of literature
10	no 521	5 Apr 1840	MHC
10	no 528	24 May 1840	MHC
10	no 541	23 Aug 1840	MHC
10	no 543	6 Sep 1840	MHC
10	no 544	13 Sep 1840	MHC
10	no 545	20 Sep 1840	MHC
10	no 546	27 Sep 1840	MHC
10	no 548	11 Oct 1840	MHC
10	no 549	18 Oct 1840	MHC
10	no 550	25 Oct 1840	MHC
10	no 552	8 Nov 1840	MHC
10	no 554	15 Nov 1840	MHC

10	no 557	6 Dec 1840	MHC
10	no 558	13 Dec 1840	MHC
10	no 559	20 Dec 1840	MHC (2)
10	no 560	27 Dec 1840	MHC
11	no 561	3 Jan 1841	MHC
11	no 562	17 Jan 1841	MHC
11	no 563	24 Jan 1841	MHC
11	no 564	31 Jan 1841	MHC
11	no 567	21 Feb 1841	MHC
11	no 568	28 Feb 1841	MHC
11	no 569	7 Mar 1841	MHC
11	no 570	14 Mar 1841	MHC
11	no 573	4 Apr 1841	MHC
11	no 574	11 Apr 1841	MHC
11	no 575	18 Apr 1841	Boz
11	no 577	2 May 1841	MHC
11	no 578	9 May 1841	MHC
11	no 180*	23 May 1841	MHC*[sic; shd be 580]
11	no 581	30 May 1841	MHC
11	no 582	6 Jne 1841	MHC
11	no 583	13 Jne 1841	MHC
11	no 584	20 Jne 1841	MHC
11	no 585	27 Jne 1841	MHC

11	no 589	1 Aug 1841	MHC
11	no 590	8 Aug 1841	MHC
11	no 592	22 Aug 1841	MHC
11	no 600	24 Oct 1841	MHC

Notes:
Set up by John Browne Bell in 1832 as a Radical paper (price eight-and-a-half pence) in opposition to Bell's Weekly Messenger (established in 1796 by his father, the famous printer John Bell [DNB 1745-1831]). The last year of cumulative numbering is 1837: Jan-Jul = pp. 1-436; Jul-Dec = pp. 1-205. The "Enlarged Series" containing six columns (instead of four) begins in the same year. After that, each issue consists of eight pages per issue, and the reviews are regularly located on p. 6. Headings for reviews include "The Reviewer," "New Books," and "The Drama." There are no more reviewing supplments from 4 Jan 1835. The "reviews" of Dickens's works are merely extracts and often appear under their own headings.

BELL'S WEEKLY MAGAZINE

"Journal of English and Foreign Literature, Science, and the Fine Arts"

nos 1 - 6	18 Jan - 22 Feb 1834: 1-96	[complete]

1	(1834): 83-84	Contemporary periodical literature

Notes:
Price twopence.

BELL'S WEEKLY MESSENGER

1833:	nos 1918 - 1969	6 Jan - 30 Dec
1834:	nos 1970 - 2020	5 Jan - 29 Dec
1835:	nos 2021 - 2071	4 Jan - 28 Dec
1836:	nos 2072 - 2123	3 Jan - 26 Dec
1837:	nos 2124 - 2176	1 Jan - 31 Dec
1838:	nos 2177 - 2228	1 Jan - 31 Dec
1839:	nos 2229 - 2280	6 Jan - 30 Dec
1840:	nos 2281 - 2331	4 Jan - 28 Dec
1841:	nos 2332 - 2383	2 Jan - 27 Dec

no 1975	10 Feb 1834: 46	MM
no 1996	6 Jul 1834: 209	Periodicals
no 2000	3 Aug 1834: 245-46	MM
no 2010	12 Oct 1834: 323	MM
no 2022	11 Jan 1835: 10	MM
no 2027	15 Feb 1835: 50	MM
no 2111	2 Oct 1836: 314	SG
no 2121	11 Dec 1836: 398	VC
no 2129	5 Feb 1837: 47	BM
no 2138	9 Apr 1837: 119	PP
no 2151	9 Jul 1837: 222	BM
no 2155	6 Aug 1837: 251	BM
no 2164	8 Oct 1837: 326	BM
no 2168	5 Nov 1837: 355	BM

no 2177	8 Jan 1838: 14	BM
no 2182	11 Feb 1838: 46	BM
no 2190	8 Apr 1838: 110	BM
no 2194	6 May 1838: 142	BM
no 2203	8 Jul 1838: 214	BM
no 2207	5 Aug 1838: 246	BM
no 2216	7 Oct 1838: 315	BM
no 2221	11 Nov 1838: 355	BM
no 2229	6 Jan 1839: 3	BM / NN
no 2294	4 Apr 1840: 110	Fraser's on Dickens
no 2366	28 Aug 1841: 282	PNP

Notes:
One of the oldest Sunday papers. The quality of the printing
is outstanding, as is to be expected from a paper published
by John Bell (DNB 1745-1831). Its "Literature" column reviews
mostly non-fiction. Price eight-and-a-half pence.

BLACKWOOD'S EDINBURGH MAGAZINE

1833:	33	nos 203 - 209	Jan - Jne
	34	nos 210 - 216	Jul - Dec
1834:	35	nos 217 - 223	Jan - Jne
	36	nos 224 - 229	Jul - Dec
1835:	37	nos 230 - 236	Jan - Jne
	38	nos 237 - 242	Jul - Dec
1836:	39	nos 243 - 248	Jan - Jne
	40	nos 249 - 254	Jul - Dec
1837:	41	nos 255 - 260	Jan - Jne
	42	nos 261 - 266	Jul - Dec
1838:	43	nos 267 - 272	Jan - Jne
	44	nos 273 - 278	Jul - Dec
1839:	45	nos 279 - 284	Jan - Jne
	46	nos 285 - 290	Jul - Dec
1840:	47	nos 291 - 296	Jan - Jne
	48	nos 297 - 302	Jul - Dec
1841:	49	nos 303 - 308	Jan - Jne
	50	nos 309 - 314	Jul - Dec

4 no 22 Jan 1819: 394-96   Novel-writing

8 no 44 Nov 1820: 138-41   Critics and criticism

8 no 44 Nov 1820: 161-68   Maturin, Melmoth the
                                Wanderer

16 no 94 Nov 1824: 518-28   Influence of periodicals

25 no 153 Apr 1829: 525-48   Contemporary periodical press

48 no 297 Jul 1840: 1-17   Style

Notes:
See Wellesley Index, v. 1; British Literary Magazines, v. 2.

BRITISH AND FOREIGN REVIEW; or, European Quarterly Journal

1835:	1	nos	1	&	2	Jul & Oct
1836:	2	nos	3	&	4	Jan & Apr
	3	nos	5	&	6	Jul & Oct
1837:	4	nos	7	&	8	Jan & Apr
	5	nos	9	&	10	Jul & Oct
1838:	6	nos	11	&	12	Jan & Apr
	7	nos	13	&	14	Jul & Oct
1839:	8	nos	15	&	16	Jan & Apr
	9	nos	17	&	18	Jul & Oct
1840:	10	nos	19	&	20	Jan & Apr
	11	nos	21	&	22	Jul & Oct
1841:	12	nos	23	&	24	Jan & Apr
	13	nos	25	&	26	Jul & Oct

1 no 1   Jul 1835: 157-72   Taxes on knowledge

1 no 1   Jul 1835: 190-217   Contemporary literature

3 no 6   Dec 1836: 477-510   Fashionable novels

10 no 19   Jan 1840: 223-46   Ainsworth, Jack Sheppard;
                                  Mrs. Trollope, Michael
                                  Armstrong

Notes:
See Wellesley Index, v. 3; British and Literary Magazines,
v.2.

CARLTON CHRONICLE (AND NATIONAL CONSERVATIVE JOURNAL) OF POLITICS, LITERATURE, SCIENCE AND ARTS)

1836: nos 1 - 26   11 Jne - 31 Dec
1837: nos 27 - 45   7 Jan - 13 May*

*[Gap between 13 Aug 1836 (no 10) and 17 Sep 1836 (no 11) is only between dates; the page and issue numbers follow on consecutively.]

no 1	11 Jne 1836: 10	PP
no 4	2 Jul 1836: 57-58	PP
no 6	23 Jul 1836: 104-05	SUTH
no 9	6 Aug 1836: 131,141	PP
no 13	1 Oct 1836: 206	SG
no 23	10 Dec 1836: 365-66	VC
no 27	7 Jan 1837: 425-27	PP / BM
no 31	4 Feb 1837: 491/492-93	PP / BM
no 35	4 Mar 1837: 554-55/555-56	PP / BM
no 37	18 Mar 1837: 589	ISHW
no 39	1 Apr 1837: 615-17	PP
no 40	8 Apr 1837: 635-36	BM
no 43	29 Apr 1837: 683-84	PP
no 44	6 May 1837: 698-99	BM

Notes:
Formerly known as <u>Fraser's Literary Chronicle</u>.   See <u>The</u>
<u>Letters of Charles Dickens, Volume One 1820-39</u>, eds. Madeline
House and Graham Storey (Oxford: Clarendon Press, 1965) for
Dickens's description of this magazine: "all among the nobs"
(160n). Edited by Percival Weldon Banks (1805-50), a close
associate of William Maginn on <u>Fraser's Magazine</u>.   Dickens
began a new series of sketches with "The Hospital Patient,"
but it ended there; "Doctors' Commons" and "Scotland-Yard"
were copied in this paper from the <u>Morning Chronicle</u> without
permission (see Dickens's objections, <u>Letters</u> 188n). Whatever
the magazine's snob appeal, its price changed from one
shilling to sixpence, and it failed after less than a year.
Its criticism is vacuous, consisting mostly of extracts.

CHAMBERS'S EDINBURGH JOURNAL

1833:	2	nos 53 - 104	2 Feb - 18 Jan 1834
1834:	3	nos 105 - 156	1 Feb - 24 Jan 1835
1835:	4	nos 157 - 208	31 Jan - 23 Jan 1836
1836:	5	nos 209 - 260	30 Jan - 21 Jan 1837
1837:	6	nos 261 - 312	28 Jan - 20 Jan 1838
1838:	7	nos 313 - 364	27 Jan - 19 Jan 1839
1839:	8	nos 365 - 416	26 Jan - 18 Jan 1840
1840:	9	nos 417 - 468	25 Jan - 16 Jan 1841
1841:	10	nos 469 - 520	23 Jan - 15 Jan 1842

6   no 274   29 Apr 1837: 109-10   PP

Notes:
Mainly useful knowledge; no reviews. Price three halfpence.
Spelling of title inconsistent: in some editions, it is
printed as "Chambers'." See <u>British Literary Magazines</u>, v.
2.

CHAMBERS' HISTORICAL NEWSPAPER

nos 1 - 39   2 Nov 1832 - 1 Jan 1836

no 20   Jne 1834: 158-59   Silver-fork and Newgate
                                      novelists

Notes:
Mostly political and statistical news; some "Miscellaneous"
items; no reviews. Price three halfpence.

THE CHAMPION

1836:   1 - 15   18 Sep - 25 Dec
1837:   16 - 34   1 Jan -   7 May

         ns 1 no 1   13 May - 23 Jne 1838   (octavo)

1838:   2 no 8   1 Jul   [end] (folio: no
                                                    literature)

no 3   2 Oct 1836: 22   SG

no 13   11 Dec 1836: 99   VC

no 26   12 Mar 1837: 205   ISHW

Notes:
A Radical paper. After it becomes a folio publication, there
is more country news, some "Theatricals," but no "Literature."
Price fourpence. Published by Richard Cobbett.

CHRISTIAN REMEMBRANCER, OR THE CHURCHMAN'S BIBLICAL,
ECCLESIASTICAL, & LITERARY MISCELLANY

1833:	___		Jan - Dec	
1834:	___		Jan - Dec	
1835:	17	nos 1 - 12	Jan - Dec	
1836:	18	nos 1 - 12	Jan - Dec	
1837:	19	nos 1 - 12	Jan - Dec	
1838:	20	nos 1 - 12	Jan - Dec	
1839:	21	nos 1 - 12	Jan - Dec	
1840:	22	nos 1 - 12	Jan - Dec	

Becomes:
CHRISTIAN REMEMBRANCER: A MONTHLY MAGAZINE AND REVIEW

1841:	ns 1	nos 1 - 6	Jan - Jne
	2	nos 7 - 12	Jul - Dec

ns 1	no 6	Jne 1841: 423-40	Literature and authorship in England

Notes:
Some reviews, but only of religious books.   Affiliation:
Church of England.

CHRISTIAN TEACHER: A THEOLOGICAL AND LITERARY JOURNAL

1839:	ns 1	nos 1 - 6	Jul 1838 - Dec 1839
1840:	2	nos 7 - 10	[no months given]
1841:	3	nos 11 - 14	[no months given]

ns 1 no 1   (1839): 1-20 Influence of periodical
                                      literature

Notes:
In its original form, as published from 1835-38 (vols. 1-4),
this journal does not concern itself with reviewing.
Affiliation: Unitarian, with an especial concern for
education. See British Literary Magazines, v. 3.

CHURCH OF ENGLAND QUARTERLY REVIEW

1837	1	nos 1 & 2	Jan & Apr
	2	nos 3 & 4	Jul & Oct
1838	3	nos 5 & 6	Jan & Apr
	4	nos 7 & 8	Jul & Oct
1839:	5	nos 9 & __*	Jan & Apr
	6		Jul & Oct
1840:	7		Jan & Apr
	8		Jul & Oct
1841:	9		Jan & Apr
	10		Jul & Oct

*[no numbers given after no 9]

6	Oct 1839: 348-83	The periodical press
9	Jan 1841: 33-52	The Church and the novelists
9	Apr 1841: 506	General literature

Notes:
Tory. Some secular literature reviewed. No index.

COBBETT'S POLITICAL REGISTER

1833:	79		5 Jan – 30 Mar
	80		6 Apr – 29 Jne
	81		6 Jul – 28 Sep
	82		5 Oct – 28 Dec
1834:	83		4 Jan – 29 Mar
	84		5 Apr – 28 Jne
	85		5 Jul – 26[7] Sep
	86		4 Oct – 27 Dec
1835:	87	nos 1-13	3 Jan – 28 Mar
	88	nos 1-13	4 Apr – 27 Jne
	89	nos 1-11	4 Jul – 12 Sep

Death of W. Cobbett
Oct 1835 – Feb 1836   Edited by W.
Cobbett, Jr.

1836:	89	no 12	20 Feb
	2s	nos 1 – 10	16 Jul – 12 Sep

79   2 Mar 1833:   cols. 564-70   The newspaper press

Notes:
Purely political. Price varies (generally around one shilling
and twopence).

THE COURIER

1833:	nos 12,921 – 13,233	1 Jan – 31 Dec
1834:	nos 13,234 – 13,545	1 Jan – 31 Dec
1835:	nos 13,546 – 13,857	1 Jan – 31 Dec
1836:	nos 13,858 – 14,166	1 Jan – 31 Dec
1837:	nos 14,167 – 14,477	2 Jan – 30 Dec
1838:	nos 14,478 – 14,794	1 Jan – 31 Dec
1839:	nos 14,795 – 15,100	1 Jan – 31 Dec
1840:	nos 15,101 – 15,410	1 Jan – 31 Dec
1841:	nos 15,411 – 15,715	1 Jan – 31 Dec

no 13,642	24 Apr 1835	Bentley's Standard Novels
no 13,801	27 Oct 1835	Journalists in society
no 14,090	30 Sep 1836	SG
no 14,091	1 Oct 1836	SG
no 14,219	3 Mar 1837	PP
no 14,278	11 May 1837	PP
no 14,322	1 Jul 1837	PP
no 14,375	1 Sep 1837	PP / BM
no 14,408	10 Oct 1837	PP
no 14,508	5 Feb 1838	BM
no 14,530	2 Mar 1838	BM
no 14,553	29 Mar 1838	OT (dramatisation)
no 14,554	30 Mar 1838	NN
no 14,581	1 May 1838	NN
no 14,068*	1 Jne 1838	NN*[sic;shd be no 14,608]
no 14,631	28 Jne 1838	NN
no 14,658	2 Aug 1838	BM
no 14,708	1 Oct 1838	NN
no 14,711	4 Oct 1838	Edinburgh Review
no 14,735	1 Nov 1838	NN
no 14,761	1 Dec 1838	BM
no 14,762	3 Dec 1838	OT
no 14,795	1 Jan 1839	NN

no 14,796	2 Jan 1839	NN
no 14,821	31 Jan 1839	NN
no 14,822	1 Feb 1839	NN
no 14,845	1 Mar 1839	BM
no 14,871	1 Apr 1839	NN
no 14,873	3 Apr 1839	NN (2)
no 14,874	4 Apr 1839	NN
no 14,904	9 May 1839	NN
no 14,974	1 Aug 1839	NN
no 15,000	3 Sep 1839	NN
no 15,025	3 Oct 1839	NN
no 15,026	4 Oct 1839	NN
no 15,045	28 Oct 1839	NN
no 15,212	14 May 1840	MHC
no 15,223	27 May 1840	MHC
no 15,295	19 Aug 1840	MHC
no 15,572	14 Jul 1841	BR (dramatisation)

Notes:
Tory; converted to Whiggism in 1830. Editors: Gibbons Merle
(1830); James Stuart (1833). "Literature" reviews are mostly
of non-fiction. New fiction works are dealt with in
"Miscellaneous"/"Advertisement" quotations from the monthlies,
in other words, puffs. In the 1840s, Dickens was offered the
editorship of this paper. There is no systematic attempt at
reviews; extracting is preferred. During the earlier years
of the decade, there is more attention given to the magazines.
In the 1840s, the extracts are generally printed under their
own headings. No page numbers given; each issue consists
of two leaves/four pages. Price fivepence.

COURT MAGAZINE AND BELLE ASSEMBLÉE

1832:	1	nos 1 – 6		Jul – Dec	
1833:	2	nos 1 – 6		Jan – Jne	
	3	nos 1 – 6		Jul – Dec	
1834:	4	nos 1 – 6		Jan – Jne	
	5	nos 1 – 6		Jul – Dec	
1835:	6	nos 1 – 6		Jan – Jne	
	7	nos 1 – 6		Jul – Dec	
1836:	8	[ns 1]	nos 1 – 6	Jan – Jne	
	9	[ns 2]	nos 1 – 6	Jul – Dec	

9	no 5	May 1836: 227	Library of Fiction

then
COURT MAGAZINE AND MONTHLY CRITIC

1837:	10	[ns 3]	nos 1 – 6	Jan – Jne
	11	[ns 4]	nos 1 – 6	Jul – Dec

and **The Lady's Magazine and Museum**

1838:	12	("United Series"	No 1)	Jan – Jne
	13	"	2	Jul – Dec
1839:	14	"	1	Jan – Jne
	15	"	2	Jul – Dec
1840:	16	"	1	Jan – Jne
	17	"	2	Jul – Dec
1841:	18	"	1	Jan – Jne
	19	"	2	Jul – Dec

10	no 1	Jan 1837: 4-13	Books of the past year
10	no 4	Apr 1837: 185-87	Genius of Boz
10	no 5	May 1837: 201-06	Contemporary criticism
10	no 6	Jne 1837: 272-78	National and historical novels

Notes:
See <u>Waterloo Directory</u>: <u>Belle Assemblée</u> (WD 2204) (1806-32).
Then <u>Court Magazine and Belle Assemblée ⟨and Monthly Critic⟩</u>
(WD 6758) nos 1 - 32 (1832-48). There is no entry for <u>Monthly</u>
<u>Critic</u>. See <u>British Literary Magazines</u>, v. 3.

DUBLIN REVIEW

1836:	1	nos	1 & 2	May & Jul
	2	nos	3 & 4	Dec & Apr 1837
1837:	3	nos	5 & 6	Jul & Oct
1838:	4	nos	7 & 8	Jan & Apr
	5	nos	9 & 10	Jul & Oct
1839:	6	nos	11 & 12	Jan/Feb & May
	7	nos	13 & 14	Aug & Nov
1840:	8	nos	15 & 16	Feb & May
	9	nos	17 & 18	Aug & Nov
1841:	10	nos	19 & 20	Feb & May
	11	nos	21 & 22	Aug & Nov

2	no 3	Dec 1836: 111-29	Fashionable novels
8	no 15	Feb 1840: 160-88	PP

Notes:
Religious (Catholic) and intellectual. See <u>Wellesley Index</u>,
v. 2; <u>British Literary Magazines</u>, v. 2.

DUBLIN UNIVERSITY MAGAZINE: A Literary and Political Journal

1833:	1	nos	1	–	6	Jan	–	Jne
	2	nos	7	–	12	Jul	–	Dec
1834:	3	nos	13	–	18	Jan	–	Jne
	4	nos	19	–	24	Jul	–	Dec
1835:	5	nos	25	–	30	Jan	–	Jne
	6	nos	31	–	36	Jul	–	Dec
1836:	7	nos	37	–	42	Jan	–	Jne
	8	nos	43	–	48	Jul	–	Dec
1837:	9	nos	49	–	54	Jan	–	Jne
	10	nos	55	–	60	Jul	–	Dec
1838:	11	nos	61	–	66	Jan	–	Jne
	12	nos	67	–	72	Jul	–	Dec
1839:	13	nos	73	–	78	Jan	–	Jne
	14	nos	79	–	84	Jul	–	Dec
1840:	15	nos	85	–	90	Jan	–	Jne
	16	nos	91	–	96	Jul	–	Dec
1841:	17	nos	97	–	102	Jan	–	Jne
	18	nos	103	–	108	Jul	–	Dec

2	no 11	Nov 1833: 530-35	Satire of authorship
4	no 20	Aug 1834: 174-83	Decline of poetry
5	no 27	Mar 1835: 276-93	Bulwer, Last Days of Pompeii
5	no 29	May 1835: 554-72	Sketch writing
11	no 66	Jne 1838: 667-88	Lockhart, Life of Scott
12	no 67	Jul 1838: 3-39	Fashionable novels
12	no 72	Dec 1838: 699-723	OT

Notes:
Irish, serious. Ulsterish Protestant. See Wellesley Index,
v. 4; British Literary Magazines, v. 2.

ECLECTIC REVIEW

1833:	3s	9	Jan - Jne
		10	Jul - Dec
1834:		11	Jan - Jne
		12	Jul - Dec
1835:		13	Jan - Jne
		14	Jul - Dec
1836:		15	Jan - Jne
		16	Jul - Dec
1837:	ns	1	Jan - Jne
		2	Jul - Dec
1838:		3	Jan - Jne
		4	Jul - Dec
1839:		5	Jan - Jne
		6	Jul - Dec
1840:		7	Jan - Jne
		8	Jul - Dec
1841:		9	Jan - Jne
		10	Jul - Dec

1   Apr 1837: 339-55   PP

Notes:
Dissenter, completely religious and serious; surprising that
Pickwick should be considered in its pages at all. See
British Literary Magazines, v. 2.

EDINBURGH REVIEW

1833:	56	no 112 [sic]	Jan
	57	no 115	Apr
		no 116	Jul
	58	no 117	Oct
1834:		no 118	Jan
	59	no 119	Apr
		no 120	Jul
	60	no 121	Oct
1835:		no 122	Jan
	61	no 123	Apr
		no 124	Jul
	62	no 125	Oct
1836:		no 126	Jan
	63	no 127	Apr
		no 128	Jul
	64	no 129	Oct
1837:		no 130	Jan
	65	no 131	Apr
		no 132	Jul
	66	no 133	Oct
1838:		no 134	Jan
	67	no 135	Apr
		no 136	Jul
	68	no 137	Oct
1839:		no 138	Jan
	69	no 139	Apr
		no 140	Jul
	70	no 141	Oct
1840:		no 142	Jan
	71	no 143	Apr
		no 144	Jul
	72	no 145	Oct
1841:		no 146	Jan
	73	no 147	Apr
		no 148	Jul
	74	no 149	Oct

45	no 95	Sep 1828: 96-169	The fourth estate
49	no 98	Jne 1829: 439-59	Mechanical intellect
52	no 53	Oct 1830: 228-30	Bentley and Colburn's National Library
55	no 109	Apr 1832: 61-79	Waverley novels
57	no 115	Apr 1833: 239-48	Periodical press
57	no 116	Jul 1833: 403-11	Status of the novel
59	no 120	Jul 1834: 475-86	State of the novel
59	no 120	Jul 1834: 439-45	Literary men and popular politics
65	no 131	Apr 1837: 180-204	Recent romances
65	no 132	Jul 1837: 196-213	Newspaper literature
66	no 133	Oct 1837: 59-72	Disraeli's novels
67	no 136	Jul 1838: 349-57	Status of the novel
68	no 137	Oct 1838: 75-97	Charles Dickens
68	no 138	Jan 1839: 354-76	History of taste
68	no 138	Jan 1839: 433-59	Thomas Love Peacock

Notes:
See Wellesley Index, v. 1; British Literary Magazines, v, 2.

THE ERA

"Wisdom is acquired, not by the reading of books, but of men."

1838:	1	nos 1 - 14	30 Sep - 30 Dec
1839:	1	nos 15 - 52	6 Jan - 22 Sep
	2	nos 53 - 66	29 Sep - 29 Dec
1840:	2	nos 67 - 105	5 Jan - 27 Sep
	3	nos 106 - 118	4 Oct - 27 Dec
1841:	3	nos 119 - 156	3 Jan - 26 Sep
	4	nos 157 - 170	3 Oct - 26 Dec

1	no 7	11 Nov 1838: 80	BM
1	no 8	18 Nov 1838: 92	OT
1	no 23	3 Mar 1839: 272	BM
1	no 28	7 Apr 1839: 332	BM
1	no 34	19 May 1839: 404	OT
2	no 55	13 Oct 1839: 32	NN
2	no 79	5 Apr 1840: 333	Fraser's on Dickens
2	no 84	3 May 1840: 386	MHC
2	no 86	17 May 1840: 410	MHC
2	no 102	6 Sep 1840: 610	BM; tales in instalments
3	no 108	18 Oct 1840	The Dickens style
3	no 110	1 Nov 1840	Imitations of Dickens
3	no 132	4 Apr 1841	Literary remarks
3	no 134	18 Apr 1841	Weekly publications
3	no 136	2 May 1841	BM serialisation

3	no 144	27 Jne 1841	Novel-writing
3	no 147	18 Jul 1841	Periodicals
4	no 170	26 Dec 1841	Novels in instalments

Notes:
Light reading: finds the <u>Monthly Magazine</u>, for example, too "grave." Lack of moral seriousness is also suggested by the fact that it particularly enjoys <u>Bentley's Miscellany</u> during the serialisation of <u>Jack Sheppard</u> (January 1839 to February 1840). Combined with <u>True Sportsman's Gazette</u>. Cumulative pagination ends with 2 no 104 20 Sep 1840: 638. From 2 no 105 27 Sep 1840, each issue = pp. 1-12, not always numbered. Price sixpence.

THE EXAMINER

A Sunday Paper on Politics, Literature, and the Fine Arts.

1831:	nos 1196 – 1247	2 Jan – 25 Dec
1832:	nos 1248 – 1300	1 Jan – 30 Dec
1833:	nos 1301 – 1352	6 Jan – 29 Dec
1834:	nos 1353 – 1404	5 Jan – 28 Dec
1835:	nos 1405 – 1456	4 Jan – 27 Dec
1836:	nos 1457 – 1508	3 Jan – 25 Dec
1837:	nos 1509 – 1561	1 Jan – 31 Dec
1838:	nos 1562 – 1613	7 Jan – 30 Dec
1839:	nos 1614 – 1665	6 Jan – 29 Dec
1840:	nos 1666 – 1717	5 Jan – 27 Dec
1841:	nos 1718 – 1769	3 Jan – 25 Dec

| no 1263 | 15 Apr 1832: 242-43 | "Puffing" |
| no 1316 | 21 Apr 1833: 245 | Critical standards |

no 1456	2 Feb 1836:	132–33	SB
no 1471	10 Apr 1836:	234–35	SB
no 1492	4 Sep 1836:	563–65	PP
no 1497	9 Oct 1836:	647–48	PP
no 1501	6 Nov 1836:	710–11	PP
no 1505	4 Dec 1836:	775–76	PP
no 1506	11 Dec 1836:	791–92	VC
no 1519	12 Mar 1837:	165–66	BM
no 1535	2 Jul 1837:	421–22	PP
no 1545	10 Sep 1837:	581–82	BM / OT
no 1553	5 Nov 1837:	708–09	PP
no 1555	19 Nov 1837:	740–41	BM
no 1566	4 Feb 1838:	68–69	SYG
no 1572	18 Mar 1838:	164	MJG
no 1574	1 Apr 1838:	195–96	NN
no 1579	6 May 1838:	278	NN
no 1588	8 Jul 1838:	420	NN
no 1593	12 Aug 1838:	507	SYG
no 1596	2 Sep 1838:	548–49	BM
no 1599	23 Sep 1838:	595–96	NN
no 1602	14 Oct 1838:	650–51	NN
no 1607	18 Nov 1838:	723–25	OT / NN
no 1608	25 Nov 1838:	740–41	OT

no 1611	16 Dec 1838: 790	PP
no 1614	6 Jan 1839: 4	NN
no 1622	3 Mar 1839: 133-34	BM
no 1632	12 May 1839: 292-23	Romance
no 1632	12 May 1839: 299-300	NN
no 1635	2 Jne 1839: 342	NN
no 1645	11 Aug 1839: 501	NN
no 1647	25 Aug 1839: 532-33	Washington Irving
no 1653	6 Oct 1839: 629-30	NN
no 1657	3 Nov 1839: 691-93	Ainsworth, <u>Jack Sheppard</u>
no 1664	22 Dec 1839: 804-05	Daniel Defoe
no 1672	16 Feb 1840: 100-01	SYC
no 1679	5 Apr 1840: 219	MHC
no 1680	12 Apr 1840: 230	MHC
no 1683	3 May 1840: 276	MHC
no 1685	17 May 1840: 309	MHC
no 1687	31 May 1840: 340	MHC
no 1693	12 Jul 1840: 435	MHC
no 1698	16 Aug 1840: 517	MHC
no 1701	6 Sep 1840: 567	MHC
no 1756	25 Sep 1841: 614	OT
no 1766	4 Dec 1841: 772-74	MHC

190

Notes:
Founded by the Hunts. A good example of the "independent"
(Radical) stance: its motto reads, "Party is the Madness of
Many for the Gain of a Few." Literary editor: John Forster
(1812-72), Dickens's friend (from March 1836) and biographer.
Price sevenpence. See British Literary Magazines, v. 2.

FIGARO IN LONDON

1831-32:	1	nos 1 - 56	10 Dec 1831 - 29 Dec 1832
1833:	2	nos 57 - 108	5 Jan - 14 Dec
1834:	3	nos 109 - 160	4 Jan - 27 Dec
1835:	4	nos 161 - 212	3 Jan - 26 Dec
1836:	5	nos 213 - 265	2 Jan - 31 Dec
1837:	6	nos 266 - 317	7 Jan - 30 Dec
1838:	7	nos 318 - 370	6 Jan - 31 Dec
1839:	8	nos 370 - 402	7 Jan - 17 Aug

6	no 253	8 Oct 1836: 167-68	SG
6	no 262	10 Dec 1836: 204	VC
6	no 276	18 Mar 1837: 44	ISHW
6	no 301	9 Sep 1837: 141-42	PP (illustrations)
7	no 318	6 Jan 1838: 1	"Political Fat Boy"
7	no 360	5 Nov 1838: 168*	NN / "Boz"

*[sic; shd be 174]

Notes:
Tory. Cartoons by Robert Seymour. Reviews of theatricals
only. Price a penny.

THE FOREIGN QUARTERLY REVIEW

1833:	11	nos 21 & 22	Jan & Apr
	12	nos 23 & 24	Jul & Oct
1834:	13	nos 25 & 26	Feb & May
	14	nos 27 & 28	Aug & Dec
1835:	15	nos 29 & 30	Mar & Jul
	16	nos 31 & 32	Oct & Jan 1836
1836:	17	nos 33 & 34	Apr & Jul
	18	nos 35 & 36	Oct & Jan 1837
1837:	19	nos 37 & 38	Apr & Jul
	20	nos 39 & 40	Oct & Jan 1838
1838:	21	nos 41 & 42	Apr & Jul
	22	nos 43 & 44	Oct & Jan 1839
1839:	23	nos 45 & 46	Apr & Jul
	24	nos 47 & 48	Oct & Jan 1840
1840:	25	nos 49 & 50	Apr & Jul
	26	nos 51 & 52	Oct & Jan 1841
1841:	27	nos 53 & 54	Apr & Jul

16	no 32	Jan 1836: 407-37	History in fiction
19	no 37	Apr 1837: 51-61	Fiction and drama
24	no 47	Oct 1839: 168-99	Paul de Kock

Notes:
Merged with <u>Westminster Review</u> in 1846. See <u>Wellesley Index</u>,
v. 3; <u>British Literary Magazines</u>, v. 2.

FRASER'S MAGAZINE

1830:	1	nos	1	-	6	Feb	-	Jul	
	2	nos	7	-	12	Aug	-	Jan	1831
1831:	3	nos	13	-	18	Feb	-	Jul	
	4	nos	19	-	24	Aug	-	Jan	1832
1832:	5	nos	25	-	30	Feb	-	Jul	
	6	nos	31	-	36	Aug	-	Dec	
1833:	7	nos	37	-	42	Jan	-	Jne	
	8	nos	43	-	48	Jul	-	Dec	
1834:	9	nos	49	-	54	Jan	-	Jne	
	10	nos	55	-	60	Jul	-	Dec	
1835:	11	nos	61	-	66	Jan	-	Jne	
	12	nos	67	-	72	Jul	-	Dec	
1836:	13	nos	73	-	78	Jan	-	Jne	
	14	nos	79	-	84	Jul	-	Dec	
1837:	15	nos	85	-	90	Jan	-	Jne	
	16	nos	91	-	96	Jul	-	Dec	
1838:	17	nos	97	-	102	Jan	-	Jne	
	18	nos	103	-	108	Jul	-	Dec	
1839:	19	nos	109	-	114	Jan	-	Jne	
	20	nos	114	-	120	Jul	-	Dec	
1840:	21	nos	121	-	126	Jan	-	Jne	
	22	nos	127	-	132	Jul	-	Dec	
1841:	23	nos	133	-	138	Jan	-	Jne	
	24	nos	139	-	144	Jul	-	Dec	

1	no 1	Feb 1830:	1-8	Editorial Policy
1	no 1	Feb 1830:	125-28	Decline of the drama
1	no 3	Apr 1830:	318-35	Fashionable novels
1	no 5	Jne 1830:	509-32	E.L. Bulwer, novel-writing
2	no 9	Oct 1830:	282-94	Parliamentary reporting
2	no 9	Oct 1830:	347-70	National Library series
2	no 10	Nov 1830:	458-66	State of the drama

2	no 11	Dec 1830: 543-54	The annuals
3	no 13	Feb 1831: 95-113	Novels of the season (I)
3	no 16	May 1831: 493-95	<u>Metropolitan Magazine</u>
3	no 18	Jul 1831: 713-19	Edward Lytton Bulwer
4	no 19	Aug 1831: 8-25	Novels of the season (II)
4	no 20	Sep 1831: 127-42	The newspaper press
4	no 21	Oct 1831: 310-21	The newspaper press
4	no 23	Dec 1831: 520-28	Edward Lytton Bulwer
4	no 24	Jan 1832: 661-71	Maritime and parliamentary novels
5	no 25	Feb 1832: 6-19	Historical romance
5	no 26	Mar 1832: 207-17	Historical romance
6	no 31	Aug 1832: 112	Gallery: Edward Lytton Bulwer
6	no 32	Sep 1832: 249	Gallery: Allan Cunningham
6	no 33	Oct 1832: 313	Gallery: William Wordsworth
7	no 37	Jan 1833: 1-15	Periodical literature
7	no 37	Jan 1833: 80	Gallery: Prince de Talleyrand
7	no 38	Feb 1833: 159	Gallery: James Morier
7	no 39	Mar 1833: 267	Gallery: Countess of Blessington
7	no 40	Apr 1833: 436	Gallery: William Dunlop
7	no 41	May 1833: 602	Gallery: Benjamin D'Israeli
7	no 42	Jne 1833: 706	Gallery: Thomas Carlyle
7	no 43	Jul 1833: 64	Gallery: Samuel Taylor Coleridge

8	no 44	Aug 1833: 190	Gallery: George Cruikshank
8	no 45	Sep 1833: 290	Gallery: David Moir
8	no 46	Oct 1833: 433	Gallery: Letitia E. Landon
8	no 47	Nov 1833: 576	Gallery: Harriet Martineau
8	no 48	Dec 1833: 700	Gallery: Grant Thorburn
9	no 49	Jan 1834: 64	Gallery: Captain John Ross
9	no 50	Feb 1834: 146	Gallery: Sir Egerton Brydges
9	no 50	Feb 1834: 224-40	"Biographical...History"
9	no 51	Mar 1834: 300	Gallery: Daniel O'Connell
9	no 52	Apr 1834: 435	Gallery: Theodore Hook
9	no 53	May 1834: 536	Gallery: Charles Westmacott
9	no 54	Jne 1834: 644	Gallery: Leigh Hunt
9	no 54	Jne 1834: 724-38	Highwaymen novels
10	no 55	Jul 1834: 48	Gallery: W. H. Ainsworth
10	no 56	Aug 1834: 172	Gallery: Thomas Hill
10	no 57	Sep 1834: 282	Gallery: George Robert Gleig
10	no 58	Oct 1834: 463	Gallery: William Godwin
10	no 59	Nov 1834: 538	Gallery: James Smith
10	no 60	Dec 1834: 645	Gallery: Comte d'Orsay
11	no 61	Jan 1835: 1-27	Gallery: The Fraserians
11	no 62	Feb 1835: 136	Gallery: Charles Lamb
11	no 63	Mar 1835: 300	Gallery: P.-J.de Béranger
11	no 64	Apr 1835: 404	Gallery: Jane Porter

11	no 65	May 1835: 529	Gallery: Lady Morgan
11	no 66	Jne 1835: 652	Gallery: Alaric Watts
12	no 67	Jul 1835: 43	Gallery: Francis Egerton
12	no 68	Aug 1835: 154	Gallery: Henry O'Brien
12	no 69	Sep 1835: 280	Gallery: Michael Sadler
12	no 70	Oct 1835: 430	Gallery: William Cobbett
12	no 71	Nov 1835: 540	Gallery: Earl of Mulgrave
12	no 72	Dec 1835: 650	Gallery: Robert Macnish
13	no 73	Jan 1836: 1-79;80	Gallery: Fraserians; Female Fraserians
13	no 74	Feb 1836: 224	Gallery: Michael Faraday
13	no 75	Mar 1836: 300	Gallery: William Lisle Bowles
13	no 76	Apr 1836: 427	Gallery: Francis Place
13	no 77	May 1836: 568	Gallery: Sir John C. Hobhouse
13	no 77	May 1836: 620-31	Morning and evening papers
13	no 78	Jne 1836: 718	Gallery: Mrs. S.C. Hall
14	no 79	Jul 1836: 68	Gallery: Thomas Noon Talfourd
14	no 80	Aug 1836: 202	Gallery: Sir John Soane
14	no 80	Aug 1836: 242-47	Grantley Berkeley
14	no 81	Sep 1836: 272	Gallery: Sheridan Knowles
14	no 82	Oct 1836: 457	Gallery: Lord Lyndhurst
14	no 83	Nov 1836: 595	Gallery: Edmund Lodge
14	no 84	Dec 1836: 720	Gallery: J.B. Buckstone
17	no 98	Apr 1838: 468-70	Gallery: Sydney Smith

17	no	98	Apr	1838:	468-70	Gallery: Sydney Smith
17	no	99	Mar	1838:	279-90	Cheap periodicals
17	no	101	May	1838:	571-77	Naval novelists
18	no	106	Oct	1838:	379-96	Genius and the public
18	no	106	Oct	1838:	481-88	Sporting literature
20	no	119	Nov	1839:	588-603	Reminiscences of the press
21	no	121	Jan	1840:	1-31	Retrospective of the 1830s
21	no	122	Feb	1840:	190-200	Literary criticism
21	no	124	Apr	1840:	381-400	Charles Dickens
23	no	136	Apr	1841:	433-50	The contemporary press

Notes:
"Gallery of Literary Characters," a semi-regular feature, offers biographical and pictorial sketches of the personalities of the day; mostly attributed to William Maginn. See the Wellesley Index, v. 2; British Literary Magazines, v. 2; Miriam Thrall, Rebellious Fraser's (1934).

THE GLOBE AND TRAVELLER

1833:	nos 9422 − 9722	1 Jan − 31 Dec
1834:	nos 9723 − 10,030	1 Jan − 31 Dec
1835:	nos 10,031 − 10,341	1 Jan − 31 Dec
1836:	nos 10,342 − 10,655	1 Jan − 31 Dec
1837:	nos 10,656 − 11,016	2 Jan − 30 Dec
1838:	nos 11,017 − 11,328	1 Jan − 31 Dec
1839:	nos 11,329 − 11,638	1 Jan − 31 Dec
1840:	nos 11,639 − 12,042	1 Jan − 31 Dec
1841:	nos 12,043 − 12,356	1 Jan − 31 Dec

no 10,478	8 Jne 1836	PP
no 10,576	30 Sep 1836	SG
no 10,634	7 Dec 1836	VC
no 10,661	7 Jan 1837	BM
no 10,680	30 Jan 1837	BM
no 10,710	6 Mar 1837	PP
no 10,756	28 Apr 1837	PP / BM
no 10,829	22 Jul 1837	BM
no 10,891	5 Aug 1837	BM
no 10,922	12 Sep 1837	PP
no 10,962	28 Oct 1837	BM
no 10,964	31 Oct 1837	BM
no 10,966	2 Nov 1837	BM
no 10,968	4 Nov 1837	BM
no 11,003	15 Dec 1837	BM
no 11,013	27 Dec 1837	BM
no 11,015	29 Dec 1837	BM
no 11,070	5 Mar 1838	MJG
no 11,083	20 Mar 1838	MJG
no 11,133	18 May 1838	BM
no 11,202	7 Aug 1838	BM
no 11,203	8 Aug 1838	NN
no 11,226	4 Sep 1838	NN

no 11,241	21 Sep 1838	BM
no 11,249	1 Oct 1838	NN
no 11,335	8 Jan 1839	BM
no 11,393	16 Mar 1839	BM
no 11,433	2 May 1839	NN
no 11,440	10 May 1839	NN
no 11,492	12 Jul 1839	NN
no 11,524	19 Aug 1839	General literary remarks
no 11,544	11 Sep 1839	NN
no 11,545	12 Sep 1839	NN
no 11,566	8 Oct 1839	NN
no 11,570	12 Oct 1839	NN
no 11,716	31 Mar 1840	SYC
no 11,735	22 Apr 1840	MHC
no 11,754	14 May 1840	MHC
no 11,764	26 May 1840	MHC
no 11,900	18 Jul 1840	MHC
no 11,941	4 Sep 1840	MHC
no 11,945	9 Sep 1840	MHC
no 11,956	22 Sep 1840	MHC
no 11,970	8 Oct 1840	MHC
no 11,991	2 Nov 1840	MHC
no 12,109	19 Mar 1841	MHC

no 12,125	7 Apr 1841	MHC
no 12,232	10 Aug 1841	MHC
no 12,234	12 Aug 1841	MHC
no 12,281	6 Oct 1841	MHC

Notes:
Avowed Ministerial organ after 1830, apparently through
connection with Palmerston. "Literature" column very
infrequent, particularly after 1833; mostly extracts under
"Fashion and Table-Talk." Bentley's Miscellany is excerpted
a good deal, even after Dickens has departed its pages; on the
other hand, it is perhaps telling that Chapman and Hall do not
advertise much in this paper. Price sevenpence; fivepence
after 1836.

JOHN BULL

1833:	13	nos	630 –	681	6 Jan – 30 Dec
1834:	14	nos	682 –	733	6 Jan – 29 Dec
1835:	15	nos	734 –	785	5 Jan – 27 Dec
1836:	16	nos	786 –	837	4 Jan – 26 Dec
1837:	17	nos	838 –	890	1 Jan – 31 Dec
1838:	18	nos	891 –	942	7 Jan – 29 Dec
1839:	19	nos	943 –	994	6 Jan – 30 Dec
1840:	20	nos	995 –	1046	5 Jan – 26 Dec
1841:	21	nos	1047 –	1098	2 Jan – 25 Dec

15	no 734	5 Jan 1835: 6	Political excitement
15	no 777	2 Nov 1835: 350	Modern Novelists series
16	no 809	13 Jne 1836: 190	PP
16	no 822	12 Sep 1836: 295	PP
17	no 843	5 Feb 1837: 72	BM
17	no 847	5 Mar 1837: 117	Monthly magazines
17	no 852	9 Apr 1837: 76	BM
17	no 856	7 May 1837: 224	PP
17	no 882	5 Nov 1837: 537	BM
18	no 912	3 Jne 1838: 261	NN
19	no 952	10 Mar 1839: 116	Novels in illus. nos.
19	no 969	7 Jul 1839: 320-21	BM
20	no 1010	19 Apr 1840: 188	MHC
21	no 1052	6 Feb 1841: 69	BM
21	no 1092	13 Nov 1841: 549	MHC

Notes:
Price sixpence.

LEIGH HUNT'S LONDON JOURNAL

"To Assist the Enquiring, Animate the Struggling, and
Sympathize with All."

1834:	1	nos 1 - 40	2 Apr - 31 Dec
1835:	2	nos 41 - 91	7 Jan - 26 Dec +
			Supplement (31 Dec)

1 no 1   2 Apr 1834: 1-2   Address

1 no 12   18 Jne 1834: 101   "Unsocial Readers of
                                    Periodicals"

1 no 38   17 Dec 1834: 296   Contemporary magazines

2 no 87   28 Nov 1835: 416   Henry Colburn, publisher

Notes:
From 2 no 62 6 Jne 1835, becomes Leigh Hunt's <u>London Journal</u>
<u>and the Printing Machine</u>. Apolitical, compares itself to
<u>Chambers's Edinburgh Journal</u>. Price one-and-a-half pence,
putting it in the category of "cheap" or democratic
literature. See <u>British Literary Magazines</u>, v. 2.

LITERARY GAZETTE AND JOURNAL OF BELLES LETTRES, ARTS, SCIENCES, ETC.

1833:	17	nos 833	- 884	5 Jan - 28 Dec
1834:	18	nos 885	- 936	4 Jan - 27 Dec
1835:	19	nos 937	- 988	3 Jan - 26 Dec
1836:	20	nos 989	- 1041	2 Jan - 31 Dec
1837:	21	nos 1042	- 1093	7 Jan - 30 Dec
1838:	22	nos 1094	- 1145	6 Jan - 29 Dec
1839:	23	nos 1146	- 1197	5 Jan - 28 Dec
1840:	24	nos 1198	- 1249	4 Jan - 26 Dec
1841:	25	nos 1250	- 1301	2 Jan - 25 Dec

17   no 837   2 Feb 1833: 75   Poverty of authors

17   no 839   16 Feb 1833: 102-03   Bentley's <u>Standard Novels</u>

17   no 851   11 May 1833: 297   <u>Modern Novelists</u> series

17   no 866   24 Aug 1833: 539   "Serious" writing

17   no 868   7 Sep 1833: 563-65   Calamities of authors

17   no 869   14 Sep 1833: 580-82   Calamities of authors

17	no 870	21 Sep 1833:	596-98	Calamities of authors
20	no 995	13 Feb 1836:	102	SB
20	no 1003	9 Apr 1836:	233	PP / LF
20	no 1016	9 Jul 1836:	442	PP
20	no 1021	13 Aug 1836:	520	PP
20	no 1025	10 Sep 1836:	584	PP
20	no 1028	1 Oct 1836:	637	SG
20	no 1034	12 Nov 1836:	727-28	PP
20	no 1038	10 Dec 1836:	795-96	VC
20	no 1040	24 Dec 1836:	822-23	SB
21	no 1051	11 Mar 1837:	164	ISHW
21	no 1055	8 Apr 1837:	228	PP
22	no 1100	17 Feb 1838:	97-99	MJG
22	no 1101	24 Feb 1838:	118-19	MJG
22	no 1106	31 Mar 1838:	203	OT (dramatisation)
22	no 1107	7 Apr 1838:	214	NN
22	no 1140	24 Nov 1838:	741	OT
22	no 1140	24 Nov 1838:	748	OT / NN (dramatisations)
24	no 1204	15 Feb 1840:	98-100	SYC
24	no 1211	4 Apr 1840:	211	MHC
25	no 1283	21 Aug 1841:	540-41	PNP

Notes:
See British Literary Magazines, v. 2.

LONDON REVIEW

1835:	1	nos 1 & 2	Apr & Jul
	2	nos 3 & 4	Jul & Jan 1836
1836:	3/25	nos 1 & 2	Apr & Jul
	4/26	nos 1 & 2	Oct & Jan 1837

then
LONDON AND WESTMINSTER REVIEW

	4/26	nos 7-8/50-51	Oct 1836 / Jan 1837
1837:	5/27	nos 9-10/52-53	Apr & Jul
	6/28	nos 11-12/54-55	Oct & Jan 1838
1838:	7/29	nos 1/2	Apr & Aug
	32	nos 1 [& 2]	Dec [& Apr 1839]
1839:	32	nos [1 &]2	[Dec 1838 &] Apr
	33	nos 1 & 2	Oct & Mar 1840
1840:	34	nos 1 & 2	Jne & Sep
1841:	35	nos 1 & 2	Jan & Apr
	36	nos 1 & 2	Jul & Oct

1	no 1	Feb 1829: 1-9	Journals
1	no 1	Feb 1829: 11-14	Sir Walter Scott
1	no 2	Jul 1835: 476-87	Prose fictions
2	no 4	Jan 1836: 336-355	Stamp-duty
3	no 1	Apr 1836: 60-71	Contemporary poets
3	no 1	Apr 1836: 234-64	English literature of 1835
3	no 2	Jul 1836: 300-10	French novels
5/27	nos 9/52	Apr 1837: 65-98	Status of journalists
5/27	nos 10/53	Jul 1837: 194-215	SB / PP / BM
6/28	nos 11/54	Oct 1837: 169-98	Theodore Hook

6/28	nos 12/55	Jan 1838: 293-345	Lockhart, Life of Scott
7/29	no 1	Apr 1838: 119-45	Thomas Hood
32	no 1	Apr 1839: 261-81	Literary lionism
33	no 1	Oct 1839: 101-37	Arabian Nights
33	no 1	Oct 1839: 137-62	Literature of childhood
34	no 1	Jne 1840: 1-61	George Cruikshank

Notes:
See Wellesley Index, v. 3; British Literary Magazines, v. 2.

THE MAGNET; AGRICULTURAL AND COMMERCIAL GAZETTE

"The Largest of the Largest, the Cheapest of the Cheapest"

"Only True Representative and Advocate of the Party of the
    People"

| 1837: | 1 | nos 1 - 42 | 13 Mar - 25 Dec |
| 1838: | 1-2 | nos 43 - 93 | 1 Jan - 31 Dec |

[2 no 44   8 Jan 1838 begins new volume;
each issue thereafter is numbered separately]

1839:	3	nos 94 - 145	7 Jan - 30 Dec
1840:	3	nos 146 - 170	6 Jan - 22 Jne
	4	nos 171 - 195	29 Jne - 28 Dec
1841:	5	nos 196 - 245	4 Jan - 27 Dec

1	no	1	13 Mar 1837: 5	ISHW
1	no	4	3 Apr 1837: 26-27	PP
1	no	17	3 Jul 1837: 133	PP
1	no	22	7 Aug 1837: 171	PP
1	no	35	6 Nov 1837: 283	PP
2	no	48	5 Feb 1838	BM
2	no	51	26 Feb 1838	MJG
2	no	52	5 Mar 1838	MJG
2	no	56	9 Apr 1838	NN
2	no	60	7 May 1838	NN
2	no	64	4 Jne 1838	NN
2	no	65	11 Jne 1838	BM
2	no	69	9 Jul 1838	NN
2	no	73	6 Aug 1838	NN
2	no	78	10 Sep 1838	NN
2	no	80	24 Sep 1838	BM
2	no	82	8 Oct 1838	NN
2	no	86	5 Nov 1838	NN
2	no	91	10 Dec 1838	NN
2	no	93	31 Dec 1838	SB
3	no	94	7 Jan 1839	NN
3	no	95	14 Jan 1839	BM
3	no	99	11 Feb 1839	NN

3	no 102	4 Mar 1839	NN
3	no 111	6 May 1839	NN
3	no 115	3 Jne 1839	NN
3	no 124	5 Aug 1839	NN
3	no 133	7 Oct 1839	NN
3	no 166	25 May 1840	MHC
4	no 179	24 Aug 1840	MHC
4	no 181	7 Sep 1840	MHC
4	no 182	14 Sep 1840	MHC
4	no 183	21 Sep 1840	MHC
4	no 183*	28 Sep 1840	MHC *[sic; shd be no 184]
4	no 185	12 Oct 1840	MHC
4	no 186	19 Oct 1840	MHC
4	no 187	26 Oct 1840	MHC
4	no 189	9 Nov 1840	MHC
4	no 189*	16 Nov 1840	MHC *[sic; shd be no 190]
4	no 192	7 Dec 1840	MHC
4	no 193	14 Dec 1840	MHC
4	no 194	21 Dec 1840	MHC
4	no 195	28 Dec 1840	MHC
5	no 196	4 Jan 1841	MHC
5	no 198	18 Jan 1841	MHC
5	no 200	1 Feb 1841	MHC

5	no 203	22 Feb 1841	MHC
5	no 204	1 Mar 1841	MHC
5	no 205	8 Mar 1841	MHC
5	no 206	15 Mar 1841	MHC
5	no 209	5 Apr 1841	MHC
5	no 210	12 Apr 1841	MHC
5	no 211	19 Apr 1841	MHC
5	no 213	3 May 1841	MHC
5	no 214	10 May 1841	MHC
5	no 216	24 May 1841	MHC
5	no 217	31 May 1841	MHC
5	no 218	7 Jne 1841	MHC
5	no 219	14 Jne 1841	MHC
5	no 220	21 Jne 1841	MHC
5	no 221	28 Jne 1841	MHC
5	no 226	2 Aug 1841	MHC
5	no 229	23 Aug 1841	MHC
5	no 236	25 Oct 1841	MHC

Notes:
Edited by John Browne Bell (see <u>Bell's New Weekly Messenger</u>).
Radical: see prospectus "To the Public" 1 no 1 13 Mar 1837:
1. "Varieties" begins as a feature from 23 Mar 1840.   Price
fourpence.

MARK LANE EXPRESS

1833:	?	nos	54	–	105	7 Jan	–	30 Dec
1834:	2	nos	106	–	157	6 Jan	–	29 Dec
1835:	3	nos	158	–	209	5 Jan	–	28 Dec
1836:	4/5*	nos	210	–	261	4 Jan	–	26 Dec
1837:	6	nos	262	–	313	2 Jan	–	25 Dec
1838:	7	nos	314	–	366	1 Jan	–	31 Dec
1839:	8	nos	367	–	418	7 Jan	–	30 Dec
1840:	9	nos	419	–	470	6 Jan	–	28 Dec
1841:	10	nos	471	–	522	4 Jan	–	27 Dec

*[5 no 247 19 Sep 1836 begins new volume; each issue
thereafter numbered pp. 1-16, and paper size is reduced]

4	no 225	18 Apr 1836: 126	PP
4	no 242	15 Aug 1836: 262	PP
4	no 248	26 Sep 1836	SG
5	no 250	10 Oct 1836	PP (2)
5	no 251	17 Oct 1836	PP
6	no 259	12 Dec 1836	VC
6	no 264	16 Jan 1837	PP
6	no 272	13 Mar 1837	ISHW
6	no 279	1 May 1837	PP
6	no 289	10 Jul 1837	BM
6	no 294	14 Aug 1837	PP
6	no 299	18 Sep 1837	PP
6	no 302	9 Oct 1837	BM

6	no 306	6 Nov 1837	PP
7	no 315	8 Jan 1838	PP / BM
7	no 320	12 Feb 1838	PP
7	no 327	2 Apr 1838	PP / NN
7	no 328	9 Apr 1838	PP
7	no 338	18 Jne 1838	NN
7	no 341	9 Jul 1838	BM
7	no 347	20 Aug 1838	BM
7	no 356	22 Oct 1838	NN
8	no 389	10 Jne 1839	NN
9	no 438	18 May 1840	MHC
9	no 442	15 Jne 1840	MHC
9	no 460	19 Oct 1840	MHC
10	no 476	8 Feb 1841	MHC
10	no 486	19 Apr 1841	MHC / BR

Notes:
No literary reviews; instead, extracts from Dickens's works
appear under "Miscellaneous." Occasionally there is a short
column under "Literature." Price sevenpence.

THE METROPOLITAN

A Monthly Journal of Literature, Science, and the Fine Arts

1831:	1	nos	1 –	4	May – Aug
	2	nos	5 –	8	Sep – Dec
1832:	3	nos	9 –	12	Jan – Apr
	4	nos	13 –	16	May – Aug
	5	nos	17 –	20	Sep – Dec
1833:	6	nos	21 –	24	Jan – Apr
	7	nos	25 –	28	May – Aug
	8	nos	29 –	32	Sep – Dec
1834:	9	nos	33 –	36	Jan – Apr
	10	nos	37 –	40	May – Aug
	11	nos	41 –	44	Sep – Dec
1835:	12	nos	45 –	48	Jan – Apr
	13	nos	49 –	52	May – Aug
	14	nos	53 –	56	Sep – Dec
1836:	15	nos	57 –	60	Jan – Apr
	16	nos	61 –	64	May – Aug
	17	nos	65 –	68	Sep – Dec
1837:	18	nos	69 –	72	Jan – Apr
	19	nos	73 –	76	May – Aug
	20	nos	77 –	80	Sep – Dec
1838:	21	nos	81 –	84	Jan – Apr
	22	nos	85 –	88	May – Aug
	23	nos	89 –	92	Sep – Dec
1839:	24	nos	93 –	96	Jan – Apr
	25	nos	97 –	100	May – Aug
	26	nos	101 –	104	Sep – Dec
1840:	27	nos	105 –	108	Jan – Apr
	28	nos	109 –	112	May – Aug
	29	nos	113 –	116	Sep – Dec
1841:	30	nos	117 –	120	Jan – Apr
	31	nos	121 –	124	May – Aug
	32	nos	125 –	128	Sep – Dec

6	no 21	Jan 1833: 53–66	The newspapers
6	no 22	Feb 1833: 176–85	The newspapers

8	no 30	Oct 1833: 123-28	Magazines
15	no 59	Mar 1836: 77	SB
16	no 61	May 1836: 15	PP / LF
16	no 62	Jne 1836: 46-47	PP
16	no 63	Jul 1836: 76	PP
16	no 64	Aug 1836: 110-11	PP / LF
16	no 64	Aug 1836: 111	SUTH
17	no 65	Sep 1836: 13	PP
17	no 67	Nov 1836: 84	PP
18	no 69	Jan 1837: 6	PP
18	no 70	Feb 1837: 46	PP
18	no 71	Mar 1837: 77	PP
18	no 72	Apr 1837: 106-07	PP
19	no 73	May 1837: 16	PP
28	no 110	Jne 1840: 51-52	MHC
28	no 112	Aug 1840: 101-02	MHC
29	no 116	Dec 1840: 111	MHC
30	no 119	Mar 1841: 78-79	MHC
31	no 123	Jne 1841: 55-56	MHC
32	no 125	Sep 1841: 25	MHC
32	no 128	Dec 1841: 111-12	MHC

Notes:
Title becomes Metropolitan Magazine with v. 6 (1833); subtitle
dropped at the same time. See British Literary Magazines, v.
2.

MIRROR OF LITERATURE, AMUSEMENT AND INSTRUCTION

1833:	21	nos	585 - 611	5 Jan - 29 Jne	+ Suppl. 612
	22	nos	613 - 640	6 Jul - 28 Dec	641
1834:	23	nos	642 - 668	4 Jan - 28 Jne	669
	24	nos	670 - 698	5 Jul - 27 Dec	699
1835:	25	nos	700 - 726	3 Jan - 27 Jne	727
	26	nos	728 - 755	4 Jul - 26 Dec	756
1836:	27	nos	757 - 783	2 Jan - 25 Jne	784
	28	nos	785 - 813	2 Jul - 31 Dec	814
1837:	29	nos	815 - 840	7 Jan - 24 Jne	841
	30	nos	842 - 871	1 Jul - 30 Dec	872
1838:	31	nos	873 - 899	6 Jan - 30 Jne	900
	32	nos	901 - 928	7 Jul - 29 Dec	929
1839:	33	nos	930 - 955	5 Jan - 29 Jne	956
	34	nos	957 - 984	6 Jul - 28 Dec	No Suppl.
1840:	35	nos	985 - 1011	4 Jan - 27 Jne	1012
	36	nos	1013 - 1038	4 Jul - 26 Dec	1039
1841:	37	nos	1040 - 1065	2 Jan - 26 Jne	?

27	no 762	6 Feb 1836: 88-89	Historical novels
27	no 772	16 Apr 1836: 249-51	SB
29	no 815	7 Jan 1837: 13-16	BM
29	no 822	25 Feb 1837: 125-27	BM
29	no 824	11 Mar 1837: 153-55	PP
29	no 825	18 Mar 1837: 170-71	BM
29	no 831	29 Apr 1837: 526*-66	BM*[sic;shd be 265]
29	no 834	20 May 1837: 313-15	BM
30	no 843	8 Jul 1837: 27-28	PP
30	no 845	22 Jul 1837: 62-63	PP
30	no 846	29 Jul 1837: 74-76	BM

30	no 850	26 Aug 1837: 143-44	PP
30	no 851	2 Sep 1837: 156-58	PP
30	no 853	16 Sep 1837: 192	PP
30	no 857	14 Oct 1837: 254-55	BM
30	no 858	21 Oct 1837: 270-71	BM
30	no 859	28 Oct 1837: 285-87	PP
30	no 868	16 Dec 1837: 407-08	PP
30	no 870	23 Dec 1837: 437-38	PP
31	no 874	13 Jan 1838: 25-27	BM
31	no 882	10 Mar 1838: 155-57	BM
31	no 883	17 Mar 1838: 169-71	MJG
31	no 885	31 Mar 1838: 202-04	MJG
31	no 886	7 Apr 1838: 222-23	NN
31	no 887	14 Apr 1838: 238-39	NN
31	no 891	5 May 1838: 302-03	DM
31	no 897	16 Jne 1838: 394-95	BM
32	no 904	21 Jul 1838: 60-63	NN
32	no 907	11 Aug 1838: 109-10	NN
32	no 916	13 Oct 1838: 251	NN
33	no 931	12 Jan 1839: 31	NN
33	no 943	6 Apr 1839: 220-23	NN
35	no 995	7 Mar 1840: 166-68	SYC
37	no 1046	13 Feb 1841: 99-101	Literary news

Notes:
A middlebrow miscellany, cheaply produced (price twopence);
there is no table of contents. Most of the features about the
magazines (see heading "Public Journals") are extracts, a
common way of filling up vacant columns. See British Literary
Magazines, v. 2.

MONTHLY CHRONICLE

A National Journal of Politics, Literature, Science and Art

1838:	1	Mar - Jne
	2	Jul - Dec
1839:	3	Jan - Jne
	4	Jul - Dec
1840:	5	Jan - Jne
	6	Jul - Dec
1841:	7	Jan - Jne [end]

4 Dec 1839: 502-08   Influence of periodical literature
                        on fine arts

5 Jan 1840: 33-38   Novel-writing and newspaper
                        criticism

5 Feb 1840: 138-50   The press

Notes:
Only "serious" literature reviewed: poetry and non-fiction.
No fiction, no Dickens. See Wellesley Index, v. 3; British
Literary Magazines, v. 2.

MONTHLY MAGAZINE, OR BRITISH REGISTER OF POLITICS, LITERATURE, ART, SCIENCE, AND THE BELLES-LETTRES

1833:	ns	15	nos	85 - 90	Jan - Jne
		16	nos	91 - 96	Jul - Dec
1834:		17	nos	97 - 102	Jan - Jne
		18	nos	103 - 108	Jul - Dec
1835:	ns	1	nos	1 - 6	Jan - Jne
		2	no	7	Jul
		20	no	116*	Aug *[signature = "M.M. No. 8"]
			no	[117]*	Sep *[signature = "M.M. No. 9"]
			nos	118 - 120*	Oct - Dec
					*[signature nos 10-12]
1836:		21	nos	121 - 126	Jan - Jne
		22	nos	127 - 129	Jul - Sep
			nos	140 - 142*	Oct - Dec
					*[sic;shd be 130-32]
1837:		23	nos	133 - 138	Jan - Jne
		24	nos	139 - 144	Jul - Dec
1838:		25	nos	145 - 150	Jan - Jne
		26	nos	151 - 156	Jul - Dec*
					*[signatures = months only]
1839:		1	nos	1 - 6	Jan - Jne
		2	nos	7 - 12	Jul - Dec
1840:		3	nos	13 - 18	Jan - Jne
		4	nos	19 - 24	Jul - Dec
1841:		5	nos	25 - 30	Jan - Jne
		6	nos	31 - 36	Jul - Dec

15	no 86	Feb 1833:	129-47	George Cruikshank
16	no 94	Oct 1833:	173-76	Fashionable novels
16	no 94	Oct 1833:	374-82	Edward Lytton Bulwer
17	no 97	Jan 1834:	25-28	John Galt
17	no 99	Mar 1834:	331-32	Bentley's Standard Novels
17	no 102	Jne 1834:	668-75	Ainsworth, Rookwood

18	no 104	Aug 1834: 211		Sentimentalism and useful knowledge
18	no 104	Aug 1834: 223-26		Decline in poetry reading
22	no 5	Nov 1836: 522-24		PP
25	nos 145-50	Jan-Jne 1838		Reynolds, "Pickwick Abroad"
25	no 148	Apr 1838: 434-35		MJG
3	no 15	Mar 1840: 229-33		Jack Sheppardism
3	no 16	Apr 1840: 433-37		Poetry
3	no 17	May 1840: 498-506		Dramatic reform
3	no 18	Jne 1840: 665-71		Dramatic reform
5	no 28	Apr 1841: 412-24		Henry Fielding

Notes:
See Geoffrey Carnall, "The Monthly Magazine" Review of English Studies ns 5 no 18 (1954): 158-64; British Literary Magazines, v. 2. The irregularity in numbering coincides with changes in publishers.

MONTHLY REPOSITORY

1833:	ns 7	nos 73 - 84	Jan - Dec
1834:	8	nos 85 - 96	Jan - Dec
1835:	9	nos 97 - 108	Jan - Dec
1836:	10	nos 109 - 120	Jan - Dec
1837:	11	nos 121 - 126	Jan - Jne

```
"Enlarged Series" 1 no    127        Jul (I)
                          221        Aug (II) ?
                          222        Sep (III)?
                          382        Oct (IV) ?
                          383        Nov (V)  ?
                          384        Dec (VI) ?
1838:                     385        Jan (VII)?
                          386        Feb (VI)?
                          386        Mar (VIII)?
                          387        Apr (IX)?
                          388        May (X)?
                   [Last page number = p. 288]
```

```
7   no 77   [May?] 1833: 305-13      Morality of authors

8   no 87   [Mar?] 1834: 172-73      Status of journalists

9   no 97   Jan    1835: 1-8         True spirit of reform

10 no 113   [May]  1836: 271-76      Modern publishers
```

Notes:
Edited by W.J. Fox to Jne 1836; R.H. Horne to Jne 1837; Leigh Hunt Jul 1837-Apr 1838. Radical (professedly apolitical). See Francis Mineka, The Dissendence of Dissent (1972).

MONTHLY REVIEW

```
1833:      1     nos 1 - 4        Jan - Apr
           2     nos 1 - 4        May - Aug
           3     nos 1 - 4        Sep - Dec
1834:      1     nos 1 - 4        Jan - Apr
           2     nos 1 - 4        May - Aug
           3     nos 1 - 4        Sep - Dec
1835:      1     nos 1 - 4        Jan - Apr
           2     nos 1 - 4        May - Aug
           3     nos 1 - 4        Sep - Dec
```

```
1836:      1     nos 1 - 4        Jan - Apr
           2     nos 1 - 4        May - Aug
           3     nos 1 - 4        Sep - Dec
1837:      1     nos 1 - 4        Jan - Apr
           2     nos 1 - 4        May - Aug
           3     nos 1 - 4        Sep - Dec
1838:      1     nos 1 - 4        Jan - Apr
           2     nos 1 - 4        May - Aug
           3     nos 1 - 4        Sep - Dec
1839:      1     nos 1 - 4        Jan - Apr
           2     nos 1 - 4        May - Aug
           3     nos 1 - 4        Sep - Dec
1840:      1     nos 1 - 4        Jan - Apr
           2     nos 1 - 4        May - Aug
           3     nos 1 - 4        Sep - Dec
1841:      1     nos 1 - 4        Jan - Apr
           2     nos 1 - 4        May - Aug
           3     nos 1 - 4        Sep - Dec
```

2	no 1	May 1835: 93-101	State of the novel
1	no 2	Feb 1836: 181-92	Novels of the season
1	no 3	Mar 1836: 350-57	SB
2	no 2	Jne 1836: 276-79	Paper-duty
1	no 1	Jan 1837: 53-69	Ainsworth, Crichton
1	no 2	Feb 1837: 153-63	SB / PP / BM
3	no 3	Nov 1837: 307-27	History of taste
2	no 1	May 1838: 98-109	NN
ns 3	no 4	Dec 1839: 457-72	The drama
1	no 1	Jan 1839: 29-41	OT
1	no 2	Feb 1840: 178-92	Paul de Kock
2	no 1	May 1840: 35-43	MHC
2	no 3	Jul 1840: 398-411	Imitations of Dickens

Notes:
See **British Literary Magazines**, v. 3.

MORNING ADVERTISER

1833:	nos 13,009	-	13,341	1 Jan	-	31 Dec
1834:	nos 13,342	-	13,654	1 Jan	-	31 Dec
1835:	nos 13,655	-	13,967	1 Jan	-	31 Dec
1836:	nos 13,968	-	14,272	1 Jan	-	31 Dec
1837:	nos 14,273	-	14,583	2 Jan	-	30 Dec
1838:	nos 14,584	-	14,896	1 Jan	-	31 Dec
1839:	nos 14,897	-	15,218	1 Jan	-	31 Dec
1840:	nos 15,219	-	15,532	1 Jan	-	31 Dec
1841:	nos 15,533	-	15,828	1 Jan	-	31 Dec

no 13,344	3 Jan 1834	MM
no 13,379	13 Feb 1834	MM
no 13,421	3 Apr 1834	MM
no 13,446	2 May 1834	MM
no 13,555	6 Sep 1834	American periodicals
no 13,576	1 Oct 1834	SB
no 13,963	26 Dec 1835	Periodical literature
no 14,003	11 Feb 1836	SB
no 14,022	4 Mar 1836	MM
no 14,052	8 Apr 1836	PP
no 14,202	30 Sep 1836	SG
no 14,209	8 Oct 1836	PP

no 14,214	25 Oct 1836	PP
no 14,251	7 Dec 1836	VC
no 14,281	11 Jan 1837	BM
no 14,327	6 Mar 1837	PP
no 14,350	1 Apr 1837	PP
no 14,375	1 May 1837	PP
no 14,480	1 Sep 1837	PP
no 14,534	3 Nov 1837	SB / PP
no 14,586	3 Jan 1838	PP
no 14,614	5 Feb 1838	BM
no 14,638	5 Mar 1838	BM
no 14,666	6 Apr 1838	NN
no 14,673	14 Apr 1838	BM
no 14,677	19 Apr 1838	Literary property
no 14,692	7 May 1838	BM
no 14,718	6 Jne 1838	BM
no 14,737	28 Jne 1838	NN
no 14,744	6 Jul 1838	BM
no 14,768	3 Aug 1838	BM / NN
no 14,795	4 Sep 1838	BM / NN
no 14,820	3 Oct 1838	NN
no 14,827	11 Oct 1838	BM
no 14,848	5 Nov 1838	NN

no 14,849	6 Nov 1838	BM
no 14,861	20 Nov 1838	OT / NN (dramatisations)
no 14,873	4 Dec 1838	NN
no 14,881	13 Dec 1838	BM / OT
no 14,902	7 Jan 1839	BM
no 14,931	9 Feb 1839	BM / NN
no 14,962	7 Mar 1839	Imitations of Dickens
no 14,991	10 Apr 1839	NN
no 15,016	9 May 1839	BM / NN
no 15,143	4 Oct 1839	NN
no 15,146	8 Oct 1839	BM
no 15,200	10 Dec 1839	BM
no 15,312	18 Apr 1840	BM / MHC
no 15,313	20 Apr 1840	Fraser's on Dickens
no 15,382	9 Jul 1840	MHC
no 15,472	22 Oct 1840	MHC (illustrations)
no 15,562	4 Feb 1841	MHC (illustrations)

Notes:
Whig, Reformist, commercial middle classes (quotes Westminster
Review). Literary section called "Progress of Publication"
or "Magazines"; after 1839, all literary matters reviewed
under "Literature." Coincident with a change of typeface in
Feb 1841, there are fewer reviews, and these are of a higher
character. Gives thoughtful attention to the magazines. Each
issue = four pages. Price sevenpence (fivepence after 15 Sep
1836).

MORNING CHRONICLE

1833:	nos 19,765 - 20,077	1 Jan - 31 Dec
1834:	nos 20,078 - 20,388	1 Jan - 31 Dec
1835:	nos 20,389 - 20,660	1 Jan - 31 Dec
1836:	nos 20,661 - 20,956	1 Jan - 31 Dec
1837:	nos 20,957 - 21,257	2 Jan - 30 Dec
1838:	nos 21,258 - 21,565	1 Jan - 31 Dec
1839:	nos 21,566 - 21,872	1 Jan - 31 Dec
1840:	nos 21,873 - 22,183	1 Jan - 31 Dec
1841:	nos 22,184 - 22,501	1 Jan - 31 Dec

no 20,696	11 Feb 1836	SB
no 20,791	7 Jne 1836	PP
no 20,843	18 Aug 1836	PP
no 20,880	30 Sep 1836	SG
no 20,884	5 Oct 1836	PP
no 20,937	7 Dec 1836	VC
no 20,970	19 Jan 1837	BM
no 21,005	7 Mar 1837	ISHW
no 21,054	4 May 1837	Literary Fund Dinner
no 21,156	2 Sep 1837	BM
no 21,181	3 Oct 1837	PP
no 21,183	5 Oct 1837	BM
no 21,391	5 Jne 1838	NN
no 21,441	2 Aug 1838	NN

no 21,533	20 Nov 1838	OT (dramatisation)
no 21,621	6 Mar 1839	BM
no 21,664	27 Apr 1839	NN

Notes:
Regular theatrical notices; literary notices rare and perfunctory (often consisting of reprints of Examiner notices). Price sevenpence, then fivepence. See Michael MacDonagh, The Reporters' Gallery (1913).

MORNING HERALD

1833:	nos 15,726 – 16,030	1 Jan – 31 Dec
1834:	nos 16,031 – 16,344	1 Jan – 31 Dec
1835:	nos 16,345 – 16,650	1 Jan – 31 Dec
1836:	nos 16,651 – 16,959	1 Jan – 31 Dec
1837:	nos 16,960 – 17,262	2 Jan – 30 Dec
1838:	nos 17,263 – 17,574	1 Jan – 31 Dec
1839:	nos 17,575 – 17,887	1 Jan – 31 Dec
1840:	nos 17,888 – 18,195	1 Jan – 31 Dec
1841:	nos 18,196 – 18,512	1 Jan – 31 Dec

no 16,266	4 Oct 1834	SB
no 16,285	30 Oct 1834	Fashionable literature
no 16,735	9 Apr 1836	PP
no 16,869	14 Sep 1836	Magazines (Metropolitan)
no 16,883	30 Sep 1836	SG

no 16,911	2 Nov 1836	PP
no 16,919	11 Nov 1836	Annuals
no 16,939	7 Dec 1836	VC
no 17,019	7 Mar 1837	PP / ISHW
no 17,031	1 Apr 1837	PP
no 17,185	2 Oct 1837	BM
no 17,630	6 Mar 1839	BM
no 17,965	3 Apr 1840	_Fraser's_ on Dickens
no 17,986	30 Apr 1840	Literary Fund
no 18,007	25 May 1840	MHC
no 18,073	11 Aug 1840	MHC (illus. by Sibson)
no 18,127	13 Oct 1840	MHC (illus. by Sibson)
no 18,133	20 Oct 1840	Leigh Hunt on drama
no 18,152	11 Nov 1840	MHC (illus. by Sibson)
no 18,502	21 Dec 1841	Adelphi Theatre

Notes:
When Parliament is sitting, the paper regularly runs to eight
pages of small print. "Literature" and "Drama" notices are
irregular and superficial. Carries more extracts from
Dickens's works in 1840–41 than in 1839. Price sevenpence,
then fivepence.

MORNING POST

1833:	nos 19,365 – 19,677	1 Jan – 31 Dec
1834:	nos 19,678 – 19,989	1 Jan – 31 Dec
1835:	nos 19,990 – 20,301	1 Jan – 31 Dec
1836:	nos 20,302 – 20,612	1 Jan – 31 Dec
1837:	nos 20,613 – 20,912	2 Jan – 30 Dec
1838:	nos 20,913 – 21,214	1 Jan – 31 Dec
1839:	nos 21,215 – 21,509	1 Jan – 31 Dec
1840:	nos 21,510 – 21,829	1 Jan – 31 Dec
1841:	nos 21,830 – 22,139	1 Jan – 31 Dec

no 19,446	5 Apr 1833	Periodical writing
no 19,576	4 Sep 1833	MM
no 19,630	6 Nov 1833	Blackwood's
no 20,363	12 Mar 1836	SB
no 20,386	8 Apr 1836	PP
no 20,413	11 May 1836	PP / LF
no 20,401	10 Aug 1836	SUTH
no 20,496	16 Aug 1836	PP
no 20,535	30 Sep 1836	SG
no 20,536	1 Oct 1836	SG
no 20,537	3 Oct 1836	PP
no 20,590	5 Dec 1836	PP
no 20,617	6 Jan 1837	BM
no 20,637	30 Jan 1837	BM
no 20,638	31 Jan 1837	BM

no 20,640	2 Feb 1837	BM
no 20,668	7 Mar 1837	ISHW
no 20,669	8 Mar 1837	BM
no 20,837	3 Oct 1837	BM
no 20,860	31 Oct 1837	<u>Quarterly Review</u> on Dickens
no 20,948	10 Feb 1838	SYG
no 20,980	20 Mar 1838	MJG
no 20,990	31 Mar 1838	NN
no 21,063	6 Jul 1838	NN
no 21,086	2 Aug 1838	NN
no 21,226	14 Jan 1839	BM / NN
no 21,247	7 Feb 1839	BM
no 21,263	26 Feb 1839	OT (dramatisation)
no 21,269	5 Mar 1839	BM
no 21,292	1 Apr 1839	BM
no 21,346	3 Jne 1839	Imitations of Dickens
no 21,360	19 Jne 1839	Status of the novel
no 21,385	8 Aug 1839	BM
no 21,400	26 Aug 1839	Poetry criticism
no 21,413	10 Sep 1839	NN
no 21,434	4 Oct 1839	Speech of the lower classes
no 21,458	1 Nov 1839	Literary criticism
no 21,553	24 Feb 1840	Contemporary literary taste

no 21,712   27 Aug 1840   "Table-Talk" essays

no 21,719   4 Sep 1840   BM (continuations)

no 21,751   12 Oct 1840   MHC

no 21,832   4 Jan 1841   Journalism

no 21,994   14 Jul 1841   BR

no 22,072   13 Oct 1841   Literature as merchandise

Notes:
Conservative, especially in its feature called "Table-Talk."
Shows fondness for Blackwood's, Fraser's, Dublin University
Magazine, and Bentley's Magazine.   The Monthly Magazine is
praised in 1834-35, but none of Dickens's articles is singled
out.   Price sevenpence, then fivepence.

NEW MONTHLY MAGAZINE AND HUMORIST

1833:	37	pt 1 nos 145 - 148	Jan - Apr
	38	2 nos 149 - 152	May - Aug
	39	3 nos 153 - 156	Sep - Dec
1834:	40	1 nos 157 - 160	Jan - Apr
	41	2 nos 161 - 164	May - Aug
	42	3 nos 165 - 168	Sep - Dec
1835:	43	1 nos 169 - 172	Jan - Apr
	44	2 nos 173 - 176	May - Aug
	45	3 nos 177 - 180	Sep - Dec
1836:	46	1 nos 181 - 184	Jan - Apr
	47	2 nos 185 - 188	May - Aug
	48	3 nos 189 - 192	Sep - Dec
1837:	49	1 nos 193 - 196	Jan - Apr
	50	2 nos 197 - 200	May - Aug
	51	3 nos 201 - 204	Sep - Dec

1838:	52	1 nos 205 - 208	Jan - Apr
	53	2 nos 209 - 212	May - Aug
	54	3 nos 213 - 216	Sep - Dec
1839:	55	1 nos 217 - 220	Jan - Apr
	56	2 nos 221 - 224	May - Aug
	57	3 nos 225 - 228	Sep - Dec
1840:	58	1 nos 229 - 232	Jan - Apr
	59	2 nos 233 - 236	May - Aug
	60	3 nos 237 - 240	Sep - Dec
1841:	61	1 nos 241 - 244	Jan - Apr
	62	2 nos 245 - 248	May - Aug
	63	3 nos 249 - 252	Sep - Dec

38	no 150	Jne 1833: 135-42	Modern novelists
39	no 156	Dec 1833: 424-31	Periodicals
40	no 160	Apr 1834: 497-505	Literature in 1834
47	no 185	May 1836: 105	SB
48	no 189	Sep 1836: 102-04	PP
50	no 100	Aug 1837: 473-79	Status of authors
51	no 203	Nov 1837: 418	Fiction writing
51	no 203	Nov 1837: 427-31	Cheap literature
63	no 249	Sep 1841: 129-30	PNP

Notes:
In January 1837, "Critical Notices" becomes "Literature." See
Wellesley Index, v. 3; British Literary Magazines, v. 2.

NEW MORAL WORLD or, Gazette of the University Community
Society of Rational Religionists

1	nos	1 – 52	1 Nov 1834 – 24 Oct 1835
2	nos	53 – 104	31 Oct 1835 – 21 Oct 1836
3	nos	105 – 156	29 Oct 1836 – 21 Oct 1837
4	nos	157 – 208	28 Oct 1837 – 21 Oct 1838
5	nos	1 – 37	27 Oct 1838 – 6 Jul 1839
6	nos	38 – 62	11 Jul 1838*– 28 Dec 1839
7	nos	63 – 88	4 Jan 1840 – 27 Jne 1840

*[sic; shd be 1839]

"Enlarged Series"

1	(os 8)	nos 1 – 26	4 Jul 1840 – 26 Dec 1840
2	(os 9)	nos 1 – 26	2 Jan 1841 – 26 Jan 1841

1	no 3	18 Jul 1840: 34–35	Boz's sketches

Notes:
Undergoes frequent changes of subtitle.   Price twopence;
threepence from 7 no 83 (23 May 1840).

OBSERVER

1833:	nos 2101 – 2152	6 Jan – 30 Dec
1834:	nos 2153 – 2195	5 Jan – 28 Dec

[numbering ends 19 Oct 1834]

1835:		4 Jan – 27 Dec
1836:		3 Jan – 26 Dec
1837:		1 Jan – 31 Dec
1838:		1 Jan – 31 Dec
1839:		6 Jan – 30 Dec
1840:		5 Jan – 28 Dec
1841:		3 Jan – 27 Dec

no 2185	10 Aug 1834	SB
no 2198	5 Oct 1834	SB
	3 May 1835	SB
	2 Oct 1836	SG
	11 Dec 1836	VC
	12 Mar 1837	ISHW
	30 Apr 1837	PP
	4 Jne 1837	BM
	2 Jul 1837	BM
	7 Aug 1837	BM
	13 Aug 1837	BM
	3 Sep 1837	PP / BM
	8 Oct 1837	PP
	29 Oct 1837	PP
	3 Dec 1837	BM
	1 Apr 1838	NN
	6 May 1838	BM
	5 Aug 1838	NN
	9 Sep 1838	BM
	7 Oct 1838	NN
	25 Nov 1838	OT
	6 Jan 1839	NN
	13 Jan 1839	NN

3 Feb 1839	BM / NN
3 Mar 1839	BM
2 Jne 1839	BM / NN
30 Jne 1839	BM / NN
1 Jul 1839	BM / NN
4 Aug 1839	NN
1 Sep 1839	NN
29 Sep 1839	NN
6 Oct 1839	BM / NN
5 Apr 1840	MHC / Fraser's on Dickens
9 Aug 1840	Henry Fielding
6 Dec 1840	MHC
12 Dec 1841	W.H. Ainsworth
26 Dec 1841	BR (dramatisation)

Notes:
Pirates Dickens's sketches "Cockney Pleasures on a Sunday" (20 Sep 1835), "The Dancing Academy" (12 Oct 1835), and "The Parlour" (13 Dec 1835) to fill columns. Price sevenpence, fivepence from 1838.

PUBLIC LEDGER
GUARDIAN AND PUBLIC LEDGER

1833:	73	nos	134 - 448	1 Jan - 31 Dec
1834:	74	nos	449 - 541	1 Jan - 19 Apr

then
MORNING NEWS AND PUBLIC LEDGER

1834:   74   nos 542 - 760   21 Apr - 31 Dec
                       [ns nos 1 - 219]
1835:   74   nos 761 - 778   1 Jan - 31 Dec
                       [ns no 220 - no 24,120]

Jumps from 74 no 782 [ns no 241] (26 Jan 1835) to 76 no 23,834
[ns no 242] (27 Jan 1835).

then
PUBLIC LEDGER
1836: 78   nos 24,121 - 24,339   1 Jan - 14 Sep

then
CONSTITUTIONAL AND PUBLIC LEDGER

1836:   1   nos 1 - 93   15 Sep - 31 Dec
1837:   1   nos 94 - 249   2 Jan - 1 Jul

78	no 24,312	13 Aug 1836	PP
1	no 2	16 Sep 1836	Spirit of criticism
1	no 14	30 Sep 1836	SG
1	no 72	7 Dec 1836	VC
1	no 88	26 Dec 1836	Spirit of criticism
1	no 98	6 Jan 1837	BM
1	no 120	1 Feb 1837	BM

1	no 120	1 Feb 1837	BM
1	no 206	12 May 1837	BM
1	no 210	17 May 1837	PP
1	no 249	1 Jul 1837	Last editorial

Notes:
Occasional "Literature" and "Periodicals" columns. Editorial announcing change of policy in 74 no 542 (21 Apr 1834) says that the paper's emphasis will shift from matters of political interest to commercial news; this seems to mean more attention to literature. Speaks of "the general good" and professes political neutrality. Well printed. Price sevenpence until 1836; with change of title on 15 September, four-and-a-half pence.

QUARTERLY REVIEW

1833:	49	nos 97 & 98	Apr & Jul
	50	nos 99 & 100	Oct & Jan 1834
1834:	51	nos 101 & 102	Mar & Jne
	52	nos 103 & 104	Aug & Nov
1835:	53	nos 105 & 106	Feb & Apr
	54	nos 107 & 108	Jul & Sep
	55	nos 109 & 110	Dec & Feb 1836
1836:	56	nos 111 & 112	Apr & Jul
	57	nos 113 & 114	Sep & Dec
1837:	58	nos 115 & 116	Feb & Apr
	59	nos 117 & 118	Jul & Oct
1838:	60	General indexes to volumes 41-59 (pub. 1839)
	61	nos 121 & 122	Jan & Apr
	62	nos 123 & 124	Jul & Oct
1839:	63	nos 125 & 126	Jan & Mar
	64	nos 127 & 128	Jne & Oct
	65	nos 129 & 130	Dec & Mar 1840
1840:	66	nos 131 & 132	Jne & Sep
	67	nos 133 & 134	Dec & Mar 1841
1841:	68	nos 135 & 136	Jne & Sep
	69	nos 137 & 138	Dec & Mar 1842

11	no 22	Jul 1814: 354-77	Sir Walter Scott
34	no 68	Sep 1826: 349-78	Scott, <u>Lives of the Novelists</u>
46	no 92	Jan 1832: 544-622	Reform crisis and the book trade
49	no 97	Apr 1833: 228-47	Fashionable novels
51	no 102	Jne 1834: 481-93	State of the novel
56	no 111	Apr 1836: 65-131	French novels
58	no 116	Apr 1837: 297-333	German literature
59	no 118	Oct 1837: 484-518	SB / PP
64	no 127	Jne 1839: 83-102	OT

Notes:
See <u>Wellesley Index</u>, v. 1; <u>British Literary Magazines</u>, v. 2.

RAILWAY TIMES

1837:	nos 1 - 10	29 Oct - 31 Dec
1838:	nos 11 - ns no 62*	7 Jan - 29 Dec
1839: 2	nos 52 - 104	5 Jan - 28 Dec
1840: 3	nos 105 - 156	4 Jan - 26 Dec

*[<u>sic</u>;shd be ns 51]

no 2   5 Nov 1837: 10   PP / BM / OT

Notes:
Price sixpence until no 13 (Jan 1838), when the size changes
to quarto, and then price to fourpence. Price goes back up
to sixpence with no 40 [ns no 29] (28 Jul 1838). On 7 Jan
1838 (no 11), "Partial Alteration of Plan" announces that the
general newspaper section is to be discarded, because the
public wants only railway news in a railway journal; at this
point, it becomes exclusively technical.

ST. JAMES'S CHRONICLE AND GENERAL EVENING POST

1833: nos 11,728 - 11,885	29 Dec 1832/1 Jan - 31 Dec
1834: nos 11,886 - 12,041	31 Dec 1833/2 Jan - 30 Dec
1835: nos 12,042 - 12,198	30 Dec 1834/1 Jan - 31 Dec
1836: nos 12,199 - 12,355	31 Dec 1835/2 Jan - 31 Dec
1837: nos 12,356 - 12,561*	13 Dec 1836/3 Jan - 30 Dec
1838: nos 12,512 - 12,667	2 Jan - 29 Dec
1839: nos 12,668 - 12,824	1 Jan - 31 Dec
1840: nos 12,825 - 12,981	2 Jan - 31 Dec
1841: nos 12,982 - 13,137	2 Jan - 30 Dec

*[sic] shd be 511]

no 12,316	1 Oct 1836	PP
no 12,365	24 Jan 1837	BM
no 12,368	31 Jan 1837	BM
no 12,395	4 Apr 1837	BM
no 12,500	5 Dec 1837	BM
no 12,539	6 Mar 1838	BM
no 12,934	12 Sep 1840	Novels in magazines

Notes:
Tory. Old-fashioned appearance. Price fivepence. No "Literature" or "Magazine Day" columns, only extracts and ads. Much Colburn and Bentley advertising (puffs).

SHIPPING AND MERCANTILE GAZETTE

1838:	nos 1 - 249	12 Mar - 31 Dec
1839:	nos 250 - 562	1 Jan - 31 Dec
1840:	nos 563 - 874	1 Jan - 31 Dec
1841:	nos 875 - 1187	1 Jan - 31 Dec

no 19	2 Apr 1838	NN
no 21	4 Apr 1838	BM
no 47	4 May 1838	BM
no 48	5 May 1838	NN
no 73	4 Jne 1838	NN
no 90	23 Jne 1838	NN
no 98	3 Jul 1838	BM / NN
no 112	19 Jul 1838	NN
no 126	4 Aug 1838	NN
no 129	8 Aug 1838	BM
no 148	30 Aug 1838	NN
no 166	20 Sep 1838	BM
no 197	31 Oct 1838	NN
no 209	14 Nov 1838	SB
no 238	18 Dec 1838	OT
no 245	26 Dec 1838	OT
no 270	24 Jan 1839	NN
no 271	25 Jan 1839	NN
no 289	15 Feb 1839	NN
no 320	23 Mar 1839	NN
no 368	18 May 1839	NN
no 372	23 May 1839	NN
no 378	30 May 1839	Boz

no 384   6 Jne 1839   Boz

no 454   27 Aug 1839   Dickens imitations

<u>Notes</u>:
No regular notices of theatricals or periodicals.   Price
sixpence.

SPECTATOR

A Weekly Journal of News, Politics, Literature, and Science

1833:	6	nos 236 - 287	5 Jan - 28 Dec
1834:	7	nos 288 - 339	4 Jan - 27 Dec
1835:	8	nos 340 - 391	3 Jan - 26 Dec
1836:	9	nos 392 - 444	2 Jan - 31 Dec
1837:	10	nos 445 - 496	7 Jan - 30 Dec
1838:	11	nos 497 - 548	6 Jan - 29 Dec
1839:	12	nos 549 - 600	5 Jan - 28 Dec
1840:	13	nos 601 - 652	4 Jan - 26 Dec
1841:	14	nos 653 - 704	2 Jan - 25 Dec

6	no 239	26 Jan 1833: 91	The book trade
7	no 289	11 Jan 1834: 33	<u>Modern Novelists</u>
7	no 289	11 Jan 1834: 38-39	Cheap literature
7	no 292	1 Feb 1834: 112	Periodicals price
9	no 399	20 Feb 1836: 182-83	SB
9	no 407	16 Apr 1836: 373	PP

9	no 423	6 Aug 1836: 755–56	The quarterlies
9	no 425	20 Aug 1836: 805	PP
9	no 441	10 Dec 1836: 1183	VC
9	no 443	26 Dec 1836: 1234–35	SB
10	no 479	2 Sep 1837: 835	BM
11	no 504	24 Feb 1838: 184–86	MJG
11	no 509	31 Mar 1838: 304–05	NN
11	no 532	8 Sep 1838: 854–55	BM
11	no 543	24 Nov 1838: 1114–116	OT
12	no 591	26 Oct 1839: 1020–21	Ainsworth, Jack Sheppard
13	no 606	8 Feb 1840: 137	SYC
13	no 616	18 Apr 1840: 380	MHC
14	no 701	4 Dec 1841: 1170	MHC / OCS / BR

Notes:
See British Literary Magazines, v. 2; Thomas, William Beach, The Story of the Spectator 1828-1928 (1928). Price one shilling; ninepence from 1837.

SPORTING MAGAZINE or Monthly Calendar of the Transactions of
the Turf, The Chase, and Every Other
Diversion Interesting to the Man of
Pleasure, Enterprize & Spirit

1833: 2s	6	os 81	nos	31 – 36	Nov 1832 – Apr
	7	os 82	nos	37 – 42	May – Oct
	8	os 83	nos	43 – 48	Nov – Apr 1834
1834:	9	os 84	nos	49 – 54	May – Oct
	10	os 85	nos	54 – 60	Nov – Apr 1835
1835:	11	os 86	nos	61 – 66	May – Oct
	12	os 87	nos	67 – 72	Nov – Apr 1836
1836:	13	os 88	nos	73 – 78	May – Oct
	14	os 89	nos	79 – 84	Nov – Apr 1837
1837:	15	os 90	nos	85 – 90	May – Oct
	16	os 91	nos	91 – 96	Nov – Apr 1838
1838:	17	os 92	nos	97 – 102	May – Oct
	18	os 93	nos	103 – 108	Nov – Apr 1839
1839:	19	os 94	nos	109 – 114	May – Oct
	20	os 95	nos	115 – 120	Nov – Apr 1840
1840:	21	os 96	nos	121 – 126	May – Oct
	22	os 97	nos	127 – 132	Nov – Apr 1841
	23	os 98	nos	133 – 138	May – Oct
	24	os 99	nos	139 – 144	Nov – Apr 1842

2s   14   no 80   Dec 1836: 141–47   PP

Notes:
"Literary notices" generally consist purely of books about
sports and animals.

STANDARD

1833:	nos 1759 – 2071	1 Jan – 31 Dec
1834:	nos 2072 – 2384	1 Jan – 31 Dec
1835:	nos 2385 – 2697	1 Jan – 31 Dec
1836:	nos 2698 – 3010	1 Jan – 31 Dec
1837:	nos 3011 – 4222	2 Jan – 30 Dec
1838:	nos 4223 – 4533	1 Jan – 31 Dec
1839:	nos 4534 – 4846	1 Jan – 31 Dec
1840:	nos 4847 – 5159	1 Jan – 31 Dec
1841:	nos 5160 – 5463	1 Jan – 31 Dec

no 2931	30 Sep 1836	SG
no 3066	7 Mar 1837	ISHW
no 5115	10 Nov 1840	OCS (dramatisation)

Notes:
No "Literature" column or a very infrequent one; some scattered theatrical notices. A good number of puffs for Bentley and Colburn and quotations from other newspapers.

SUN

1833:	nos 12,577 – 12,888	1 Jan – 31 Dec
1834:	nos 12,889 – 13,201	1 Jan – 31 Dec
1835:	nos 13,202 – 13,511	1 Jan – 31 Dec
1836:	nos 13,512 – 13,820	1 Jan – 31 Dec
1837:	nos 13,821 – 14,134	2 Jan – 30 Dec
1838:	nos 14,135 – 14,450	1 Jan – 31 Dec
1839:	nos 14,451 – 14,762	1 Jan – 31 Dec
1840:	nos 14,763 – 15,075	1 Jan – 31 Dec
1841:	nos 15,076 – 15,388	1 Jan – 31 Dec

no 12,607	5 Feb 1833	Bentley's Standard Novels
no 12,785	2 Sep 1833	State of publishing
no 12,812	3 Oct 1833	Monthly Magazine
no 12,863	2 Dec 1833	MM
no 12,889	1 Jan 1834	MM
no 12,915	1 Feb 1834	MM
no 12,940	1 Mar 1834	New Monthly Magazine
no 12,966	1 Apr 1834	MM
no 13,096	30 Aug 1834	Bentley's Standard Novels
no 13,126	4 Oct 1834	MM
no 13,202	1 Jan 1835	MM
no 13,230	4 Feb 1835	MM
no 13,296	22 Apr 1835	Bentley's Standard Novels
no 13,460	2 Nov 1835	MM
no 13,550	15 Feb 1836	SB
no 13,615	2 May 1836	PP
no 13,642	2 Jne 1836	PP / LF
no 13,669	4 Jul 1836	PP
no 13,719	2 Sep 1836	PP
no 13,744	1 Oct 1836	PP
no 13,770	1 Nov 1836	PP
no 13,796	3 Dec 1836	PP
no 13,799	7 Dec 1836	VC

no 13,821	2 Jan 1837	PP / BM
no 13,848	1 Feb 1837	BM
no 13,873	2 Mar 1837	BM
no 13,900	1 Apr 1837	PP / BM
no 13,925	1 May 1837	BM
no 13,978	1 Jul 1837	PP / BM
no 14,004	1 Aug 1837	BM
no 14,005	2 Aug 1837	PP
no 14,031	1 Sep 1837	BM
no 14,057	2 Oct 1837	BM
no 14,081	30 Oct 1837	<u>Quarterly Review</u>
no 14,083	1 Nov 1837	BM
no 14,109	1 Dec 1837	BM
no 14,135	1 Jan 1838	BM
no 14,167	7 Feb 1838	BM
no 14,186	1 Mar 1838	BM
no 14,201	19 Mar 1838	MJG
no 14,215	2 Apr 1838	BM / NN
no 14,238	1 May 1838	BM
no 14,239	2 May 1838	NN
no 14,267	2 Jne 1838	BM
no 14,270	6 Jne 1838	NN
no 14,293	2 Jul 1838	BM

no 14,319	1 Aug 1838	BM
no 14,323	5 Aug 1838	NN
no 14,347	1 Sep 1838	BM
no 14,373	2 Oct 1838	BM
no 14,375	4 Oct 1838	Edinburgh Review on Dickens
no 14,399	1 Nov 1838	BM
no 14,415	20 Nov 1838	OT
no 14,425	1 Dec 1838	BM / OT
no 14,454	4 Jan 1839	BM / OT
no 14,479	1 Feb 1839	BM
no 14,529	1 Apr 1839	BM
no 14,530	2 Apr 1839	NN
no 14,582	1 Jne 1839	BM
no 14,610	4 Jul 1839	NN
no 14,644	13 Aug 1839	NN
no 14,665	6 Sep 1839	NN
no 14,689	4 Oct 1839	NN
no 14,789	3 Feb 1840	BM, W.H. Ainsworth
no 14,839	1 Apr 1840	Fraser's on Dickens
no 14,850	14 Apr 1840	MHC
no 14,853	20 Apr 1840	MHC
no 15,230	1 Jul 1841	Public Dinner at Edinburgh
no 15,385	28 Dec 1841	BR (dramatisation)

Notes:
"Magazine Day" appears first few days of every month; there is regular and generous attention paid to periodical literature. Universally praised for its literary criticism, which is as serious as that found in the quarterlies and often shows more acuteness. Dickens seems to have known its reviewer, William Deacon (DNB 1777-1845), who reviewed for the paper from the early 1830s until his death; Dickens's work receives some of its best criticism here. See James Grant <u>The Great Metropolis</u> (1836). Price sevenpence; fivepence after 1836.

SUNDAY TIMES

1833:	nos 533	–	584	6 Jan	–	29 Dec
1834:	nos 585	–	636	5 Jan	–	28 Dec
1835:	nos 637	–	688	4 Jan	–	27 Dec
1836:	nos 689	–	740	3 Jan	–	25 Dec
1837:	nos 741	–	793	1 Jan	–	31 Dec
1838:	nos 794	–	845	7 Jan	–	30 Dec
1839:	nos 846	–	897	6 Jan	–	29 Dec
1840:	nos 898	–	949	5 Jan	–	27 Dec
1841:	nos 950	–	1001	3 Jan	–	26 Dec

no 624	5 Oct 1834	MM
no 696	21 Feb 1836	SB
no 703	10 Apr 1836	PP
no 728	2 Oct 1836	SG
no 738	11 Dec 1836	VC

no 751	12 Mar 1837	ISHW
no 757	23 Apr 1837	SB
no 769	16 Jul 1837	BM
no 781	8 Oct 1837	BM
no 798	4 Feb 1838	BM
no 801	25 Feb 1838	BM
no 805	25 Mar 1838	Gov't patronage
no 806	1 Apr 1838	OT (dramatisation)
no 807	8 Apr 1838	BM / NN
no 811	6 May 1838	BM / NN
no 819	1 Jul 1838	NN
no 820	8 Jul 1838	BM
no 824	5 Aug 1838	BM / NN
no 825	12 Aug 1838	BM
no 829	9 Sep 1838	BM
no 830	16 Sep 1838	BM / NN
no 833	7 Oct 1838	BM / NN
no 837	4 Nov 1838	BM / NN
no 841	2 Dec 1838	OT
no 842	9 Dec 1838	BM / NN
no 846	6 Jan 1839	BM / NN
no 850	3 Feb 1839	NN
no 854	3 Mar 1839	BM / NN

no 859	7 Apr 1839	NN
no 861	21 Apr 1839	Shilling numbers
no 864	12 May 1839	NN
no 868	9 Jne 1839	NN
no 872	7 Jul 1839	NN
no 876	4 Aug 1839	NN
no 881	8 Sep 1839	NN
no 886	13 Oct 1839	NN
no 851	10 Feb 1840	SYC
no 911	5 Apr 1840	Fraser's on Dickens
no 914	3 May 1840	MHC
no 922	28 Jne 1840	MHC
no 938	11 Oct 1840	MHC
no 943	15 Nov 1840	MHC
no 982	15 Aug 1841	BR (dramatisation)
no 1001	26 Dec 1841	BR (dramatisation)

Notes:
Has both Town and Country editions. Price sixpence.

TABLET

1840:	nos 1 - 33	6 May - 31 Dec
1841:	nos 34 - 85	2 Jan - 25 Dec

no 19	19 Sep 1840: 308	MHC
no 63	28 Aug 1841: 565-66	PNP
no 76	23 Oct 1841: 698-94	MHC; the Dickens machine

Notes:
Catholic gentleman's weekly. "Review" and "Miscellaneous" sections; there are extracts from periodicals but no regular review space is given to them. Quarto. Price sixpence.

TAIT'S EDINBURGH MAGAZINE

1833:	2	nos 10 - 12	Jan - Mar
	3	nos 13 - 18	Apr - Sep
	4	nos 19 - 22	Oct - Jan 1834
1834:	ns 1 nos	1 - 11	Feb - Dec + Suppl. 12
1835:	2 nos	13 - 24	Jan - Dec
1836:	3 nos	25 - 36	Jan - Dec
1837:	4 nos	37 - 48	Jan - Dec
1838:	5 nos	49 - 60	Jan - Dec
1839:	6 nos	61 - 72	Jan - Dec
1840:	7 nos	73 - 84	Jan - Dec
1841:	8 nos	85 - 96	Jan - Dec

2	no 11	Feb 1833: 662	Crisis in literature
3	no 14	May 1833: 256-58	Magazine writing
3	no 16	Jul 1833: 491-96	Periodical literature
3	no 18	Sep 1833: 727-28	French authorship
3	no 18	Sep 1833: 729-31	Fashionable novels
4	no 22	Jan 1834: 490-500	Growth in weeklies
1	no 1	Feb 1834: 54-59	Fashionable literature
1	no 12	Suppl. 1834: 788-92	London newspaper press
2	no 13	Jan 1835: 3-10	Samuel Taylor Coleridge
5	no 51	Mar 1838: 196	SYG

Notes:
Scottish and religious. More poetry than fiction considered.
After 1834, format becomes more like that of a miscellany than
a quarterly. See Wellesley Index, v. 4; British Literary
Magazines, v. 2.

THE TIMES

1833:	nos 15,050 - 15,362	1 Jan - 31 Dec
1834:	nos 15,363 - 15,675	1 Jan - 31 Dec
1835:	nos 15,676 - 15,987	1 Jan - 31 Dec
1836:	nos 15,988 - 16,301	1 Jan - 31 Dec
1837:	nos 16,302 - 16,613	2 Jan - 30 Dec
1838:	nos 16,614 - 16,926	1 Jan - 31 Dec
1839:	nos 16,927 - 17,239	1 Jan - 31 Dec
1840:	nos 17,240 - 17,555	1 Jan - 31 Dec
1841:	nos 17,556 - 17,868	1 Jan - 31 Dec

no 15,162	11 May 1833	Status of the novel
no 16,178	10 Aug 1836	PP
no 16,222	30 Sep 1836	SG
no 16,223	1 Oct 1836	PP
no 16,280	7 Dec 1836	VC
no 16,327	31 Jan 1837	BM
no 16,407	4 May 1837	Literary Fund Dinner
no 16,539	5 Oct 1837	PP / BM
no 16,541	7 Oct 1837	BM
no 16,564	3 Nov 1837	BM
no 16,891	20 Nov 1838	NN
no 16,892	21 Nov 1838	OT (dramatisation)
no 16,929	3 Jan 1839	NN
no 16,977	28 Feb 1839	Copyright bill

| no 17,796 | 8 Oct 1841 | Imitations of Dickens |
| no 17,859 | 21 Dec 1841 | BR (dramatisation) |

Notes:
Achieved under Thomas Barnes (1817-41) unprecedented political
power for a daily newspaper, particularly when the
Conservatives consulted The Times on formation of its brief
government in 1835. Its attitude towards literary affairs was
set out on 27 February 1835: "We are not in the habit of
noticing the novels which are issuing in an almost continued
stream from the press--not, certainly, that we undervalue a
species of literature adorned by Fielding and Smollett or
Scott and Edgeworth, but because we have little time for
amusing ourselves with any romance except the extravagant
romance of political life." Scholarly and historical works
were more likely to be noticed. Price sevenpence.

TOWN; Journal of Original Essays, Characteristic of the
Manners, Social, Domestic, and Superficial, of London
and the Londoners.

1837:	1	nos	1 - 31	3 Jne - 30 Dec
1838:		nos	32 - 52	6 Jan - 26 May
	2	nos	53 - 83	2 Jne - 29 Dec
1839:	1	nos	84 - 104	5 Jan - 25 May
	3	nos	105 - 156	1 Jne - 23 May 1840
			[Missing 23 May 1840 - 27 Jan 1841]	
1841:		nos	192 - 240	27 Jan - 29 Dec
1842:		nos	241 - 244	5 Jan - 26 Jne

no	39	24 Feb 1838: 306	Mr. Harley the actor
no	44	31 Mar 1838: 349	Imitations of Boz
no	123	5 Oct 1839: 983	NN
no	129	16 Nov 1839: 1028	Ainsworth, Jack Sheppard
no	152	25 Apr 1840: 1213	MHC satire
no	153	2 May 1840: 1221	MHC satire
no	154	9 May 1840: 1229-30	MHC satire
no	155	16 May 1840: 1237	MHC satire
no	156	23 May 1840: 1245	MHC satire
no	192	27 Jan 1841: 1521	"Familiar Epistle" satire
no	196	24 Feb 1841: 1554	OCS
no	233	10 Nov 1841: 1852	MHC satire
no	234	17 Nov 1841: 1861	MHC satire
no	235	24 Nov 1841: 1869	MHC satire
no	236	1 Dec 1841: 1877	MHC satire
no	237	8 Dec 1841: 1885-86	MHC satire
no	239	22 Dec 1841: 1901	MHC satire
no	240	29 Dec 1841: 1909	MHC satire
no	241	5 Jan 1842: 1917	MHC satire
no	242	12 Jan 1842: 1925	MHC satire
no	243	19 Jan 1842: 1934	MHC satire
no	244	26 Jan 1842: 1939	MHC satire

Notes:
Shows marked attention to <u>Bentley's Miscellany</u>, especially
after <u>Jack Sheppard</u> begins to appear there. Carries no
literary advertisements. In its emphasis on London characters,
it covers much of Dickens's famous territory but is not
suitable for the young reader; its articles on cigar shops are
less euphemistic than Dickens's own <u>Sketches by Boz</u>. By the
time of <u>Master Humphrey's Clock</u>, the paper is scornful of
Dickens's increasingly moralistic perspective on London. Price
twopence, until 1841, when it goes up to fourpence. See Louis
James, <u>Fiction for the Working Man 1830-50</u> (1963) for a
summary of this scurrilous journal.

TRUE SUN

1832:	nos	1 – 259	5 Mar – 31 Dec	
1833:	nos	260 – 572	1 Jan – 31 Dec	
1834:	nos	573 – 905	1 Jan – 31 Dec	
1835:	nos	906 – 1210	1 Jan – 31 Dec	
1836:	nos	1211 – 1386	1 Jan – 23 Jul	
ns	nos	1 – 138	25 Jul – 31 Dec	
1837:	nos	139 – 442	2 Jan – 23 Dec	

no 84	9 Jne 1832	MM
no 87	13 Jne 1832	Magazines
no 103	2 Jul 1832	MM
no 156	1 Sep 1832	MM
no 188	9 Oct 1832	MM
no 236	4 Dec 1832	Magazines

no 261	2 Jan 1833	MM
no 585	15 Jan 1834	MM
no 827	1 Oct 1834	MM
no 1258	25 Feb 1836	SB
no 1316	3 May 1836	MM
ns 15	10 Aug 1836	PP
ns 57	28 Sep 1836	Newspapers
ns 60	1 Oct 1836	PP
ns 65	7 Oct 1836	PP
ns 72	15 Oct 1836	PP
ns 87	2 Nov 1836	PP
ns 97	14 Nov 1836	PP
ns 117	7 Dec 1836	VC
ns 141	4 Jan 1837	BM
ns 206	24 Mar 1837	PP
ns 240	4 May 1837	BM

Notes:
Dickens is thought to have worked for this paper from March
to July 1832. John Forster was its drama critic at the same
time, and Leigh Hunt wrote briefly as its literary critic.
The physical format closely resembles that of the Sun, with
whom this paper is in competition. During 1833, it is sued
for libel by the government and runs excerpts from other
papers in support of its case; in January 1834, the
proprietors are sentenced to six months' imprisonment. See
Weekly True Sun. Price sevenpence.

UNITED SERVICES GAZETTE, and Naval and Military Chronicle

1833:	nos 1 - 47	9 Feb - 28 Dec
1834:	nos 48 - 99	4 Jan - 27 Dec
1835:	nos 100 - 151	3 Jan - 26 Dec
1836:	nos 152 - 204	2 Jan - 31 Dec
1837:	nos 205 - 258	7 Jan - 30 Dec
1838:	nos 259 - 311	6 Jan - 29 Dec
1839:	nos 312 - 364	5 Jan - 28 Dec
1840:	nos 365 - 417	4 Jan - 26 Dec
1841:	nos 418 - 468	2 Jan - 25 Dec

no 109	7 Mar 1835	MM
no 115	18 Apr 1835	Bentley, the publisher
no 191	1 Oct 1836	SG
no 209	4 Feb 1837	PP / BM
no 272	7 Apr 1838	PP / BM
no 277	12 May 1838	BM
no 300	13 Oct 1838	NN
no 304	10 Nov 1838	NN
no 312	5 Jan 1839	BM / NN
no 316	2 Feb 1839	BM
no 317	9 Feb 1839	NN
no 322	9 Mar 1839	BM
no 324	23 Mar 1839	NN
no 326	6 Apr 1839	BM / NN
no 331	11 May 1839	NN

no 335	8 Jne 1839	NN
no 339	6 Jul 1839	BM / NN
no 343	3 Aug 1839	NN
no 348	7 Sep 1839	NN
no 352	5 Oct 1839	NN
no 354	19 Oct 1839	Imitations of Dickens
no 364	28 Dec 1839	Bentley's "puffing"
no 373	23 Feb 1840	Dickens and Bentley
no 374	7 Mar 1840	BM
no 377	28 Mar 1840	Ainsworth, Jack Sheppard
no 408	24 Oct 1840	MHC
no 411	14 Nov 1840	MHC
no 415	12 Dec 1840	MHC
no 436	8 May 1841	MHC
no 454	11 Sep 1841	PNP
no 465	11 Dec 1841	MHC

Notes:
Inarticulate and respectable; a military readership. Its readers subscribe to Blackwood's and the annuals, and the major quarterlies are regularly reviewed (see under "A Parthian Glance"). Scornful of Colburn's less respectable United Service Journal. Each issue = eight pages. Price sevenpence.

WEEKLY DISPATCH

1833:	nos 1631 – 1682	6 Jan – 30 Dec
1834:	nos 1683 – 1734	5 Jan – 28 Dec
1835:	nos 1735 – 1785	4 Jan – 27 Dec
1836:	nos 1786 – 1836	3 Jan – 25 Dec
1837:	nos 1837 – 1889	1 Jan – 31 Dec
1838:	nos 1890 – 1941	7 Jan – 30 Dec
1839:	nos 1942 – 1993	6 Jan – 29 Dec
1840:	nos 1994 – 2045	5 Jan – 27 Dec
1841:	nos 2046 – 2096	3 Jan – 26 Dec

no 1696	6 Apr 1834: 106	MM
no 1700	4 May 1834: 142	MM
no 1713	3 Aug 1834: 252	MM
no 1722	5 Oct 1834: 332	The book trade
no 1735	4 Jan 1835: 8	MM
no 1740	8 Feb 1835: 54	MM
no 1793	28 Feb 1836: 78	SB
no 1799	10 Apr 1836: 134	PP
no 1800	17 Apr 1836: 146	The book trade
no 1811	3 Jul 1836: 246	SUTH
no 1818	21 Aug 1836: 320	PP
no 1824	2 Oct 1836: 368	SG
no 1831	20 Nov 1836: 452	PP
no 1839	15 Jan 1837: 34	BM

no 1842	5 Feb 1837: 70	PP
no 1847	12 Mar 1837: 130	BM
no 1851	9 Apr 1837: 178	SB
no 1855	7 May 1837: 226	BM
no 1864	9 Jul 1837: 334	BM
no 1865	16 Jul 1837: 346	BM
no 1866	23 Jul 1837: 356	PP
no 1868	6 Aug 1837: 382	Continuations
no 1869	13 Aug 1837: 394	BM
no 1872	3 Sep 1837: 430	BM
no 1877	8 Oct 1837: 488	BM
no 1882	12 Nov 1837: 550	BM
no 1895	11 Feb 1838: 70	SYG
no 1899	11 Mar 1838: 118	MJG
no 1903	8 Apr 1838: 166	NN
no 1908	13 May 1838: 226	NN
no 1913	17 Jne 1838: 286	NN
no 1916	8 Jul 1836: 322	NN
no 1935	18 Nov 1838: 550	NN
no 1936	25 Nov 1838: 562	OT
no 1942	6 Jan 1839: 10	NN
no 1951	10 Mar 1839: 118	BM
no 1954	31 Mar 1839: 154	BM

no 1964	9 Jne 1839: 274	Dickens imitations
no 2007	5 Apr 1840: 166	Fraser's on Dickens
no 2008	12 Apr 1840: 178	MHC
no 2047	10 Jan 1841: 22	Newspaper criticism
no 2063	2 May 1841: 214	Stories in parts
no 2077	15 Aug 1841: 394	W.H. Ainsworth
no 2096	26 Dec 1841: 620	BR (dramatisation)

Notes:
Inclined to extracts as part of its reviews. Favourable towards Bentley's Miscellany and not squeamish about Jack Sheppard, except at the beginning of 1840, when it delivers diatribes against "vulgarity." Well printed, like most Bell's newspapers. Both Town and Country editions. Price eight-and-a-half pence; sixpence after 1836.

WEEKLY TRUE SUN

| 1833: | nos 1 - ns 18 | 10 Feb - 29 Dec |

| ns 2 | 8 Sep 1833: 9-10 | Criticism |

Notes:
See "Statement of Facts Regarding the 'Sun' Newspaper" by Patrick Grant, who set up the Weekly True Sun in competition with that paper. Price sevenpence.

WESTMINSTER REVIEW

1833:	18	nos 35 & 36	Jan & Apr
	19	nos 37 & 38	Jul & Oct
1834:	20	nos 39 & 40	Jan & Apr
	21	nos 41 & 42	Jul & Oct
1835:	22	nos 43 & 44	Jan & Apr
	23	nos 45 & 46	Jul & Oct
1836:	24	no 47	Jan
	3/25		Apr & Jul

[see **London and Westminster Review**]

1	no 1	Jan 1824: 206-49	Periodicals
10	no 19	Jan 1829: 173-91	Fashionable novels
10	no 19	Jan 1829: 216-37	Newspaper press
10	no 20	Apr 1829: 466-80	Weekly newspapers
18	no 35	Jan 1833: 31-43	Dramatic literature
18	no 35	Jan 1833: 195-208	Journalism
22	no 44	Apr 1835: 314-21	Fashionable novels

Notes:

See Wellesley Index, v. 3; British Literary Magazines, v. 2.

IV.   SECONDARY SOURCES

Nineteenth Century

Ainsworth, William Harrison. Jack Sheppard. London: Bentley, 1840.

_____. Rookwood: A Romance. London: Bentley, 1834. 3 vols.

Andrews, Alexander. The History of British Journalism. London: Bentley, 1859. 2 vols.

The Author's Printing and Publishing Assistant. 2nd ed. London: Saunders & Otley, 1839.

Babbage, Charles. On the Economy of Machinery and Manufactures. London: Charles Knight, 1832.

Bell's Edition. The Poets of Great Britain Complete from Chaucer to Churchill. London: John Bell, 1782. 109 vols.

[Bentley.] Publishers' Archives: Richard Bentley & Son 1829-98. Cambridge: Chadwyck-Healey, 1976.

Bentley, Richard. List of Principal Publications Issued from New Burlington Street 1829-98. London: Richard Bentley and Son, 1893-1920.

Blanchard, S.L. Sketches of Life, London: Colburn, 1846. 3 vols.

Bourne, H.R. Fox. English Newspapers. London: Chatto & Windus, 1887. 2 vols.

Bulwer, Edward Lytton. England and the English. London: Bentley, 1833.

_____. England and the English. Ed. with an introduction by Standish Meacham. Chicago: U of Chicago Pr, 1970.

_____. Eugene Aram: A Tale. London: Richard Bentley, 1832. 3 vols.

_____. Paul Clifford. London: Henry Colburn and Bentley, 1830. 3 vols.

____. <u>Pelham; or, the Adventures of a Gentleman</u>. London: Colburn, 1828. 3 vols.

Carlyle, Thomas. <u>Reminiscences</u> (1881). Ed. C.E. Norton. Intro. Ian Campbell. 1887; London: Dent, 1972.

____. <u>Collected Works</u>. <u>Centenary Edition</u>. London: Chapman and Hall. 1896-99. 30 vols.

Carlyle, Thomas and Jane Welsh. <u>The Collected Letters of Thomas and Jane Welsh Carlyle</u>. <u>Duke-Edinburgh Edition</u>. Eds. C.R. Sanders, K.J. Fielding. Durham: Duke U Pr, 1977-81. 9 vols.

Cockburn, Henry. <u>The Life of Lord Jeffrey</u>. Edinburgh: Adam and Charles Black, 1852. 2 vols.

[Collier, John Payne.] <u>An Old Man's Diary, Forty Years Ago</u>. London: Thomas Richards, 1871-72. 4 vols.

Croal, David. <u>Early Recollections of a Journalist 1832-59</u>. Edinburgh: Andrew Elliot, 1898.

Cross, Wilbur L. <u>The Development of the English Novel</u>. New York: Macmillan, 1899.

Egan, Pierce. <u>Life in London</u>. London: Sherwood, Neely, and Jones, 1821.

Espinasse, Francis. <u>Literary Recollections and Sketches</u>. London: Hodder and Stoughton, 1893.

Forster, John. <u>The Life of Charles Dickens</u> (1872). Ed. A.J. Hoppé. London: Dent, 1966. 2 vols.

____. <u>The Life and Times of Oliver Goldsmith</u>. London: Bradbury & Evans, 1848. 2 vols.

Francis, John, comp. <u>John Francis, Publisher of the Athenaeum</u>. London: Bentley, 1888, 2 vols.

Froude, James Anthony. <u>Thomas Carlyle: A History of His Life in London 1834-81</u>. London: Longmans, Green, 1884. 2 vols.

262

Gillies, R.P. Memoirs of a Literary Veteran. London: Richard
    Bentley, 1851. 3 vols.

[Grant, James.] The Great Metropolis. London: Saunders and
    Otley, 1836. 2 vols.

Grant, James. The Newspaper Press. London: Tinsley Brothers,
    1871-72. 3 vols.

[Grant, James.] Random Recollections of the House of Commons
    1830-35. London: Smith, Elder, 1836.

_____. Random Recollections of the House of Lords 1830-36.
    London: Smith, Elder, 1836.

Greville, Charles Cavendish Fulke. The Greville Memoirs. Ed.
    R. Fulford. New York: Macmillan, 1963.

Hall, S.C. A Book of Memories of Great Men and Women of the
    Age. London: Virtue, 1871.

_____. Retrospect of a Long Life 1815-83. London: Richard
    Bentley & Son, 1883. 2 vols.

Horne, R.H. Exposition of the False Medium and Barriers
    Excluding Men of Genius from the Public. London:
    Effingham Wilson, 1833.

_____. A New Spirit of the Age. London: Smith, Elder, 1844.
    2 vols.

Howard, Edward. Rattlin the Reefer. 1834-36; London: Oxford
    U Pr, 1971.

Hunt, F.Knight. The Fourth Estate. London: David Bogue,
    1850. 2 vols.

Jerdan, William. The Autobiography of William Jerdan.
    London: Arthur Hall, 1852. 4 vols.

Knight, Charles. The Old Printer and the Modern Press.
    London: John Murray, 1854.

Lackington, James. Memoirs of the Forty-five First Years of
    the Life of James Lackington, Bookseller. London: Hunt
    and Clarke, 1827.

Lewes, George Henry. <u>Ranthorpe</u>. London: Chapman and Hall, 1847.

The London Catalogue of Books 1814-1839. London: Robert Bent, 1839.

The London Catalogue of Books 1814-1846. London: Thomas Hodgson, 1846

The London Catalogue of Books: Supplement January 1839-January 1844. London: Thomas Hodgson, 1844.

Mackay, Charles. <u>Forty Years' Recollections of Life, Literature and Public Affairs 1830-70</u>. London: Chapman and Hall, 1877. 2 vols.

Miller, Thomas. <u>Godfrey Malvern; or, The Life of an Author</u>. London: Thomas Miller, 1842. 2 vols.

Montgomery, James. <u>Lectures on Poetry and General Literature</u>. London: Longman, Rees, Orme, Brown, Green & Longman, 1833.

Poole, John. <u>Sketches and Recollections</u>. London: Colburn, 1835.

Porter, G.R. <u>The Progress of the Nation</u>. London: Charles Knight, 1836. 3 vols.

Redding, Cyrus. <u>Fifty Years' Recollections, Literary and Personal</u>. 2nd ed. London: Charles J. Skeet, 1858. 3 vols.

Rees, Thomas. <u>Reminiscences of Literary London from 1779 to 1853</u>. London: Suckling and Galloway, 1896.

Ritchie, Leitch, ed. <u>Library of Romance</u>. London: Smith, Elder, 1833. 15 vols.

Roscoe, Thomas, ed. <u>Novelist's Library</u>. London: Cochrane & Pickergill, 1831-32. 14 vols.

Smiles, Samuel. <u>A Publisher and His Friends: Memoir and Correspondence of the Late John Murray</u>. London: John Murray, 1891. 2 vols.

"Statistics of Newspapers in Various Countries" Journal of the Statistical Society of London 4 Jul 1841: 111-16.

Stirling, Edward. Nicholas Nickleby: A Farce in Two Acts. London: Chapman and Hall, n.d.

___. Oliver Twist: A Serio-Comic Burletta. In Three Acts. London: Chapman and Hall, n.d.

Thackeray, William Makepeace. The History of Pendennis. London: Bradbury & Evans, 1849. 2 vols.

___. The Letters of William Makepeace Thackeray. Ed. Gordon N. Ray. Cambridge: Harvard U Pr, 1946. 4 vols.

Thomson, H. Byerley. The Choice of a Profession. London: Chapman and Hall, 1857.

Timperley, C.H. A Dictionary of Printers and Printing, with the Progress of Literature, Ancient and Modern. London: H. Johnson, 1839.

___. Encyclopedia of Literary and Typographical Anecdote. London: H. Bohn, 1842.

Trollope, Frances. The Life and Adventures of Michael Armstrong, Factory Boy. London: Colburn, 1840. 3 vols.

Webster, Benjamin, ed. The Acting National Drama. London: Chapman and Hall, 1837-47. 13 vols.

Weller, Sam [pseud]. The Beauties of Pickwick. London: W. Morgan, 1838.

Wight, John. Mornings at Bow Street. London: Charles Baldwyn, 1824.

___. More Mornings at Bow Street. London: James Robins, 1827.

Twentieth Century

Adburgham, Alison. Silver Fork Society: Fashionable Life and
    Literature from 1814 to 1840. London: Constable, 1983.

Altick, Richard. The English Common Reader. Chicago: U of
    Chicago Pr, 1957.

Appleman, Philip, et al., eds. 1859: Entering an Age of
    Crisis. Bloomington: Indiana U Pr, 1959.

Armstrong, Isobel. Victorian Scrutinies: Reviews of Poetry
    1830-1870. London: Athlone, 1972.

Aspinall, Arthur. Politics and the Press c.1780-1850. London:
    Holme & Van Thal, 1949.

___. "The Social Status of Journalists at the Beginning of
    the Nineteenth Century" Review of English Studies 21
    no 83   Jul 1945: 216-32.

___. "Statistical Accounts of the London Newspapers 1800-36"
    English Historical Review 65   Apr 1950: 222-34.

Barnes, James J. Free Trade in Books: A Study of the London
    Book Trade since 1800. Oxford: Clarendon Pr, 1964.

Bennett, Scott.   "John Murray's Family Library and the
    Cheapening   of Books in Early Nineteenth   Century
    Britain" Studies in Bibliography 29 (1976): 139-66.

Blakey, Dorothy.   The Minerva Press 1790-1820.   London:
    Bibliographical Society, 1939.

Brice, Alex W.   "Reviewers of Dickens in the Examiner:
    Fonblanque, Forster, Hunt, and Morley" Dickens Studies
    Newsletter 3   Sep 1972: 68-80.

Butler, Marilyn. Romantics, Rebels and Reactionaries: English
    Literature and Its Background 1760-1830. London: Oxford
    U Pr, 1981.

Carnall, Geoffrey. "The Monthly Magazine" Review of English
    Studies ns 5   no 18   (1954): 158-64.

Churchill, R.C., comp. <u>A Bibliography of Dickensian Criticism</u> <u>1836-75</u>. London: Macmillan, 1975.

Colby, Robert. <u>Fiction with a Purpose</u>. Bloomington: Indiana U Pr, 1967.

Collins, A.S. <u>The Profession of Letters: A Study of the</u> <u>Relation of Author to Patron, Publisher, and Public,</u> <u>1780-1832</u>. London: George Routledge & Sons, 1928.

Collins, Philip. "Dickens and the <u>Edinburgh Review</u>" <u>Review</u> <u>of English Studies</u> ns 14 no 54 (1963): 167-72.

____. <u>Dickens: The Critical Heritage</u>. New York: Barnes & Noble, 1971.

____. "Significance of Dickens's Periodicals" <u>Review of</u> <u>English Literature</u> 2 Jul 1961: 55-64.

Cooper, F. Renad. <u>Nothing Extenuate: The Life of Frederick</u> <u>Fox Cooper</u>. London: Barrie and Rockliff, 1964.

Cox, R.G. "The Great Reviews" <u>Scrutiny</u> 6 no 1 Jne 1937: 2-20; 6 no 2 Sep 1937: 155-75.

____. "The Reviews and Magazines" in <u>The Pelican Guide to</u> <u>English Literature: From Dickens to Hardy</u>, ed. Boris Ford. Harmondsworth: Penguin, 1958. 188-204.

Cross, Nigel. <u>The Common Writer: Life in Nineteenth-Century</u> <u>Grub Street</u>. Cambridge: Cambridge U Pr, 1985.

____. <u>The Royal Literary Fund 1790-1918</u>. London: World Microfilms Publications, 1984.

Darton, R.J. Harvey. <u>Dickens: Positively the First</u> <u>Appearance</u>. London: Argonaut Pr, 1933.

Davis, Lennard J. <u>Factual Fictions: The Origins of the</u> <u>English Novel</u>. New York: Columbia U Pr, 1983.

Day, Geoffrey. <u>From Fiction to the Novel</u>. London: Routledge & Kegan Paul, 1987.

DeVries, Duane. <u>Dickens's Apprentice Years</u>. Brighton: Harvester Pr, 1976.

Dexter, Walter. "Bentley's Miscellany" <u>Dickensian</u> 33 no 244 Autumn 1937: 232-38.

____. "Contemporary Opinion of Dickens's Earliest Work" <u>Dickensian</u> 31 no 234 Spring 1935: 105-08.

____. "How Press and Public Received 'The Pickwick Papers'" <u>Nineteenth Century</u> 119 Mar 1936: 318-29.

____. "The Reception of Dickens's First Book" <u>Dickensian</u> 32 no 237 Winter 1935-36: 43-50.

____. "The Rise to Fame" <u>Dickensian</u> 32 no 239 Summer 1936: 193-202.

____. "Some Early Reviews of <u>Pickwick</u>" <u>Dickensian</u> 32 no 239 Summer 1936: 216-18; continued in 32 no 240 Autumn 1936: 281-85.

____. "A Stage Aside: Dickens's Early Dramatic Productions" <u>Dickensian</u> 33 no 244 Autumn 1937: 251-56.

Dexter, W. and Ley, J.W.T. <u>The Origin of Pickwick</u>. London: Chapman and Hall, 1936.

Ellis, S.W. <u>William Harrison Ainsworth and His Friends</u>. London: John Lane, The Bodley Head, 1910. 2 vols.

Engel, Elliot and King, Margaret F. <u>The Victorian Novel before Victoria: British Fiction during the Reign of William IV 1830-37</u>. London: Macmillan, 1984.

____. "Pickwick's Progress: The Critical Reception of <u>The Pickwick Papers</u> from 1836 to 1986" <u>Dickens Quarterly</u> 3 no 1 Mar 1986: 56-66.

Feltes, N. N. "The Moment of <u>Pickwick</u>, or the Production of a Commodity Text" <u>Literature and History</u> 10 no 2 Autumn 1984: 203-17.

Fielding, K.J. and Brice, A.W. "Forster: Critic of Fiction" <u>Dickensian</u> 70 no 734 Sep 1974: 159-70.

Ford, G.H. <u>Dickens and His Readers: Aspects of Novel-Criticism since 1836</u>. Princeton: Princeton U Pr, 1955.

Gash, Norman. Aristocracy and People: Britain 1815-65. London: Edward Arnold, 1979.

Gettmann, Royal A. A Victorian Publisher: A Study of the Bentley Papers. Cambridge: Cambridge U Pr, 1960.

Jack, Ian. English Literature 1815-1832. Oxford: Clarendon Pr, 1963.

Kincaid, James R. and Kuhn, Albert J., eds. Victorian Literature and Society: Essays presented to Richard D. Altick. Akron: Ohio State U Pr, 1983.

Koss, Stephen. The Rise and Fall of the Political Press in Britain. Volume I: The Nineteenth Century. London: Hamish Hamilton, 1981.

Landon, Richard, ed. Book Selling and Book Buying: Aspects of the Nineteenth-Century British and North American Book Trade. Chicago: American Library Association, 1978.

Lounsbury, Thomas R. The Life and Times of Tennyson 1809-50. New Haven: Yale U Pr, 1915.

Marchand, Leslie A. The Athenaeum: A Mirror of Victorian Culture. 1941; New York: Octagon Books, 1971.

Maxted, Ian. The London Book Trades 1775-1800. Surrey: Dawson, 1977.

Mineka, Francis E. The Dissidence of Dissent: The Monthly Repository 1806-38. 1944: New York: Octagon Books, 1972.

Morison, Stanley. The English Newspaper 1622-1932. Cambridge: Cambridge U Pr, 1932.

Olmsted, John Charles. A Victorian Art of Fiction: Essays on the Novel in British Periodicals 1830-1850. New York: Garland, 1979.

Patten, Robert L. Charles Dickens and His Publishers. London: Clarendon, 1978.

Patten, Robert L. "The Story-Weaver at His Loom: Dickens and the Beginning of The Old Curiosity Shop" in Dickens the Craftsman: Strategies of Presentation, ed. Robert L. Partlow, Jr. Carbondale & Edwardsville: Southern Illinois U Pr, 1970.

Pitcher, Edward S. "The Serial Publication and Collecting of Pamphlets 1790-1815" The Library 5th ser 30 no 4 Dec 1975: 323-29.

Raleigh, John Henry. "What Scott Meant to the Victorians" Victorian Studies 7 no 1 Sep 1963: 7-34.

Sadleir, Michael. Things Past. London: Constable, 1944.

Schachterle, Lance. "Oliver Twist and its Serial Predecessors" Dickens Studies Annual 3 (1973): 1-13.

Shattock, Joanne, and Wolff, Michael. The Victorian Periodical Press: Samplings and Soundings. Leicester: Leicester U Pr, 1982.

Slater, Michael, ed. The Catalogue of the Suzannet Charles Dickens Collection. London and New York: Sotheby Parke Bermt Publications/Dickens House, 1975.

Smith, Walter E. Charles Dickens in the Original Cloth. Los Angeles: Heritage Book Shop, 1982. 2 vols.

Stange, Richard. The Theory of the Novel in England 1850-70. New York: Columbia U Pr, 1959.

Sutherland, J.A. "Henry Colburn, Publisher" Publishing History 19 (1986): 59-84.

___. "John Macrone: Victorian Publisher" Dickens Studies Annual 13 (1984): 243-59.

___. Victorian Novelists and Publishers. London: Athlone, 1976.

Thomas, William Beach. The Story of the Spectator 1828-1928. London: Methuen, 1928.

Thrall, Miriam M.H. Rebellious Fraser's. New York: Columbia U Pr, 1934.

Turner, Michael L.   Index and Guide to the Lists of the
    Publications of Richard Bentley & Son 1829-98.   Bishops
    Stortford: Chadwyck-Healey, 1975.

Vann, J.Don.   "The Early Success of Pickwick"   Publishing
    History 2 (1977): 51-55.

____.   "Pickwick in the London Newspapers"   Dickensian   70
    no 372   Jan 1974: 49-52.

____.   Victorian Novels in Serial.   New York: MLA, 1985.

Vivian, Charles H.   "Dickens, the 'True Sun,' and Samuel Laman
    Blanchard"   Nineteenth-Century Fiction 4 no 4   Mar 1950:
    328-30.

Waugh, Arthur.   A Hundred Years of Publishing.   London:
    Chapman and Hall, 1930.

Weimann, Robert.   Structure and Society in Literary History:
    Studies in the History and Theory of Historical
    Criticism.   1976; Baltimore and London: Johns Hopkins
    U Pr, 1984.

Williams, Ian.   Sir Walter Scott on Novelists and Fiction.
    London: Routledge and Kegan Paul, 1968.

Woodruff, James F.   "The Background and Significance of The
    Rambler's Format" Publishing History 4 (1978): 113-33.

Young, G.M.   Early Victorian England 1830-65.   London: Oxford
    U Pr, 1934.

V. LIST OF PERIODICALS CONSULTED

NCB = New Cambridge Bibliography   WD = Waterloo Directory

( ) = Year of inception   * = not in Key Serials

List

        n/a = not applicable. Usually denotes a specialized
           technical or religious publication.

Age (1825) NCB 1810 WD 323   Weekly

Archaeologia (1770)   Annual   n/a

Architectural Magazine (1834)   NCB 1846 WD 1126 Monthly
        n/a

Art-Union (1839) NCB 1846 WD 1269   Monthly

Asiatic Journal and Monthly Register (1816) NCB 1844 WD 1361
        Monthly n/a

Athenaeum (1828) NCB 1821 WD 1495   Weekly

Atlas (1826)   NCB 1810 WD 1559   Weekly

Baptist Magazine (1809) NCB 1843 WD 1846   Monthly   n/a

Bell's Life in London and Sporting Chronicle (1822) NCB 1809
        WD 2217   Weekly

Bell's Literary Intelligence (1834) WD 2218   Weekly   n/a

Bell's New Weekly Messenger (1832) NCB 1810 WD 2220   Weekly

Bell's Weekly Magazine (1834) WD 2224   Weekly

Bell's Weekly Messenger (1796) NCB 1808 WD 2225 Weekly n/a

Blackwood's Edinburgh Magazine (1817)   NCB 1844   WD 2659
Monthly

British and Foreign Review (1835)   NCB 1856   WD 3381 Quarterly

British Critic (1827)   NCB 1855   WD 3475   Quarterly

Bronterre's National Reformer (1837)   NCB 1818   WD 3784
Weekly   n/a

Cambridge Quarterly Review (1833)   NCB 1865   WD 4164 Quarterly
n/a

Carlton Chronicle (and National Conservative Journal)* (1836)
WD 4332   Weekly

Chambers's Edinburgh Journal (1832)   NCB 1813   WD 4593
Weekly   n/a

Chambers's Historical Newspaper (1832)   NCB 1845   WD 4605
Monthly   n/a

Champion (1836)   NCB 1811   WD 4620   Weekly

Christian Observer (1802)   NCB 1842   WD 5207   Monthly   n/a

Christian Remembrancer (1819)   NCB 1844   WD 5238   Monthly

Christian Teacher (1835)   NCB 1856   WD 5267   Monthly/Quarterly

Church of England Quarterly Review (1837)   NCB 1856   WD 5516
Quarterly

Cobbett's Political Register (1802)   NCB 1817   WD 5992
Weekly

Comic Annual (1830)   NCB 1874   WD 6162   Annual   n/a

Companion to the Newspaper (1833) NCB 1846 WD 6279 Monthly

    n/a

Constitutional and Public Ledger (1836) NCB 1790 WD 6400

    Daily

Courier (1792) NCB 1792 WD 6723 Daily

Court Magazine and Belle Assemblée [and Monthly Critic] (1832)

    NCB 1842 WD 2204 Monthly

Destructive and Poor Man's Conservative (1833) NCB 1818

    WD 7394 Weekly n/a

Dublin Review (1836) NCB 1856 WD 7801 Quarterly

Dublin University Magazine (1833) NCB 1845 WD 7815 Monthly

Eclectic Review (1805) NCB 1842 WD 8186 Monthly

Edinburgh Review (1802) NCB 1853 WD 8296 Quarterly

Era (1838) NCB 1826 WD 8692 Weekly

Evangelical Magazine (1793) NCB 1840 WD 8815 Monthly n/a

Evening Chronicle* (1835) NCB 1807 WD 8847 Tri-weekly

Examiner (1808) NCB 1809 WD 8991 Weekly

Figaro in London (1831) NCB 1825 WD 9384 Weekly

Fisher's Drawing Room Scrapbook (1832) NCB 1875 WD 9514

    Annual n/a

Fisher's Juvenile Scrapbook (1836) NCB 1877 WD 9517 Annual

    n/a

Foreign Quarterly Review (1827) NCB 1855 WD 9687 Quarterly

Fraser's Magazine (1830) NCB 1845 WD 9777 Monthly

Friendship's Offering (1824) NCB 1873 WD 9950 Annual n/a

Gardener's Chronicle (1841) NCB 1827 WD 10087 Weekly n/a

General Baptist Repository and Missionary Observer (1802)

    NCB 1842 WD 10199 Monthly n/a

Gentleman's Magazine (1731) NCB 1839 WD 10246 Monthly

Globe (1803) NCB 1792 WD 10457 Daily

Heath's Book of Beauty (1833) NCB 1875 WD 11409 Annual n/a

Hetherington's Twopenny Dispatch and People's Police Register

    (1834) NCB 1818 WD 11574 Weekly n/a

Jewish Chronicle (1841) NCB 1822 WD 13248 n/a

John Bull (1820) NCB 1809 WD 13289 Weekly

Keepsake (1828) NCB 1874 WD 13616 Annual n/a

Lancet (1823) NCB 1826 WD 14179 Weekly n/a

Law Magazine (1828) NCB 1856 WD 14296 Quarterly n/a

Leigh Hunt's London Journal (1834) NCB 1821 WD 14582

    Weekly

Library of the Fine Arts (1831) WD 14742 Monthly n/a

Literary Gazette (1817) NCB 1821 WD 14998 Weekly

London Review (1835) NCB 1856 WD 15715 Monthly

London Gazette (1665) NCB 1808 WD 19704 Bi-weekly n/a

Magazine of Natural History (1829) NCB 1845 WD 16068

    Monthly n/a

Magazine of Zoology and Botany (1837)   NCB 1846   WD 16085

    Monthly   n/a

Magnet: Agricultural and Commercial Gazette (1837)   NCB 1823

    WD 16099   Weekly

Mark Lane Express (1832)   NCB 1823   WD 16410   Weekly

Mechanics' Magazine (1823)   NCB 1827   WD 16585   Weekly   n/a

Medical Times (1839)   NCB 1826   WD 16654   Weekly   n/a

Metropolitan (1831)   NCB 1845   WD 16862   Monthly

Mining Journal (1835)   NCB 1827   WD 17130   Weekly

Minutes of Proceedings, Institution of Civil Engineers(1837)

    WD 17161   Weekly   n/a

Mirror (1822)   NCB 1816   WD 17186   Weekly

Monthly Chronicle (1838)   NCB 1846   WD 17373   Monthly

Monthly Magazine and British Register (1796)   NCB   1841

    WD 17425   Monthly

Monthly Repository of Theology and General Literature (1806)

    NCB 1843   WD 17495   Monthly

Monthly Review (1749)   NCB 1839   WD 17506   Monthly

Morning Advertiser (1794)   NCB 1789   Daily

Morning Chronicle (1769)   NCB 1789   WD 17572   Daily

Morning Herald (1780)   NCB 1789   WD 17575   Daily

Morning Post (1772)   NCB 1789   WD 17594   Daily

New Monthly Magazine and Universal Register (1814)   NCB 1843
    WD 18331   Monthly

New Moral World (1834)   NCB 1818   WD 18338   Weekly

Nonconformist (1841)   NCB 1822   WD 18627   Weekly   n/a

Observer (1791)   NCB 1807   WD 19135   Weekly

Penny Magazine (1832)   NCB 1813   WD 20197   Weekly   n/a

Peter Parley's Annual (1839)   NCB 1878   Annual   n/a

Philosophical Magazine (1798)   NCB 1841   WD 20485   Monthly
    n/a

Pierce Egan's Book of Sports and Mirror of Life*   (1824)
    NCB 1810   WD 20702   Weekly

Poor Man's Guardian (1831)   NCB 1818   WD 20985   Weekly

Public Ledger (1760)   NCB 1789   WD 21575   Daily

Punch (1841)   NCB 1825   WD 21624   Weekly

Quarterly Review (1809)   NCB 1855   WD 21737   Quarterly

Railway Magazine and Annals of Science (1835)   WD 21939
    Weekly   n/a

Railway Times (1837)   NCB 1827   WD 21977   Weekly

Record (1828)   NCB 1822   WD 22099   Bi-weekly   n/a

Repertory of Arts and Manufactures (1794)   NCB 1841   WD 22290
    Monthly   n/a

St. James's Chronicle (1761)   NCB 1808   WD 24749   Tri-weekly

Servant's Magazine (1838)   NCB 1846   WD 23601   Monthly   n/a

Shipping and Mercantile Gazette (1838)   NCB 1793   WD 23773

    Daily

Spectator (1828)   NCB 1813   WD 24490   Weekly

Sporting Magazine (1792)   NCB 1840   WD 24601   Monthly

Sportsman (1833)   NCB 1846 WD 24636   Monthly   n/a

Standard (1827)   NCB 1793   WD 24903   Daily

Sun (1792)   NCB 1792   WD 25270   Daily

Sunday Times (1822)   NCB 1810   WD 12442   Weekly

Tablet (1840)   NCB 1822   WD 25625   Weekly

Tait's Edinburgh Magazine (1832)   NCB 1845   WD 23178   Monthly

The Times (1788)   NCB 1789   WD 7165   Daily

Town (1837)   NCB 1813   WD 26196   Weekly

True Sun* (1832)   NCB 1793   WD 26429   Daily

United Services Gazette (1833)   NCB 1826   WD 26692   Weekly

United Service Journal (1829)   NCB 1845   WD 6017   Monthly

    n/a

Weekly Dispatch (1801)   NCB 1808   Weekly

Weekly True Sun* (1833)   NCB 1810   WD 27555   Weekly

Wesleyan-Methodist Magazine (1838)   NCB 1846   WD 27657

    Monthly   n/a

Westminster Review (1824)   NCB 1855   WD 27968   Quarterly

Working Man's Friend (1832)   NCB 1818   WD 28492   Weekly   n/a